Embedded Sustainability

EMBEDDED
SUSTAINABILITY
THE NEXT BIG
COMPETITIVE ADVANTAGE

Chris Laszlo and **Nadya Zhexembayeva**

Stanford Business Books
an Imprint of Stanford University Press
Stanford, California

Published in the USA by
Stanford University Press
Stanford, California

Library of Congress Cataloging-in-Publication Data

Laszlo, Christopher, author.
    Embedded sustainability : the next big competitive advantage / Chris Laszlo and Nadya
Zhexembayeva.
       pages cm
    Published simultaneously in the UK by: Sheffield : Greenleaf Publishing.
    Includes bibliographical references and index.
    ISBN 978-0-8047-7554-0 (cloth : alk. paper)
  1. Industrial management--Environmental aspects. 2. Sustainability. 3. Social
responsibility of business. I. Zhexembayeva, Nadya, author. II. Title.
    HD30.255.L396 2011
    658.4'083--dc22

                    2011002646

Published simultaneously in the UK by
Greenleaf Publishing Limited
Aizlewood's Mill
Nursery Street
Sheffield S3 8GG
www.greenleaf-publishing.com

British Library Cataloguing in Publication Data:
  A catalogue record for this book is available from the British Library.
    ISBN-13: 978-1-906093-58-7 (hardback)

Cover by LaliAbril.com

MIX
From responsible
sources
FSC® C113845
FSC
www.fsc.org

To our parents
Carita Laszlo and Ervin Laszlo
Lydia Zhexembayeva and Timur Zhexembayev

Contents

Foreword

Greg Babe[1]

A century ago, Gifford Pinchot – one of the environmental movement's most important early champions – wrote:

> The outgrowth of conservation, the inevitable result, is national efficiency. In the great commercial struggle between nations which is eventually to determine the welfare of all, national efficiency will be the deciding factor. So from every point of view conservation is a good thing for the American people.[2]

Pinchot's words were no doubt mystifying to his early 20th-century readers. How could conservation – an important component of what we today call sustainability – promote "efficiency" in the sense of how Frederick Winslow Taylor, the father of industrial efficiency, had popularized the term? Pinchot's ideas about conservation and wilderness preservation must have struck many as far removed, literally and figuratively, from the world of Taylor's time-motion studies on the factory floor.

Indeed, it has taken nearly a hundred years for us to reach the point where we can fully grasp Pinchot's vision of sustainability as part of a broader struggle for worldwide competitiveness in every sense of the word. Today, as businesses work to recover from the biggest recession since the Great Depression, those who look on sustainability, not merely as a management "fad du jour," but as the key to future prosperity, are rapidly gaining a powerful advantage over their domestic and international competition.

Today, the concept of sustainability has matured from the concept of conservation in the 20th century to the concept of stewardship in all its forms – social, economic, and environmental. True sustainability involves applying systems thinking to anticipate unintended consequences that can occur when the entire system is not taken into account.

In this book, Chris Laszlo and Nadya Zhexembayeva offer a practical guide to the power and necessity of weaving sustainability into the DNA of an organization. They show how, over the years, three once-distinct trends – declining natural resources, increasing transparency of business practices, and a rising tide of social and commercial expectations – have converged to make sustainability the most urgent issue of the contemporary business agenda. In this sense, they are heirs to the legacy of Pinchot and Taylor. But they bring to their cause, a century later, an even greater sense of urgency.

Professors Laszlo and Zhexembayeva well understand that embedding sustainability into the corporate culture – which is to say, into the hearts and minds of employees, customers, suppliers, shareholders, and other stakeholders – represents a long and difficult journey. And while our sustainability journey at Bayer in North America is far from over, we have already learned much along the way. Those lessons can be summarized in three words: **awareness**, **involvement**, and **innovation**.

Awareness. Companies must begin their change journey by recognizing that reputation is their biggest asset or their biggest potential liability. Companies who fail to adhere to sustainability thinking and principles – everywhere and always – can garner, practically overnight, negative media attention, lost stakeholder trust, and enormous unplanned costs. BP's disaster in the Gulf of Mexico is the most recent and costly example of this phenomenon, but it is far from the only one. As the authors argue, "Managing sustainability-related business risks is not so much about value creation as it is about avoiding its destruction" (page 61). It's an important point.

Bayer has launched an employee education program to advance sustainability throughout the corporation. It's called STEP – for Sustainability Thinking Education Program. Chris Laszlo was instrumental in designing STEP and preparing Bayer executives for the key leadership role they must play in making the program a success.

Involvement. Beyond awareness, embedding sustainability means mobilizing the active involvement, not just of employees, but of all stakeholders in the adoption of sustainable business practices. The authors cite the example of Australia's Yellow Tail wines, which "raised the retail store involvement relative to table wines" (page 85), creating in the process a product almost beyond category. As of this writing, Yellow Tail is the best selling wine in the United States, outselling all French producers combined. Sustainability is embedded in Yellow Tail's brand image, which includes recycling all irrigation water, cardboard, plastic, and glass. And the involvement of both employees and consumers in its sustainability efforts is one of the keys to the company's success.

Similarly, a patent-pending idea by a Bayer employee trained in process control led to a decrease in greenhouse gas emissions equivalent to 13,000 metric tons of carbon a year. That single change will save our company some $2 million in operating costs annually.

Innovation. As we increase organizational awareness of sustainability and engage our stakeholders in our vision, we find that we also unlock the power of company-wide innovation. At Bayer MaterialScience, that has led, for example, to innovative products for retrofitting buildings to make them more energy-efficient and to combat one of the bigger sources of greenhouse gas emissions in North America. In our CropScience group, we have developed seed treatment technology to help growers produce more output per acre of land without extra steps. Producing more per acre equates to using fewer natural resources such as water and arable land to feed a growing population. Our HealthCare group has likewise developed such innovative products as the Contour USB meter for patients on insulin therapy. Helping them better manage their disease over a lifetime means not only a better quality of life for the individual but lower costs to society as a whole.

The journey to embedded sustainability isn't one that can be traversed over a matter of several quarters or even several years. But ideas that underlie it have evolved to the point where we can fully grasp and employ them to transform both business and society.

Likewise, the meaning of sustainability itself will continue to unfold over time. As Gifford Pinchot wrote:

> While at first conservation was supposed to apply only to forests, we see now that its sweep extends even beyond the natural resources . . . I recall very well indeed how, in the early days of forest fires, they were considered simply and solely as acts of God, against which any opposition was hopeless and any attempt to control them not merely hopeless but childish. It was assumed that they came in the natural order of things, as inevitably as the seasons or the rising and setting of the sun. Today we understand that forest fires are wholly within the control of men. So we are coming in like manner to understand that the prevention of waste in all other directions is a simple matter of good business. The first duty of the human race is to control the earth it lives upon.[3]

The time has come for business to understand that duty and, what is more important, to act on it.

Greg Babe
President and Chief Executive Officer
Bayer Corporation and Bayer MaterialScience LLC

Foreword

Andrew J. Hoffman[4]

This book recognizes one overriding reality: sustainability represents a market shift. The simple fact is that you can be completely agnostic about the science of many environmental issues such as climate change and still see them as business issues, ones that will alter the market environment.

Consider the issue of climate change; companies will find that their raw material and energy costs will go up as government sets policies to reduce greenhouse gas emissions (whether a price for carbon; fuel economy, appliance or building standards; renewable portfolio standards; subsidies for renewable energy sources or simply regulating CO_2 as a pollutant). In addition, consumers are becoming more aware of energy conservation, investors are starting to get excited about investment potential of renewables, and new college graduates are looking more carefully at a company's values (environmental and otherwise) before accepting a job. Jeffrey Immelt freely admits that his company's Ecomagination initiative has vastly improved GE's ability to attract and retain the best candidates. And with the reframing of the climate change issue as a market shift, it becomes an issue of straight business strategy.

Market shifts create winners and losers; and companies must innovate to survive. They must divest some businesses, acquire others, and alter the ones they keep. The question "does it pay to be green?" becomes nonsensical. It is the same as asking "does it pay to innovate?" The answer depends on who does it, when they do it, and how they do it. As this book explains, to answer these questions, the business executive must put aside "green" considerations and concentrate on business fundamentals. And so, when it comes to "green" jobs, we are talking about new demographics and skill sets in the face of new competitive realities. When we talk of "green-tech" we are talking about new innovation and investment opportunities. And when we talk of "green buildings" we are talking about buildings that use improved technologies that lead to lower operating costs and more productive workforces.

But the problem is that green is presently everywhere! For many companies, it has become a fad without much substance behind it. "Green jobs;" "Green-tech"; "Green buildings"; and on it goes! CSX boasts of the greenness of train hauling; IBM touts its green mainframe computers; trucking companies are pushing for tandem trailers as a way to reduce greenhouse gas emissions. Like the broader term "sustainability," everyone is jumping on the "green" bandwagon and using the term ad nauseam. For many, the term "green" is becoming too undefined, ambiguous, and universal. And for others, the term is like waiving a red flag in front of a bull, yielding resistance and outright antagonism. For example, Christian Evangelicals who have begun to engage climate change as a moral issue are loath to call themselves "environmentalists," which they see as synonymous with a left-leaning, liberal agenda: one that in their minds elevates nature over humans and disrespects property rights to protect it. Instead, they call themselves "caring creationists." Similarly, in the area of green architecture, surveys have found that many consumers and business executives will answer "no" when asked if they want a "green building," but answer "yes" when asked if they want a hyper-efficient building or smart building. And concern over mainstreaming goes beyond semantics. In 2009, the *New York Times* pointed out that, in the same home improvement store, one can buy a plastic-handled paint brush that is "green" because it does not use trees to make the handle. In the next bin, you can buy a wooden-handled paintbrush that is "green" because the handle is not made from fossil fuels.

This can only breed confusion, cynicism, and contempt, both in the general public and in the corporate sector. The problem became vivid for me in 2008 when I was talking with an auto industry executive (before the fiscal crisis hit the industry). He told me that the hybrid market was a temporary blip because it made no economic sense. His logic ran that, once consumers realized that they will never recoup their initial investment in the hybrid drive train through gas savings, they will stop buying them.

I countered that the psychology of buying a hybrid car was no different than that of buying other cars. It was tied to a personal decision-making process; it wasn't merely an economic choice. On that count, I told him, he should see very little difference between his company selling a hybrid to someone who wants to project his or her environmental values and selling a Corvette to a middle-aged guy who wants to pick up chicks. He smiled, but I sensed I was not getting past his resistance that this whole green thing was just a liberal fad, soon to die. As is now obvious, he was wrong.

The problem is that the continual drum beat of "green" perpetuates the kind of resistance that this experience illustrates. Certainly the Detroit auto sector would be better off right now had it invested more in energy-efficient autos (not ignoring other issues such as health care and legacy costs). But in seeing hybrids as merely an "irrational" blip of the moment that is driven by a social and nonbusiness agenda, auto executives could not see the market shift coming. It is reminiscent of Thomas Watson, CEO of IBM, famously predicting "a world market for maybe five computers"; or H.M. Warner, CEO of Warner Brothers, asking "Who the hell wants to hear actors talk?" For their own particular reasons, these legendary business leaders could not see the market shift in their midst.

Today, we are in the midst of such a transition: what I believe future generations will look back on as an energy renaissance. So, rather than talking of "green" jobs, tech or building, we need to talk of the next generation of innovations in each of these sectors. This is not an issue of "corporate social responsibility." This is an issue of market economics and business strategy. In the end, as green becomes more mainstream, it becomes less "green." When Clorox introduces its new line of Green Works™ cleaners, GE develops wind turbines under its Ecomagination program, Toyota develops its Hybrid Synergy Drive train, or Matsushita increases lithium-ion battery production, these are not examples of "green" products; they are examples of companies attacking new and profitable market segments and hastening the market shift under way. "Green" goes away. I can see it in my MBA classes on environmental strategy: no longer is this the domain of a fringe group of socially minded students. Attendance has exploded with the entry of mainstream business students who see environmental issues as critical to the corporate success and that of their careers. It is just becoming the way we do business. That is the overriding message of this book.

Andrew J. Hoffman
Holcim (U.S.) Professor of Sustainable Enterprise
University of Michigan
Ann Arbor, Michigan

Acknowledgments

This book is the culmination of hundreds of conversations and interactions that helped shape our research and provide incisive glimpses into the future of sustainable business. It started as a search for new answers to new questions insistently probed by our colleagues, clients, and students, many of whom have taken countless hours to read the manuscript in its emergent stages and provide rigorous feedback and encouragement.

We are particularly grateful to Henry Mintzberg, the Cleghorn Professor of Management Studies at the Desautels Faculty of Management of McGill University; Jim Ellert, former Academic Dean and Professor of Strategy and Finance, IMD and EMBA Director at IEDC-Bled School of Management; Jean-Pierre Lehmann, Professor of International Political Economy, IMD and Founding Director, The Evian Group; Derek F. Abell, Founding President and Professor Emeritus of the European School of Management and Technology and former Professor at Harvard Business School and IMD; Andrew J. Hoffman, the Holcim (U.S.) Professor of Sustainable Enterprise at the University of Michigan; Ervin Laszlo, Founder-President of The Club of Budapest and Chancellor of the Giordano Bruno GlobalShift University; Ira A. Jackson, Dean, Peter F. Drucker and Masatoshi Ito Graduate School of Management, Claremont Graduate University; Vijay Sathe, Professor of Strategy, Peter F. Drucker and Masatoshi Ito Graduate School of Management, Claremont Graduate University; James Wallace, Associate Professor of Finance, Peter F. Drucker and Masatoshi Ito Graduate School of Management, Claremont Graduate University; Valerie Patrick, Head of Sustainability at Bayer Corporation; Wilfried Grommen, Regional Technology Office, Microsoft CEE; Arnold Walravens, Chairman of the Supervisory Board, Eureko and member of the Supervisory Board, Rabobank Nederland; Mason Carpenter, the M. Keith Weikel Professor of Leadership, The University of Wisconsin School of Business; Alexander Laszlo, co-Founder and President of Syntony Quest; Martin Flash, Director, the General Management Programme (GMP), CEDEP-INSEAD; Ante Glavas, Assistant Professor, the University of Notre Dame Mendoza School of Business; Lindsey N. Godwin, Assistant Professor of Management, Morehead State University; Nigel Topping, Chief Innovation Officer, Carbon Disclosure Project; Andreja Kodrin, Founder and President, *Challenge:Future* Youth Think Tank; and Garima Sharma, PhD Candidate, Case Western Reserve University.

We are deeply indebted to the handful of leading business schools and programs that pioneered sustainability in their management curricula and allowed us to play in this space: The Weatherhead School of Management at Case Western Reserve University (USA), IEDC-Bled School of Management (Slovenia), INSEAD (France), CEDEP-INSEAD (France), The Tata Management Training Center (India), The Darden School of Management at the University of Virginia (USA), and the Johnson School of Management at Cornell University (USA).

At the Weatherhead School, the Fowler Center for Sustainable Value – on whose Advisory Board we both sit – has been a powerful source of ideas and connections. We are thankful to the Center and its associated faculty for providing us with the opportunity to collaborate and for allowing us to become a part of an amazing group of thinkers. Our warmest thanks go to David Cooperrider, the Center's Founder, who among the many roles he played for us, generously agreed to write the Afterword. Roger Saillant, Ron Fry, Dean Mohan Reddy, and Sayan Chatterjee provided ongoing thought partnership and inspiring scholarship. Special thanks go to Erin Christmas for research throughout all stages of the book, and to Erin Fields who breathed life into the book's social media outreach.

We are also indebted to the leaders of IEDC-Bled School of Management, who gave us a chance to test our ideas across courses and programs – and dared to embed sustainability deep into its management curriculum. We are particularly thankful to Danica Purg, President and Dean, for her support for our sustainability thinking and efforts, and Nenad Filipović for ongoing encouragement and insights, as well as Gorazd Planinc for his continuous support of our online presence.

Several industry leaders played a key role through their spirit of inquisitive partnership or willingness to learn with us in executive education programs. In alphabetical order these are: Arch Chemicals, Bayer Corporation, British American Tobacco, Celanese, Clarke, Coca-Cola, Erste Group Bank, Fairmount Minerals, Gojo Industries, L'Oréal, Microsoft, Orange, Portland General Electric, Renault/Nissan, Saint-Gobain, Tata, UBS Bank, Unilever, and Walmart. We thank these pioneering leaders and managers at every level who helped advance the ideas and experiences described in this book.

We've been gifted with an editorial team that recognized early on the power of *Embedded Sustainability*, even as it was just beginning to emerge as a book idea. Our gratitude goes to John Stuart and Dean Bargh at Greenleaf Publishing, and to Margo Beth Crouppen and Geoffrey Burn at Stanford University Press, for their steady support during the ten-month project. John and Dean provided us with a rare editorial partnership, assisting us every step of the way with both content and form.

A wonderful network of teachers, colleagues, clients, students, and friends dispersed across the continents deserve special thanks for all they contributed to us in one form or another. They are Nancy Adler, Sandra Waddock, Han van Dissel, David Orr, Richard Boyatzis, Bonnie Richley, Jean-François Laugel, Joe Bozada, Andrew Winston, William Shephard, Linda Robson, Peter Whitehouse, Michel Avital, Tojo Thatchenkery, Rafael Sanches Neto, Marco A. Oliveira, Dorival Donadão, Antonio Zuvela, Saidul Rahman Mahomed, Alban Aucoin, Federico Balzola, Laurent Guy, Michael Heurtevant, Mark Milstein, Karen Christensen, Loïc Sadoulet, Ram Nidumolu, Marc Major, Lauren Heine, Rich Liroff, Tony Bond, Diana Riverburgh, George Eapen, Jens Meyer, Nicholas Dungan, Bob Willard, Santiago Gowland, Rick Ramirez, Todd Baldwin, Dennis Church, Leslie Pascaud, Mike Nightingale, James Blakelock, Jennie Galbraith, Maggie Parker, Jacqui Earl, Tina Taylor, Stephen F. Grey, Rita Muci, Zaida Monell, Alibek Belyalov, Roman Finadeev, Yulia Dubrovsky, Barbara Ferjan, Judy Rodgers, Mary Grace Neville, Irina Redicheva, Olga Veligurska, Deniz Kirazci, Olga Nikulin, Svetlana Zakharchenko, Misha Uchitel, Sergey Vecher, Yulia Oleinik, Alex Meyboom, Emily Drew, and Jeanne du Plessis.

Finally, there is a very high chance that our families contributed more to this effort than we can account for ourselves. We are deeply grateful to our spouses – Lakshmi Laszlo and Vladimir Jernovoi – for the avid reactions, countless edits, and frequent mealtimes generously committed to this project. Carita Laszlo, Ervin Laszlo, Alexander Laszlo, Kathia Laszlo, Lydia Zhexembayeva, Timur Zhexembayev, Tatyana Nurgazina, Marat Zhexembayev, Vladimir Zhexembayev, Olga Zhexembayeva, Emma Jernovoi, Enessa Gucker, and Hans Gucker continue to play a huge supporting role in shaping our lives and minds. And to the three girls who will forever energize our search for meaning, happiness, and hope, we give all our love: Jenna Laszlo, Ishana Laszlo, and Lila Jernovoi.

The wasp and the frog
An introduction

George Orwell, reflecting on the terrible things that humanity did in the 1930s, mulled over . . .

> . . . a rather cruel trick I once played on a wasp. He was sucking jam on my plate, and I cut him in half. He paid no attention, merely went on with his meal . . . Only when he tried to fly away did he grasp the dreadful thing that had happened to him. It is the same with modern man. The thing that has been cut away is his soul, and there was a period – 20 years perhaps – during which he did not notice it.[5]

This metaphor has been used to describe the business approach to environmental issues in the 1990s. An overly strong focus on regulatory compliance and liability containment on the one hand, and on profits on the other, led to a total separation of environmental matters from the very heartbeat of business.

To this analogy we add another: the story of the frog placed in cold water that is heated so gradually it fails to notice and eventually dies. Companies that have succeeded in marrying environmental, health, and social issues with business strategy have done so using increasingly outdated strategy concepts and management processes. The gradual entry of sustainability into mainstream markets has led business leaders and scholars alike to adapt existing strategy frameworks in a way reminiscent of Ptolemaic efforts to keep the Earth at the center of the universe by adding epicycles. Competitive advantage today is described in the same essential terms it was 30 years ago, simply bolting on new factors of competition such as energy savings, green product features, and socially responsible branding. Sustainability ends up being an afterthought, despite good intentions and even though the external market is not just a little more ecologically and socially mindful, it is now an entirely different ball game. Companies that fail to notice are, like the frog in the story, putting their future at risk. Our premise is that declining resources, radical transparency, and rising expectations have reached a critical point where the rules of the game have changed. Embedded sustainability is not just a better environmentalist strategy; it is a response to a radically different market reality, one that unifies the profit, ecological, and social spheres into a single integrated value creation space.

Emerging values and aspirations for a sustainable world are creating a convergence of interests between business and society. Efforts to raise public awareness about global issues such as climate change and water scarcity are leading to rising expectations which, in turn, increase the demand for products that are low-cost, high-quality, and good for this world. Consumers, investors, and employees have both the desire and the technological means to verify that their expectations are being met. Global industry leaders are embracing sustainability, not as a way to serve green consumers, but as a way to achieve mainstream industry leadership. They are putting sustainability at the core of their business strategy. Those that create value for society and the environment *without trade-offs* have an opportunity to create even more value for their customers and shareholders than they otherwise would.

By contrast, other sustainability efforts are calling for the purpose of business to be redefined, such as Corporation 20/20, which seeks to impose new design principles urging all corporations to serve better the public interest while distributing wealth equitably and acting more responsibly. Such attempts often propose to limit profits or constrain competition through moral persuasion and regulation. However, we believe that it will be difficult to change the essential purpose of business as a profit-making institution. So long as capitalist markets exist, companies will pursue profits as a primary goal, even though they may have a larger societal mission.

A business strategy approach to global challenges automatically creates a more effective platform for corporate responsibility. *A theory of strategy that enables a company to pursue profit with sustainability embedded at its very core* supports greater responsibility by harnessing the profit motive in service of market-based solutions to global problems.

Our book is organized around the central themes of business strategy and change management, with two bookends. The strategy chapters (3–5) place sustainability in frameworks that have become accepted tools of the trade, offering a complete, systematic, and rigorous explanation of how embedded sustainability creates business value. The change management chapters (6–8) give the methods, competencies, and processes for embedding sustainability in the organization and its larger business system. The opening bookend provides the reason for it all: the mega-trends that are driving the new business environment. The closing bookend spells out a future vision of business as it seizes profit opportunities by addressing the many global challenges entering phases of critical instability. It concludes with an inquiry into the changing context of business, raising big questions about topics such as the desirability of growth, government regulation, and spiritual transformation.

While the metaphors of the wasp and the frog are a somewhat dark commentary on human behavior, the story of embedded sustainability is largely a positive and inspiring one. It is about the business opportunity to be more profitable and more responsible. As Patrick Cescau, the former CEO of Unilever, said, it is not only about doing well by doing good, it is about doing even better.

Chris Laszlo   *Nadya Zhexembayeva*

Part I

SUSTAINABILITY ON THE SHORES OF BUSINESS

1
Business reality reshaped
The BIG three trends

Flip through the scholarly pages of Michael Porter[6] and C.K. Prahalad,[7] or browse through the entertainment sections of *Glamour* magazine[8] and MTV,[9] and you would think the world has become obsessed with social and ecological issues. With topics ranging from CO_2 emissions, water rights, and deforestation to child labor, peace, and social equity, the needs of society and the environment present a perfect storm for the average manager: complex, disorienting, and maddeningly inscrutable. *Fortune* magazine might have already declared "green" to be the business story of the 21st century,[10] but for many managers, even its most basic points remain contentious.[11] Which issues merit consideration? How is one to understand the vast landscape of seemingly disconnected concerns? And, at the end of the day, why does it all matter to business?

Looking deeper into the economic, social, health, and ecological pressures that fall under the sustainability umbrella, one finds three distinct but interconnected trends: **declining resources**, **radical transparency**, and **increasing expectations**. Together, these trends are becoming a major market force that is redefining the way companies compete. It has now reached a critical point, changing the rules for profit and growth in almost every sector of the economy.

Here are the pieces of the new business puzzle.

Declining resources

Takeharu Jinguji has been watching a steady decline of bluefin tuna in Japanese waters for years. His longline fishing boat competes with net-fishing folk who also catch smaller species, and for Takeharu, the issue of tuna and its entire food chain is vital to his livelihood: ". . . the total number of fish has been decreasing a lot. So the biggest problem for me is that my income has been reduced."[12] His observations reflect a stark new reality: bluefin tuna has been heavily overfished in all but the Antarctic waters, with stocks at less than 10 per cent of what they once were.[13] Are you at a sushi restaurant looking for maguro or toro, the highest grade of tuna? You may be out of luck . . . or out of money. Today, bluefin tuna has become so rare that a single, healthy-sized adult recently fetched $396,000 in Tokyo's largest fish market.[14] So, staring at a picture of a fully grown specimen might soon become our only option . . .

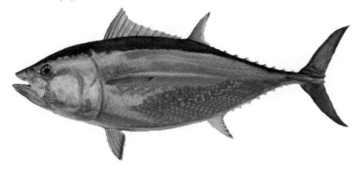

When we share the story of Takeharu Jinguji at conferences and executive education seminars, we are often met with disbelief. One manager recently told us that such exaggerations and myths weaken the cause of sustainability. "I simply can't believe that the population of bluefin tuna has declined by 90 per cent" was his response.

And yet bluefin tuna is only the tip of the iceberg. According to a Stanford University study, overfishing could take all seafood off the menu by 2048. "Unless we fundamentally change the way we manage all the oceans species together, as working ecosystems, then this [20th] century is the last century of wild seafood," notes marine biologist Stephen Palumbi of Stanford University.[15]

Companies across industries and continents are being increasingly affected by the rapid decline of natural resources. Attention to this topic is not new. Long before The Natural Step – a sustainability framework developed in the 1980s that put declining resources at the center of the business-in-society debate[16] – the issue of resource scarcity had the attention of scholars and practitioners alike. Indeed, the notion of unbounded growth in a finite world is nearly as old as economics itself,[17] tracing back to Plato's subordination of family size to the common good[18] and in later times to Thomas Malthus's warnings about the dangers of unchecked population growth.[19]

More recently, in-depth explorations such as the 1963 *Scarcity and Growth* by Harold Barnett and Chandler Morse[20] concluded that resource scarcity was virtually nonexistent, with those conclusions in turn being strongly questioned by the 1972 Club of Rome's *Limits to Growth*.[21] Since then, the two opposing groups have been endlessly debating the (in)exhaustibility of resources. First, there are the proponents of unlimited growth, sometimes called "cornucopians," in reference to cornucopia, or the horn of plenty, a symbol of abundance dating from the ancient Greeks. Most adherents to this philosophy believe in the miracles of neo-classical economics and technological progress. The cornucopians contrast with the tribe of Neo-Malthusians, who believe that growth limits are imposed by the environment. The dispute between the two factions continues to this day.[22]

While the debate is not new, recent years have seen renewed concerns about the rapid decline of natural resources, voiced by international bodies such as WWF. Its *Living Planet Report* warns that "the possibility of financial recession pales in comparison to the looming ecological credit crunch".[23] While the level of decline in certain resources such as oil remains hotly debated,[24] other data is less contested.[25] Even a brief scan across recent studies suggests a strong and clear trend at the level of the planet itself:

- Clean water supply is seeing significant mismatches with demand,[26] especially in Asia, Africa, and Europe.[27] An estimated 1.1 billion people lack access to safe drinking water, while 2.6 billion people lack adequate sanitation, and 1.8 million people die every year from diarrheal diseases, including 90 per cent of children under five who are struck by water-borne disease[28]

- Food security is emerging as a central issue of the new millennium, with food prices[29] and price volatility[30] reflecting the uncertain state of the world's food supply. But even if enough food is produced to feed everyone, it appears that the nutritional value of crops has been on the decline: a recent study shows an average decline of 6 per cent in protein, 16 per cent in calcium, 9 per cent in phosphorus, 15 per cent in iron, 38 per cent in riboflavin, and 20 per cent in vitamin C from 1950 to 1999 across 43 garden variety crops[31]

- Energy security is equally troublesome, with new energy demands largely driven by growth in the BRIC countries (Brazil, Russia, India, and China). Price volatility and geopolitical dependence on a few supplier countries located mostly in the Middle East are seen as growing risk factors.[32] By 2030, the world's primary energy demand is expected to reach a breathtaking 40 per cent higher than 2007[33]

- Biodiversity has seen a rapid decline. The Millennium Ecosystem Assessment[34] reports that, over the past few hundred years, humans have increased species extinction by as much as 1,000 times the rates typical over Earth's history; the bluefin tuna is one of many species bordering on extinction[35]

We can continue this list indefinitely at a risk of losing you to frustration or apathy, the way much of the environmental movement has done before us. We can also add to the list the many "social" resources that add market pressure, whether it is physical security, health, education, or social equity. Our purpose, however, is different. We are committed to sharing an exciting but largely invisible story of a shift in the conduct of business. In the new narrative, the gloom and doom of declining resources is also the foundation for opportunity, an emerging paradigm of business that can be more sustainable *and* more profitable.

The paradigm shift is embodied in the story of TerraCycle, a company known for producing the world's first product made from 100 per cent post-consumer garbage. It is best known for its colorfully named "Worm Poop" – an organic fertilizer created by feeding organic waste to millions of worms that consume and process the waste material, which is then packaged into recycled soda bottles. Nearly two hundred other products have been developed since the first introduction of Worm Poop, and the company is now operational in five countries.

Beyond the efforts of niche start-ups, the shadow of resource decline is finding its way into the stories of well-established mainstream companies, such as Shaw, one of the world's largest flooring manufacturers, now owned by Warren Buffett's Berkshire Hathaway. At Shaw's Evergreen closed-loop operation, old pieces of carpet are ground and processed into their original components, with nylon and other precious raw materials recycled indefinitely into new carpet, without any loss in aesthetic or performance properties.

What TerraCycle and Shaw illustrate is the resource crunch transformed into a new business opportunity. As it quietly marches through industries and continents, a wave of new thinking is entering the mind of business.

Declining resources may have been the headline news of 1798, the year of Thomas Malthus's essay on population. What is so important about this trend now? Surprisingly, the difference is rather striking: never before have we seen the speed, extent, and magnitude of resource loss that we observe now. Whether it is soil, water, nutrition, a stable climate, or social equity as measured by the rich–poor gap, the list of declining resources in question is relevant for nearly the entire global economy, with no company left unaffected. And that, in turn, creates a fundamental change in how companies compete to create enduring value.

Just consider this: for as long as we can remember, three primary factors – the three Cs – have been guiding business strategy: **customers**, **capital**, and **competition**. If meeting customer needs represented the grand prize, with access to capital as the indispensable lubricant and competitive positioning providing the unique route to victory, now there is an entirely new factor to consider: **security of the value chain**. A company might have the best product for the right customer at the right price, but a natural resource crunch upstream in the value chain could wipe out all profits, if not the entire industry. Think tuna: if we put ourselves in the shoes of the fishermen, it is not only fish lovers, wholesale markets, or fellow fishermen that we need to worry about. Now, it is the plankton and the small catch hidden in the tuna's food chain that will determine whether we sink or swim.

And that is only the beginning.

Radical transparency

While the resource crunch is reaching historic proportions, its impact is being amplified by a second big trend that itself is reshaping the business environment – **radical transparency**. Fueled by the unprecedented growth of the civil sector and enabled by rapid developments in the field of information technology, transparency has become the dynamic, immediate, and substantive force of modern corporate life.

Now, we might be using some strong language here, so let us pause for a second and examine a few facts. What is happening, exactly, to bring about radical transparency and how is it relevant for business?

First: the power of numbers

Among the many important developments that are making business increasingly transparent, the rise of civil society must be considered *primus inter pares*. From humble beginnings in Cicero's *societas civilis* to the global power of influence in the present day, the number of voluntary social and nonprofit organizations dedicated to societal and environmental concerns has surpassed the 1 million mark.[36] For the sake of simplicity, let us imagine that each of these organizations unites the efforts of only ten people – whether volunteers or employees. That means that at this very moment, at least 10 million full-time activists (!) are putting sustainability at the center of their lives – many pursuing visions of social equity or healthy ecology with as much strategy, efficiency, rigor, and innovativeness as any well-run business. It is precisely this collective strength that leads observers such as Paul Hawken to refer to this wave of civic action as "the largest movement on Earth." An author of several best-selling books, including his seminal work *The Ecology of Commerce*, Hawken explores the growing influence of the nonprofit sector on business and society in his 2007 *Blessed Unrest: How the Largest Movement in the World Came into Being, and Why No One Saw it Coming*[37] – a great resource and colorful read for those grappling with the idea. But whether it is through the pages of passionate visionaries or through daily encounters with influential NGOs, one thing becomes crystal clear: throughout the world, millions of minds are now dedicated to measuring, recording, making very visible, and ultimately improving the social and environmental well-being of society at large. And business is among their favorite leverage points.

Second: the magic of low-cost communication

As the sheer number of NGOs grew, so did the number and sophistication of their tools. Increasingly affordable global communications technologies coupled with immensely popular social media solutions have created a level of connectivity never seen or imagined before. Consider the story of Kiva.org, a nonprofit that combines the concept of micro-financing with the power of the Internet. As we are writing these very words, Greta, a scientist from Colorado, USA, is using Kiva's website to support the dream of Priyanka from Hikkaduwa, Sri Lanka, to have her own food production and sales business. Greta is among nine lenders from Canada, Netherlands, and the U.S.A. that pitched in to fund Priyanka's request for $225.

While working on this book, we were able to meet both Priyanka and Greta on the pages of Kiva.org, and you might like to meet them, too (see overleaf).

As of mid-2010, Kiva has facilitated over $135 million in loans, connecting over 346,000 entrepreneurs with more than 450,000 lenders, and assuring a remarkable 98.57 per cent repayment rate.

Empowering civil society to facilitate action the way Kiva and others do is one of the many ways that low-cost communications technologies are changing the world in which we live. Providing instant access to previously unattainable or severely restricted information is another. The example of Gapminder illustrates this point very well. A free and open online resource, Gapminder is designed to "unveil the beauty of statistics for a fact-based

world view." Want to trace CO_2 emissions since 1820? Concerned with child mortality rates? Gapminder combines good data with easy-to-follow technology and design, serving as one-stop shop for reliable data on a wide range of social and environmental issues.[38]

While the outreach of Kiva.org, Gapminder, and others like them may be limited and narrowly focused, with both organizations hardly reaching the status of a household name, efforts like these have penetrated and influenced the more traditional mass media outlets. As a result, major news providers are now churning out information previously available only via niche or barely known channels. Take, for example, the issue of pollution. Two decades ago, pollution facts for the entire planet were only available through highly specialized outlets, run by nonprofits or international organizations. Fast-forward to the present, and it is *Time* magazine that does the job, publishing feature spreads on topics such as the most polluted places on Earth.

It is precisely the combination of civic activism and low-cost global communications, along with widespread media support, that is creating a new level playing field. If at one time much of a company's social and environmental impacts could go unnoticed, now it is a matter of days, if not hours or even seconds, before their existence in Punta Arenas, Chile, becomes front-page news in Paris, France, or Topeka, Kansas.

Third: the end of us-versus-them

As the movers and shakers of the sustainability movement changed, and the tools of the trade evolved, so did their relationship with business. Long gone are the days of nonprofits that serve only as hotbeds of radical anti-business sentiment. The image of young activists chaining themselves to factory fences or riding shotgun in Zodiac boats as they attack oil rig platforms – only to be telegenically repelled by water cannons – are over. Greenpeace has come a long way since the *Rainbow Warrior*, the retrofitted trawler used to challenge nuclear testing and whaling (which eventually led the French government to dispatch commandoes to sink her in 1985).

In 2010 Greenpeace International announced that it was hiring ForestEthics founder Tzeporah Berman as director of its global climate and energy campaign. Her pro-business views are a sign of a new era in activism. "The notion of activists vs. corporations, of good vs. evil, no longer applies . . . It's about creating dialogue, and finding the solutions that will be mutually beneficial to all."[39] Another prominent NGO, the Environmental Defense Fund (EDF), now uses corporate partnerships as one of its four core strategies. "The environment is our only client," EDF states on its website, "while businesses are our allies in pursuit of common aims."[40]

Financial contributors and nonprofit watchdogs are holding these organizations accountable for constructive results. Shaping the future of markets and positively influencing business behaviors are seen as more desirable outcomes than simply condemning companies to prevent any continued activity.

Fourth: the culture of connectivity

While the decreasing cost of communication and collaboration creates an important technical infrastructure, the emerging culture of connectivity guides what we choose to do with it. Whether it is BlackBerry, Twitter, Facebook, Friendster (popular in South-east Asia), or any other medium, there is no denying that we have come to love – and expect ongoing connection with – the people in our virtual spaces. Writing this book, for example, would have been a difficult and time-consuming project across two continents, if not for the newly available modes of connecting – with chapter titles brainstormed over Skype, conceptual disagreements resolved on BlackBerries between flights, peer reviewers engaged on LinkedIn, and key ideas tested on Facebook.

As we explore the new hyper-connected world in which business, too, must operate, the work of Howard Rheingold serves as a useful reference. In 2002 Rheingold published an exploration of a new techno-cultural wave that allows all of us to be connected to anyone, anywhere, anytime. *Smart Mobs: The Next Social Revolution*[41] makes a striking point about the marriage of two technologies – cell phones and the Internet – which produced an entirely new form of media. What *Smart Mobs* illustrates so well is the emergence of a new change agent – the common man. If the social and environmental heroes of the 20th century were the activists, nonprofit leaders, media, and government heads, the turn of the millennium has seen the new power of a flat world – the collective wisdom of all of us, deeply and instantly connected. In an age where sending an SMS to one's entire address book takes only a few clicks, and viral videos have more impact than carefully orchestrated commercials, it is the connected collective that brings sustainability into every household – and every market.

In light of the many takes on the issue of transparency that we see in the media and public dialogue, let us make one significant distinction. We have repeatedly come across the view that transparency is a choice for companies to consider, a strategy to utilize, or even a competence to build and nurture. While we are delighted to see attention turning to the subject, we are absolutely sure that the radical transparency we observe today is not a choice, but a shared reality, whether executives like it or not. The question is: do we choose to ride the new wave of change on our own terms, or become its victims as the tsunami reaches our shore? That is about as much choice as we have in today's radically transparent world.

It is not surprising, then, that transparency was chosen as the cover topic of the April 2010 issue of the *Harvard Business Review*. Christopher Meyer and Julia Kirby showcase the big difference that radical transparency is making by comparing the recent history of the food industry with a decades-old story of the tobacco industry. It was seemingly yesterday that we all watched the media headlines "outing" tobacco executives' efforts to suppress scientific studies of cigarette health damage. Fast-forward a few decades, and the picture could not possibly be more different: in light of the growing evidence of the health risk of trans fats, many corporations such as Kraft, Nabisco, and Nestlé have decided to reformulate recipes well ahead of regulation.[42]

Another example from the food industry: Dole certified organic bananas now come with a sticker showing a unique "origins" code that allows any interested consumer to verify online exactly where the banana was grown and the organic certifications of its farm facilities.

By going to the Dole Organic Banana website and plugging in the code, the consumer can even "see" the plantation, using Google Earth. Talk about transparency!

Business life in a radically transparent world is a new art to master. Some, like key players of the food industry, are choosing to harness the power of transparency, fostering innovation, customer loyalty, and brand awareness for higher returns. Others may hope that poor social performance will get lost in the overwhelming sea of data, and that they will never have to wake up to scandal, customer de-selection, and a major loss of momentum.

But if there is any doubt about the business risks of trying to hide poor performance, just ask Toyota about its 2010 pedal debacle.

Increasing expectations

If the resource crunch calls into question the security of entire value chains, while transparency opens up every corporate move to instant global scrutiny, the third trend invites companies to rethink the very essence of market demand. Investors, regulators, employees, and, most importantly, customers and consumers increasingly expect sound social and environmental performance from the marketplace, which, in turn, imposes new pressure on companies and creates new opportunities for profit and growth.

The customer rising

In our quest to understand today's market reality, the story of Daniel Lubetzky and the success of his venture, PeaceWorks, is a fine place to start. Created in 1994 as a "not-only-for-profit-company," PeaceWorks produces specialty food, such as vegetable spreads and energy bars, by bringing together buyers and sellers divided by conflict, such as Israelis and Arabs. With significant growth in sales, product portfolio, and distribution network, and ongoing community support, including four consecutive wins of the Fast Company Social Capitalist Award, the company's track record speaks volumes to the new expectations of customers and society at large.[43]

Remarkably, companies such as PeaceWorks, a niche player dependent on premium prices, are not the real story behind the tectonic shift in market demand. The real story is that mainstream customers across an array of markets and geographic areas are increasingly expecting social and environmental performance from the brands, companies, and products they choose. More importantly, they want it without any green or social premium. Mainstream consumers want products that are more affordable, better-performing, healthier, longer-lasting, with added appeal – in other words, it is "smarter" rather than greener or more responsible, that they are after.

Glancing over the statement above, you have every right to ask that nagging question in the back of your mind: can you show me the facts? So, here is a short overview of the data behind our claims: a few words on consumer surveys and what they do (and don't) mean.

- **Consumers appear to say one thing . . .** As early as 2006, a National Consumers League and Fleishman-Hillard survey of U.S. consumers reported the social responsibility of a company as being the number one determining factor of brand loyalty (35 per cent of respondents), well ahead of product price and availability (each receiving 20 per cent of respondents' votes). Four years later it became clear that concerns for the environment were not limited to the consumers from developed economies; the 2010 World Economic Forum report suggested that such concern was as strong in the developing world, "and in some areas stronger as they are often more directly affected, for example water pollution."[44] A recent Deloitte report suggests that, while much of consumer behavior is still dictated by price, quality, and convenience, a whopping 95 per cent of American consumers report that they are willing to "buy green."[45] A BBMG[46] survey that combined a national poll of 2,000 consumers with ethnographic interviews supports the Deloitte findings: nearly seven in ten Americans (67 per cent) agree that "even in tough economic times, it is important to purchase products with social and environmental benefits"

- **. . . but do another!** All of the above surveys – suggesting the existence of the green consumer – are very encouraging, BUT . . . the relatively high level of *interest* in green products does not appear to be backed by *action*. In the Deloitte study, only 10 per cent strongly agree that they are in fact willing to pay more for green. The vast majority of consumers are clearly unwilling to fork over more money at the checkout counter[47]

If sustainability is on the radar screen of consumer expectations, why is it not translating into the opening of wallets in the act of purchase? From a review of consumer studies, we conclude that the gap between stated expectations and the purchase act exists for three reasons.

1. **Perceptions**. A majority of the consumers surveyed perceive green products as more costly, unavailable, and poor in quality when compared with conventional counterparts[48]

2. **Trust**. There is a gap between consumers' interest in green products and their confidence in green marketing claims. According to the BBMG study, nearly one in four U.S. consumers (23 per cent) say

they have "no way of knowing" if a product is green or if it actually does what it claims

3. **Survey language**. Plenty of evidence exists that the very surveys designed to measure consumer expectations are driving the myth of green and social premium. Here is a typical headline: "53 per cent of consumers say they would be willing to pay some type of premium for televisions with green attributes."[49] Who wants to pay a premium, and what is a green attribute anyway? Consumers are presented with two assumptions to digest and accept – sustainability comes at a price and they are getting green benefits or social responsibility in exchange

By contrast, mainstream sustainability leaders are offering competitively priced, smarter products, whether they are Clorox cleaning sprays that are biodegradable and safer for human health or GE hybrid locomotives that save 15 per cent in fuel costs for the CFO of a railroad company. Asking the question, "would you buy a green product?" is very different from offering a smarter product that is priced competitively – one that is higher-quality and better for human health and the environment.

It's no wonder that Walmart sold 190,000 organic cotton yoga outfits in ten weeks[50] on its first try. Once a company dares to debunk the myth of the green and social premium and offer a product with sustainability performance at competitive prices and quality, customers are quick to prefer them over conventional alternatives – providing an often hard-to-imitate advantage in a highly competitive world.

It is clear that consumer expectations are shifting. Yet serving the end consumer is only one part of the deal; increasingly, companies located in the middle of a value chain find the most pressure coming from their direct customers in business-to-business relationships. IBM, Pepsi, IKEA, Ford, and Kaiser Permanente are among those setting new, tougher standards. Procter & Gamble has now come out with its own Supplier Scorecard,[51] after being subjected for several years to Walmart's scorecard as a supplier itself – not particularly unexpected. But we must admit that receiving a letter from a missile manufacturing company, one of our business education clients, explaining the new sustainability demands for all suppliers to the company, was at least mildly surprising.

Customer and consumer expectations go well beyond questions about the *use* of the final product. Fueled by information on declining resources and catalyzed daily by NGOs and consumer activist groups, customers and consumers are demanding a completely new relationship to their providers of products and services. A mere satisfaction with price, quality, and availability is no longer good enough – consumers are expecting to be co-creators in nearly all aspects of business, from product development and manufacturing to packaging and sales. No, they are not eager to compromise on quality and price, but they are ready to pay for smarter solutions featuring embedded ecological and social intelligence.[52] The Trendwatching.com's "10 Crucial Consumer Trends For 2010" put it best:

> Ruthless capitalism went out of fashion way before the crisis hit. This year, prepare for "business as unusual". For the first time, there's a global understanding, if not a feeling of *urgency* that sustainability, in every possible meaning of the word, is the only way forward. How that should or shouldn't impact consumer societies is of course still part of a raging debate, but at least there *is* a debate. Meanwhile, in mature consumer societies, companies will have to do more than just embrace the notion of being a good corporate citizen. To truly prosper, they will have to "move with the culture". This may mean displaying greater transparency and honesty, or having conversations as opposed to one-way advertising, or championing collaboration instead of an us-versus-them mentality.[53]

The monumental shift in customer and consumer expectations can be best described as follows: we are increasingly moving from a focus on green products to offering customer-oriented solutions, and that makes all the difference. Let us conclude "The customer rising" with an example from a completely different domain – fast-moving consumer goods. Imagine you are a company specializing in personal hygiene products, and you are considering the development of a new shampoo. When looked at from a product perspective, a shampoo has very clear and distinct characteristics – it is a liquid substance packaged in a convenient container and used to "lather, rinse, and repeat." Now, what would happen to a shampoo if we look at it from the perspective of a total solution? Lush, a UK-based cosmetics company answered this question by developing a solid shampoo that lathers like you would not believe, and provides a clean hair equivalent of three 250-milliliter bottles. Here is the way a few of the solid shampoos would look on your bathroom shelf:

Produced without plastic packaging (and therefore eliminating all raw material, design, and processing costs related to packaging), the solid shampoo is distributed in bulk and saves tons of shelf space – it would take 15 truckloads of liquid shampoos to deliver the equivalent of one truckload of solids. As such, it is no longer a conventional product, but rather a complex solution that delivers a universe of end benefits to customers, store operators, the manufacturer, and society at large.

Mike Brown, sustainability consultant, captures this change from products to end benefits in the following way:

> The cutting edge, the thing that is getting more traction, is the effort to sell services rather than products. It's a shift in perspective that can transform a business. Companies that are able to turn their business inside out this way find that addressing sustainability issues can change from a burden or cost to an opportunity for efficiency and profit.[54]

One way or another, the customer is rising, opening new doors for those companies ready to move through them.

The employee engaging

While declining resources and radical transparency continue to fuel consumer pressures on business from the outside in, another wave of expectations is pressuring companies from the inside out. This new wave is the employees.

In 1997, McKinsey & Co published the results of a year-long study involving 77 companies and nearly 6,000 managers. The now legendary report predicted a major talent war over 20 years following its publication – whereby all-around intelligent, technologically savvy, globally aware, operationally astute professionals would become a highly fought-over resource.[55] With demand significantly outstripping supply, McKinsey offered four strategies to bring the best professionals on board:

- "Go with the Winner" – attracting those eager to join a high-performing company
- "Big Risk, Big Reward" – appealing to those who crave challenge and risk
- "Lifestyle" – focused on those attracted by a flexible work–life balance and a great quality of life
- "Save the World" – crucial for those driven by an inspiring mission and sense of purpose

Nearly three-quarters of the way through the projected timeline, it is interesting to see if "Save the World" continues to feature among the top "attractors" for potential employees. "Yes, it does!" says Net Impact, an association of sustainability-minded MBAs. Already back in 2006, Net Impact polled 2,100 MBA students in 87 programs in the U.S. and Canada, discovering that nearly 80 per cent of soon-to-be MBAs polled wanted to find socially responsible employment at some point in their careers, while 59 per cent reported they would seek such an opportunity immediately after graduation.[56]

While Net Impact focused on talent in the Western world, Douglas Ready, Linda Hill, and Jay Conger turned their attention to emerging markets. Their 2008 report, featured in the *Harvard Business Review*, suggests four key factors that determine a company's success in attracting the most talented employees:[57] "brand," "opportunity," "culture," and "purpose."

Sounds familiar? Indeed, the 2008 *HBR* report offers many parallels to the 1997 McKinsey survey. These and many other studies[58] are all starting to sing in unison: a company's contribution to making the world a better place features prominently among the distinct factors that determine whether a recruitment effort succeeds or fails. Furthermore, a business commitment to strong social and environmental performance matters even more once the coveted employees are finally recruited. At that point a completely different dimension of employment kicks in: engagement.

Engagement represents, perhaps, the most touchy-feely and fuzzy word in the lexicon of management, so let us offer a brief definition of it. An "engaged employee" is one who "is fully involved in, and enthusiastic about, his or her work, and thus will act in a way that furthers their organization's interests."[59] An estimated $300 billion is lost in the U.S. economy as a result of disengaged employees.[60] In contrast, high engagement has been shown to lead to increased self-efficacy and a nearly one-third increase in work-related performance.[61] For example, engagement studies with data-entry personnel showed a tenfold increase in productivity by engaged employees.[62] Employees that are engaged were also found to have 38 per cent higher probability of success on productivity measures and 44 per cent higher success on customer loyalty and employee retention.[63]

Now, if employee engagement is so important when it comes to company performance, how can we get more of it? Interestingly enough, embedding social and environmental considerations into the company's purpose, strategy, and operations might just be the best way to go. While the exact relationship between company commitment to social and environmental excellence and employee engagement has long been debated, it is only very recently that such a relationship was measured in a scholarly manner, proving that, when employees perceive their company to be a good corporate citizen, their engagement, along with creative involvement and deep, high-quality rela-tionships goes up.[64] Bob Stiller, Chairman of the Board of Green Mountain Coffee Roasters, describes this connection between business sustainability and employee engagement:

> I've learned that people are motivated and more willing to go the extra mile to make the company successful when there's a higher good associated with it. It's no longer just a job. Work becomes meaningful and this makes us more competitive. Everyone real-izes we can't do good unless we're profitable. The two go hand in hand.[65]

Whether we are talking about attraction, retention, or engagement, sus-tainability seems to be the cornerstone of new employee expectations. Moved by the rapidly declining availability of resources, and equipped by instantly available and highly targeted sustainability intelligence, employees are putting forth new demands to business. Some companies are quick to integrate social and environmental performance into their people strategies and policies, thus creating a source of differentiation in a highly competitive talent market. Timberland, ING, and Ford are just a few of thousands of com-panies that offer their teams up to 40 hours paid time-off to volunteer every year. Target goes a step further by sponsoring www.VolunteerMatch.org,[66] which makes it easy for any company to engage its employees or consumers in volunteer efforts; while the youth nonprofit Junior Achievement produces a comprehensive report making a strong business case for offering such ben-efits to employees.[67] But volunteer programs are among the least innovative ways to use a company's sustainability record as a new source of attraction, retention, and engagement of precious talent. A number of other ideas can be considered for your company's "social compensation" package: Burt's Bees calculates bonuses in part on how well the company meets energy conserva-tion goals,[68] which employees and management set together. The offshoot is reduced energy costs, employee engagement and buy-in because they have a hand in setting the energy reduction goal, and, of course, in providing a boon to the environment. The auditing and tax firm KPMG awards 16 service-com-mitted employees with a $1,000 donation for their favorite nonprofit.[69] Gap, Inc. was recently in the news for a series of grants that support employees' philanthropic work.[70] Pepsi takes it further and offers thousands of dollars to fund ideas for a better world submitted by everyone and anyone – and it is the community vote that makes the difference in project selection.[71]

And talent-capture innovations keep rolling in.

The investor calling

From a small fringe in the 1970s to the present-day trillions of dollars in total assets under management,[72] the rise of socially responsible investment (SRI) is remarkable. A broad-based approach to investing that includes screening, shareholder advocacy, and community investing, SRI is perhaps most known for the rapid growth in funds that exclude so-called "sin-stocks" such as tobacco, armaments, and gambling. In some countries, SRI now encompasses 11 per cent of total assets under management[73] – a hefty chunk of the investment market.

Yet it is the other 89 per cent of mainstream investment that is the real news of the day. The amount of attention coming from the "normal" investor is what companies are suddenly becoming attuned to.

The involvement of the mainstream investment community in the field of climate change illustrates the new reality. A highly contested, tension-causing topic, climate change is hardly one to incite "save-the-world" action and "Kumbaya" singing from the gray pinstripe universe of finance. Yet it is the investment community represented by the Ceres Investor Network on Climate Risk (INCR) that so proudly reported a record 95 climate change-related shareholder resolutions filed by March 2010, a whopping 40 per cent increase over the previous year's proxy period.[74] Uniting asset managers, state and city treasurers and comptrollers, public and labor pension funds, and other institutional investors, the U.S.-based INCR represents an investor group with nearly $10 trillion in assets. INCR's UK counterpart, the Carbon Disclosure Project, acts on behalf of 475 investors representing total assets of $55 trillion – and uses its power to force the world's largest publicly traded companies to disclose their emissions. In 2009, 409 out of 500 largest companies responded to Carbon Disclosure Project's request, up from 383 in the previous year. While France, Germany, Japan, the UK, and the U.S. represent 70 per cent of the total emissions disclosed, the response rate from the BRIC countries has doubled since 2008 to 44 per cent, with Brazil reaching a 100 per cent response rate.[75]

The efforts of investors are heavily influenced by the insurance industry, which might just be the most important driver of the new-found affection of business for climate change action. Imagine that you are a U.S.-based insurer, reviewing the following statistic: American insurers . . .

> . . . have experienced growth in weather-related catastrophe losses from levels of about $1 billion per year in the 1970s to an average of $17 billion per year over the past decade, far out-stripping growth in premiums, populations, and inflation during the same period.[76]

What action will you take?

While you are catching your breath, here is the Allstate response: run! In 2005, Allstate refused to renew policies with 95,000 homeowners and 16,000 commercial property owners in Florida. Allstate CEO Ed Liddy made the logic behind the decision painfully clear: "We are girding for the onslaught of the next hurricane season. What's new is the intensity of this (storm) cycle could be a lot worse than things that we've seen before."[77] If the insurers are running, no wonder that investors are calling, and as the spread of such guidelines as the Equator Principles illustrates, climate change is only one of many environmental and social concerns on the investors' agenda. These Principles, launched in 2003 with the first ten global financial institutions – ABN AMRO Bank N.V., Barclays plc, Citigroup Inc., Crédit Lyonnais, Credit Suisse First Boston, HVB Group, Rabobank Group, The Royal Bank of Scotland, WestLB AG, and Westpac Banking Corporation – offer standards for determining, assessing, and managing social and environmental risk in project financing. Seventy global players signed on to the Equator Principles in the first six years of its existence.[78]

For some, rising investor expectations can be a tough pill to swallow, but others are quick to leverage outstanding social and environmental performance as a way to attract new capital. Intermediaries are also taking notice – connecting the socially and environmentally savvy investors with top performers – and making money on it.

The regulator acting

In 2008, China launched a surprise crackdown on plastic bags, banning outright the production of some designs and forbidding shops from handing out free bags.[79] This was only a year after San Francisco became the first U.S. city to ban plastic bags in supermarkets.[80] Also in 2008, Calgary became the first city in Canada to make trans fats from restaurants and fast food chains illegal,[81] while the Brazilian state of Mato Grosso became the first Latin American state to pass a WEEE bill,[82] focused specifically on electronic waste prevention. In 2009, the U.S. National Association of Insurance Commissioners made climate change risk disclosure mandatory for all insurance companies with annual policies over $500 million.[83] In 2010, the UK launched its first mandatory carbon trading scheme, initially called the Carbon Reduction Commitment, and later renamed the CRC Energy Efficiency Scheme.[84] Also in a single month in 2010, South Africa passed 47 amendments and extensions to its sustainability legislation and regulation,[85] ranging from chemical management to atmospheric emissions to fertilizers and everything in between.

The data speaks for itself here, but let us try to make the point even more explicit: whether it is an act of leadership or a desperate reaction to the pressures of NGOs and activist voters, governments are taking social and environmental issues to heart, adding new laws and regulations to the pressures shaping the business environment. The question is: will your company ride the wave of legislative changes to get ahead of the curve, or wait until the waters drag it under?

By all accounts, the Whirlpool Corporation is keeping its head above water (no pun intended) while making the government a close friend and ally. A maker of household appliances, the company has been consistently preparing ever-stricter regulations – demanding higher energy and water efficiency – and receives government support for its pro-sustainability research and development efforts. In 2009, Whirlpool received a $19.3 million grant from the U.S. stimulus project to develop "smart appliances" with the ability to communicate with the grid, cutting the energy use during peak hours and going full steam during the low-demand periods. But it is not just future products that give the appliance maker an advantage via its relationship with new pro-sustainability regulation: in the same year, Whirlpool launched a comprehensive "Cash for Appliances" website[86] to help American consumers get reimbursed by the U.S. Department of Energy.[87]

Could it be that compliance is simply no longer enough? Is it time to readjust business attitudes to speed up (rather than slow down) sustainability regulation?

Whether it is customers, employees, investors, regulators, or society at large pushing for change, the expectations of business are going up rapidly. As the decline of resources continues to take center stage in an increasingly transparent world, sustainability is rapidly becoming a must – a new standard for business to follow, reach, and exceed.

Pieces of the puzzle

Fit them together, and it is remarkable to see how the three trends of **declining resources**, **radical transparency**, and **increasing expectations** are redefining the way business creates value. While only a decade ago concerns for society and environment would have been happily assigned to the environmental, health, and safety (EH&S) department, or prominently featured in the corporate social responsibility (CSR) report and managed by a public relations team, today they are every line manager's concern. Product design, research and development, operations, procurement, marketing, sales, logistics, finance – it is hard to find a domain of business spared the effects of changes in the external environment.

As the three trends are deeply interconnected and interdependent, they form a perfect puzzle with each piece impacting the bigger picture. Here is one way to visualize the three trends fitting together:

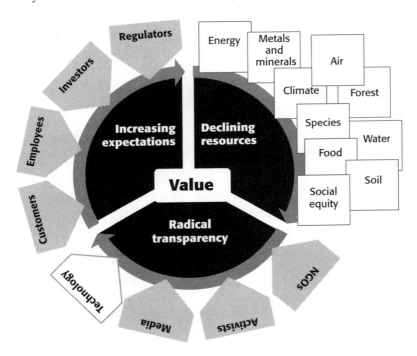

Declining resources refers to the overuse and in some cases exhaustion of resources such as fossil fuels, metals and minerals, topsoil, freshwater, clean air, rain forests, species diversity, and natural habitats. By some measures, 60 per cent of the planet's ecosystem services that provide us with climate regulation, freshwater, clean air, fertile soil, and food have already been degraded or are being used unsustainably. Even for contested resources such as oil, where the debate continues about how much remains, there can be no doubt that we are consuming it much faster than nature is able to replenish it. Regime stability and public security can also be considered declining resources given rising social inequity (such as the growth in the rich–poor gap) and social injustice.

Radical transparency is the ability to fully, accurately, and instantly obtain information about a company or product at any stage of its life cycle, from raw material extraction to product end-of-life. There is a **technological component** based on virtual communication tools that make it possible for anyone anywhere to "see" into a company or product. There is also a **behavioral component** coming from rising awareness of ecological and social issues. Greater awareness is leading to the desire by consumers, investors, and employees to know how companies and products are impacting the world around them.

Increasing expectations – by consumers, investors, employees, and other constituents of business – are transforming market demand by introducing new performance parameters such as quiet, healthy, socially equitable, or environmentally friendly for every product and service in every sector of the economy. We don't want just any household cleaning product; it must be nontoxic and biodegradable. We drink fair-trade coffee and bring reusable shopping bags to the supermarket. And we no longer accept to pay more for green and socially responsible products.

Value is at the center of the puzzle – and not by accident. Rising ecological and social pressures no longer represent what economists call externalities – the positive and negative by-products of company operations that can be neglected in making business decisions. Sustainability impacts are moving inside the boundaries of the marketplace – whether we like it or not – posing questions that companies have never had to answer before.

Consider, for example, the impact of declining resources, radical transparency, and increasing expectations on a company serving your needs this very second: the furniture business. Barely a few decades ago, the producer of the chair you sit on made decisions about the product design, raw materials, productions, packaging, distribution, and use with little, if any, consideration for social and environmental sustainability. Now, the same producer is faced with dilemmas of a totally new kind. Will the materials chosen continue to be available at an acceptable price? Are there toxic materials and are they on a shortlist for being boycotted by customers? Are the major suppliers utilizing child labor or any other unfair labor practices? What about the weight of the chair – is there room to improve transportation costs? What is the amount of water and electricity used in the production of each chair and is the level comparable to that used by competitors? And what happens to the chair once the customer is done with it – can its materials be utilized again, or will it find itself in a dreaded landfill, photographed by random nonprofit organizations searching for new symbols of our consumption-driven, over-polluted world?

In contrast to this fear-of-being-seen-as-harmful furniture company, consider a new breed of company that focuses instead on the opportunity to be seen as doing good. Aptly named A Piece of Cleveland (APOC), this player designs and constructs quality furnishings and accessories out of materials reclaimed from deconstructed buildings in the Cleveland area. It works to preserve the history of the city and its buildings by salvaging constructed materials and then turning them around as functional products that tell a story.[88] In essence, APOC transforms declining resources, radical transparency, and rising expectations from threats into opportunity, a harbinger of things to come.

Like many other examples shared throughout this chapter, APOC is giving us insight into a new story, still largely invisible, of the BIG three trends and how they are reshaping business.

Now take a look at the following pair of business shoes and the accompanying tag:

What you see in front of you is what 16,600 liters (the amount of water in a family-size swimming pool 4 feet high by 15 feet wide) looks like when embodied in the leather required to manufacture the two shoes.[89] As the security of freshwater supply comes under question, a radically transparent world makes it painfully visible – and actionable – for the whole world. Multiple sources, such as Hydrolosophy, a start-up run by a Harvard grad student,[90] already provide data on product water footprints, and it is clear that the day when all products feature a mandatory water footprint label is not far ahead. In world of declining resources, radical transparency, and increasing expectations, a simple sticker might just be the factor that makes or breaks your ability to compete.

To the story of water we add one more – the story of stuff. Sourcemap.org is an online open-source collaboration platform that fosters greater transparency in supply chains and life cycle assessments.[91] This very second, you and any other person in the world can go to the Sourcemap.org website, and see exactly where the IKEA Sultan Alsarp bed comes from, and what kind of environmental impact its ingredients have along the way. In a matter of a few clicks, you will see that in the making of one bed, 10 kilos of Polish-made indoor plywood are used, with 130.28 kg of CO_2 embedded in plywood production. Galvanized steel from Russia (39.6 kg of CO_2), cotton fabric from Africa (3.5 kg of CO_2), particle board from China (37.6 kg of CO_2) . . . the data is waiting at your fingertips.

Reproduced with permission from Sourcemap.org. This map added by jeremyjih.

A symbol of the times, Sourcemap.org will be seen by some companies as the unfair convergence of risks in a resource-hungry, transparent, and demanding world. Yet we are convinced that open-source collaboration efforts of this kind are a powerful signal of the new ways in which companies will achieve profit and growth.

Never before have the boundaries of the corporation been so clearly under siege. Tomorrow's business solutions and competencies lie outside the organization's walls. You can try to address strategic issues behind closed doors, and make every attempt to control information flows and solution development. Or you can take the new reality as a business opportunity, and use the power of collective open-source innovation to solve the toughest business challenges your company is facing. After all, some of Sourcemap. org's business users already use the site to help calculate the ideal location for international meetings and to help visualize the flow of money, resources, and ideas as their influence spreads across the world.

In summary

Three interconnected and interdependent trends – **decreasing resources**, **radical transparency**, and **increasing expectations** – are redefining the way business is creating value. The linear throwaway economy in which products and services follow a one-way trajectory, from extraction to use and trash, can no longer be supported by the Earth's natural carrying capacity. Consumers, employees, investors, and society at large are beginning to demand socially and environmentally savvy products and services without compromise on price or quality. Radical transparency, fueled by the growth of the nonprofit sector and supported by evolving technologies, makes both trends ever more present in the public eye, and, therefore, ever more present in the marketplace.

With the new reality upon us, what is business to do? How should it handle these changes? What is the best strategy for *your* business? In the following pages, we invite you to join us on a journey in search of answers, beginning with a review of some of the best-known strategy theories in existence. Building on the many discoveries we made along the way, a clean and clear path forward is emerging – one that offers a better response to a radically different game. That path is *Embedded Sustainability*.

But we are getting ahead of ourselves. Before we delve too far into the "what," "how," "who," and "when" of embedded sustainability, let us take a look at the history of the turbulent relationship between business and society, so that we can build on solid foundations.

2
To the desert and back
A brief history of value

It is 8:28 in the morning, and every seat is full for a business class at a well-known university. We are here for an advanced seminar for the soon-to-be graduates. Our gracious host, a professor of finance, announces the agenda for the day: "Today, we have a very special guest lecture. Our topic is business in society. The goal is a deeper understanding – and readiness – for the many social and environmental issues you will face as tomorrow's leaders."

Barely a second later, a hand is already up.

> With all due respect [says the eager student in the third row], I would hate for us to waste a whole hour here. Don't you think that social and environmental challenges are for government and non-profits to solve? After all, we . . . I mean the private sector already has its hands full with creating business value. Isn't that enough?

If nothing else, their punctuality and impatience should have given them away. Yes, we have a room full of future C-suite executives, high-financiers, and business unit managers, all channeling the Nobel prize-winning economist Milton Friedman.

Five hours later, the second section of the seminar is due to start. The room is barely half full, with recently woken faces slowly trickling in. Six minutes after the announced start time, the last student nearly falls into her seat, a giant-size coffee mug gripped in her hands.

Before the formal introduction, our host confides in a somewhat apologetic tone: "As you can guess, the timing of our second section attracts art history, pre-med, political science, and a few undecided majors." After an hour of corporate bashing and anti-globalization rants, the class gets serious and plans a campaign of online boycotts. Our coffee-loving friend is leading the attack: "We've had enough of speculation and using and abusing. It's time for business to go back to its roots and do something valuable for the planet." Somewhere above, Karl Marx is smiling.

And so we have it, the decades-old battle, re-enacted. At the center of the debate is a simple question: what is the role and purpose of business in society?

Surprisingly, when it comes to the essence of the matter, all parties are in violent agreement. Business is there to create value, and more of it. But, as is often the case, the problem lies in the meaning of the word.

Ask a group of managers anywhere in the world what is their definition of value, and the answers will come with astonishing speed and predictability: the business of business is to create *shareholder value.*

If you ask the same group of managers to dig a little deeper, a few of them will begin to speak in terms of *solutions* the company creates to solve particular client problems, whether the client is internal or external. The serious engineer will talk nuts and bolts, the operations manager will bring up the new IT system, while the brand manager touts next season's product line-up. Products, services, and processes – the many solutions developed by the company – add up to its value created.

And then there is the third dimension of value, perhaps less visible to the typical manager: value as a set of *end benefits and outcomes* for customers, consumers, employees, and other key constituencies – whether in the form of a product's functionality and aesthetics, or jobs, or something even less tangible. Charles Revson, the founder of Revlon Cosmetics, offered a perfect illustration of such intangible end benefit: "In the factories we manufacture cosmetics, but in the stores we sell hope."[92]

Naturally, the three dimensions of value are parts of an integrated whole. Value created by an architecture firm can be understood in terms of the returns it generates for its owners (shareholder value), the building spaces it designs (solution), and the comfort, functionality, efficiency, and safety it provides (end benefits and outcomes) – the same kind of triad any other company generates. Yet, throughout history, perceptions of the relative importance of each of the three dimensions have varied significantly, changing the relationship between business and the rest of society. While an exhaustive historical retrospective is beyond our quest, a brief look at the past is needed to better understand the capitalism of today and the forces currently driving sustainability agendas in the private sector. And thus we travel back in time to uncover where business came from and where it is going, zooming in on the many different ways business has related to its social and environmental context over time. Value is what stands at the very center of this relationship.

Barely ten generations ago: marriage

Fly back in time – say to just before the year 1800 – and you will find corporations big and small being an important but relatively small part of a diverse economic system of farmers, tradesmen, merchants, guilds, and village markets all woven into the fabric of society.[93] "Capitalism in the past (as distinct from capitalism today) only occupied a narrow platform of economic life,"[94] writes the historian Fernand Braudel about the 16th to 18th centuries. Another historian[95] describes all industrial activity during this period as falling into one of four categories: (a) the tiny family workshops, countless in number and grouped into clusters, each with a master tradesman, two or three journeymen and one or two apprentices; (b) workshops that were scattered but connected to each other; (c) "concentrated manufacture" which included water-operated forges, breweries, tanneries, and glassworks;[96] and (d) factories equipped with machinery and using energy sources such as running water and steam.

Only business activity in the last two categories can be compared in ownership or structure to the modern-day corporation. The family workshops and the interconnected network (which had merchant entrepreneurs who acted as go-betweens, for example in textile production, coordinating the flow of materials from spinner to weaver to dyer to shearer and receiving a profit for their trouble) would have been a common scene of the day. In each of the four categories, families played a major role and patriarchal systems of management were widespread. Outside of Europe, the first two categories represented an even higher proportion of activity. More concentrated forms of manufacture were exceptional.

In essence, pre-19th century, industry and the corporation were minor elements of a richly diverse economic life, "barely distinguishable from the omnipresent agricultural life which ran alongside it and sometimes submerged it."[97] Deeply interwoven into the fabric of the local community, the corporation served tangible human needs. The value created, therefore, was first and foremost understood in terms of the real and concrete end benefits and outcomes created for customers, while the other two dimensions were derived from and built on this primary purpose.[98] The end benefits and needs of society guided the life of the corporation, with the products changing to meet the needs, and shareholder value emerging as the top of the pyramid resting on a solid and far-reaching foundation. Here is the way value might have looked ten generations ago:

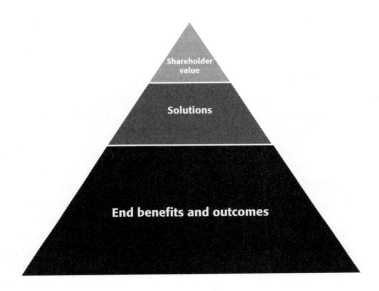

With this attention paid to end benefits and outcomes, it is not surprising to find the early language of business reflecting the role of trade, production, and profit in the larger schema of life. The ancient Swedish term for business is *narings liv*, which literally means "nourishment for life."[99] The Russian word *delo*, traditionally used to signify business, means "purpose" or "calling."[100] Even the English word *business*, which has come a long way from its relatively rare appearances in the early 1700s[101] to near universal usage today, derives its meaning from *bisig*, which means "careful," "anxious," "busy," and "occupied".[102]

In addition to the deep interconnectedness and embeddedness of business in society, the marketplace leading up to the Industrial Revolution was simultaneously transparent and obscure by today's standards. A historian of the 16th to 18th centuries spoke about this reality in the following way: "The economy was a world of transparence and regularity, in which everyone could be sure in advance, with the benefit of common experience, how the processes of exchange would operate."[103] The town marketplace (or country fair) dominated economic life, and in such markets goods were exchanged "on the spot" for money or barter – allowing both consumers and producers to see what they were getting in the moment of the transaction. This was also the case in retail shops until much later in the 20th century. The speculative economy, based on investing in shares of publicly held companies, was almost unknown; the idea of using supercomputers for nanosecond decisions would have come across as pure witchcraft.

Sounds a bit idealistic, doesn't it? Before we go overboard with romanticizing the past, let us add a few sobering details about pre-1800 capitalism.

Labor conditions and human rights were terrible . . .

There is no question that back then social expectations were relatively basic and unsophisticated by today's standards. Child labor in inhuman conditions was a regular feature of industry and commerce – remember the painful story of Oliver Twist, one of the most memorable characters of Charles Dickens? Before the 1900s, tens of thousands of Oliver Twists were working throughout the so-called civilized world. Machine-made bonnets and lace-making in the French city of Caen, for example, "consisted . . . of nothing more or less than the establishment of a number of training schools using child labor."[104] However, there was little social resistance to these practices until the 20th century – in other words, child labor was expected if not demanded by society. The Factory and Workshop Acts were passed initially to limit the hours of employment for women and children in the textile industry. Until then, a young child pulling a coal tub might have been a normal scene in the middle of the 18th century:

. . . transparency was rudimentary

While the market was more closely ruled by the sway of daily life, compared to today, technology and socio-ecological awareness were vastly more rudimentary. Information traveled slowly, whether about prices or supply and demand. The desire to know the social and ecological impacts of a given product or company barely existed. Thus, the origins of a product's raw materials and labor conditions involved in its production could not be easily known even in the unlikely event that someone wished to know such things. In this sense, markets were far less transparent than they are today.

... but environmental damage was largely limited

In the days of early capitalism, human-caused environmental disasters were rather rare. Yes, indeed, examples such as the soil erosion and deforestation of Easter Island in the 18th century, documented by scientist and author Jared Diamond in *Collapse*,[105] could be found. However, before the start of the 19th century, issues of natural resource scarcity were local rather than global in nature.

Environmental disasters were localized and temporary. Humans did not affect society or the Earth at the level of the whole – not surprising given that the world's population totaled less than 1 billion in 1800,[106] about a seventh of what it is today. The great majority lived lives of poverty with only limited access to resource-intensive lifestyles. If we think in terms of the IPAT equation[107] – Impact = Population × Affluence × Technology – all three independent variables were many times smaller than they are today, so that their multiplied impact was orders of magnitude less.

Harvard Business Review authors Chris Meyer and Julia Kirby illustrate the point:

> When the Eureka Iron Works, the first Bessemer steel mill, opened in 1854 in Wyandotte, Michigan, it probably wasn't very clean. But however inefficient it was, a single furnace wasn't going to have much effect on the earth's atmosphere ... One recent analysis shows that before 1850, global carbon emissions from fossil fuels were negligible, but by 1925 the figure had reached a billion metric tons per year. By 1950, the amount had doubled. By 2005, it had doubled twice more, to 8 billion. Simply put, commercial activity has [now] achieved planetary scale.[108]

Of course back then, sudden shortages in essential foods and materials occurred on a regular basis, leading to famine or simply exorbitant prices depending on the case. Wheat, sugar, wine, cotton, grain, wood, silver, gold, and many other commodities were transported long distances according to where they were produced in abundance and where demand yielded the highest prices. "Wheat ... travelled as little as possible, in the sense that it was grown everywhere. But if a bad harvest meant that it was in short supply for any length of time, it might be sent on very long journeys."[109] Being interconnected, however, was not the same as being in an increasingly fragile and interdependent global market. So, how did we get from there to here, finding ourselves confused and disoriented in the face of rapidly declining resources, radical transparency, and immense and rising expectations?

The intervening generations: a tale of divorce

We started our time travel with a visit to the pre-industrial world in which business and society were so interconnected as to be indistinguishable or at least difficult to disentangle from each other. It is time for us to move into the 19th and 20th centuries, when the corporation slowly acquired a distinct stature, separate from the rest of society and increasingly focused in on itself.

Modern-day corporations were invented at the end of the 16th century as a mechanism for managing colonial trade[110] – and early on they were a product of European governments, limited in scope and importance. After 1800 the corporation became a self-contained system of consumers, producers, and transactions and acquired its own set of legal rights and its own "science of management." Renowned economist and activist David Korten follows this transformation in his seminal work *When Corporations Rule the World*: "step-by-step, the court system put in place new precedents that made the protection of corporations and corporate property as a centre-piece of constitutional law."[111] By the early 1900s, the corporation is cynically defined by Ambrose Bierce as "an ingenious device for obtaining individual profit without individual responsibility."[112] Its single-minded purpose is to create wealth for its shareholders: an idea that continues to grow until Nobel prize-winning economist Milton Friedman was able to write in 1970 that "there is one and only one social responsibility of business – to use its resources and engage in activities designed to increase its profits."[113] Advocates of the shareholder value approach, led by outstanding thinkers such as Alfred Rappaport,[114] produced powerful algorithms for creating shareholder value as the strict measure of corporate performance.

And thus, a new perception of business value firmly took hold as the axiom to be built into every decision and action. Shareholder value came to rule the day, financial targets were translated into product portfolios, with end benefits and outcomes to consumers almost a secondary consideration. Value took on an entirely new shape, divorcing business from the rest of society:

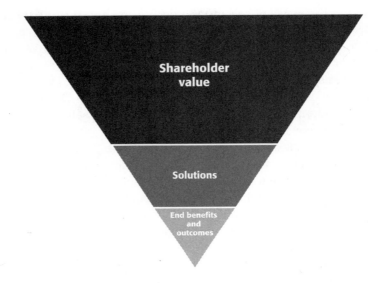

In the heat of the corporate social responsibility debates of the 1960s and 1970s, Greenpeace and Friends of the Earth were founded. These were the vanguards of a much wider nonprofit movement dedicated to reuniting business and the world – or at least to limiting the damage of wayward corporations. Remarkably, Adam Smith – rather than Karl Marx – could serve as an inspiration for the work of these activists. Already in the late 1700s, Adam Smith held the eerily prescient view that the shareholder-controlled corporation (in contrast to the partnership corporations in which the owner–manager relationship is continuous and closely interlinked) is a recipe for profit-taking at the expense of the greater good. For Adam Smith, who was first and foremost a moral philosopher, corporations such as the powerful East India Company exemplified the inevitable antisocial behavior of unchecked corporate monopoly and power. Along with civil society, environmental regulations and laws began to grow exponentially. In the U.S., the year 1970 marked the establishment of the Environmental Protection Agency as well as the passing of the Clean Air Act, following which federal and state environmental regulations multiplied rapidly.

Zooming forward to the 1980s, business became ever more freed from government regulation. Corporations continued to focus on "faster, better, and cheaper" with little regard to externalities being foisted on society. The axiom of shareholder value maximization was soon the first lesson of every self-respecting MBA program, but small, subtle indicators suggested that all was not perfect in paradise. With the vast majority of managers spending their days on profit maximization, or at best product delivery, some companies grew blind to the needs of society, and deaf to the benefits and outcomes sought by more savvy consumers. The music industry is a perfect – and very recent – illustration of this ongoing shareholder value blindness. With profit maximization as the primary concern, the industry failed to notice that traditional CD-based music albums no longer represented the best way to deliver end benefits to customers. The result: a dramatic fall of CD sales[115] and a chance to watch Apple build its product strategy on a solid foundation of well-understood consumer needs.

Throughout the 1980s, the market demand for more attention to the needs, outcomes, and end benefits for society and nature continued to grow, giving stakeholders more influence in the value equation. In 1983, Edward Freeman and David Reed published their now classic article,[116] inviting corporations to revisit the 1963 idea of stakeholders – the many groups that have a stake in the action of the enterprise. The corporation is reimagined not as "the instrument of shareholders, but as a coalition between various resource suppliers, with the intention of increasing their common wealth."[117]

Also in the 1980s, perhaps in reaction to the increasingly cavalier attitude of the Wall Streets of the world, the U.N.-sponsored Brundtland Commission provided the first widely recognized definition of sustainability.[118] With its emphasis on meeting the needs of the present without detracting from the opportunities of future generations, the Brundtland definition set a clear moral compass but failed to provide any practical guidelines on how business should reconcile its fiduciary responsibility to shareholders with its newfound responsibilities to people and planet.

In the 1990s, the triple bottom line became popular, with its widely used visual of three overlapping circles showing three sets of targets – people, profit, and planet. Yet it is the disparity – rather than overlap – that took the center stage of the decade. A plethora of thinkers – including Peter Drucker,[119] Tom Cannon,[120] Ada Demb and F.-Friedrich Neubauer,[121] Masaru Yoshimori,[122] and many others – spoke loudly to the tension and contradictions between profitability and responsibility. Value created for society was firmly held in opposition to the value created for business; the great trade-off became seen as an immutable reality. In November of 1999, the world woke up to the breaking news of the massive Seattle anti-globalization protests. Business was not just temporarily separated from society; the two were widely considered to be battling "irreconcilable differences."

Today's generation: reconciliation

By the end of the 20th century, business and the rest of society reached a peak of conflict in its troubled relationship. Yet, alongside the conflict, small, timid sprouts of reconciliation were beginning to take root.

As we zoom closer to the year 2000, a number of voices began to question the necessity of a trade-off between business profit and social good. Business associations and corporate movements for social responsibility were budding around the globe: Business for Social Responsibility emerged in 1992, the New Academy of Business launched in 1996, and the same year gave birth to CSR Europe, while 1999 saw the emergence of the United Nations Global Compact. Scholarly attention to the topic did not lag far behind: in 1997, Stuart Hart won the McKinsey Award for Best Paper for the seminal *Harvard Business Review* piece titled "Beyond Greening: Strategies for a Sustainable World,"[123] while specialized outlets, such as the *Journal of Corporate Citizenship* as well as *Ethical Corporation* magazine, were launched in 2001 alongside a number of book publishers focusing on social and environmental issues in the private sector.[124] At the center of attention (in both theory and practice) was the question of the business case: is it possible to find a commercial rationale for the social and environmental efforts of the firm? Yes, according to a number of studies with colorful titles clearly aimed at the business mainstream: the UN Global Compact's *Who Cares Wins*;[125] a private consultancy SustainAbility advertised *Buried Treasure*;[126] while the International Finance Corporation co-authored *Developing Value: The Business Case for Sustainability in Emergent Markets*.[127] Following these calls to action, an increasing number of mainstream companies began to experiment with environmental and social policies designed to contribute to shareholder value, with a focus on eco-efficiency and worker safety, while a ghetto of sustainability champions toiled in isolation. Although it was a fragmented and reactive approach to social and environmental issues, a new era for business in society was in the works.

Through the 2000s, the rapid and universal decline of resources became increasingly visible and tangible throughout the world. With global-stage events such as Katrina, the much ballyhooed IPCC reports on climate change, and Walmart's conversion to environmental sustainability, the world began to take notice, placing new expectations and demanding new outcomes from business. Radical transparency fueled the pressure, with customers leading the way. The three dimensions of value were re-envisioned once again:

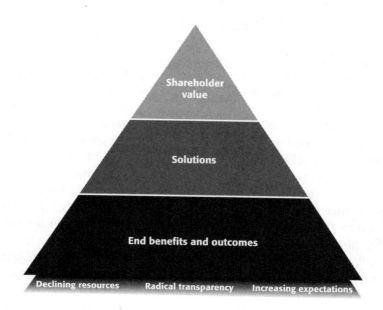

As social and environmental pressures penetrated every aspect of business reality, the assumption of a trade-off between shareholder value and stakeholder value was increasingly questioned. By mid-decade, a provocative question fundamentally challenged the necessity of war between business and the rest of society: could it be that the only way to create *sustainable value* is to find a way to satisfy both?[128]

A number of early pioneers experimented with the answer to this question – Nestlé's *Shared Value* report as well as BMW's *Sustainable Value* report are just two publications of such efforts. Yet the vast majority of corporations were keeping busy with business as usual. Even worse, in the run-up to the stock market collapse of 2008, a "casino economy" grew out of all reasonable proportion. Leading up to that year, speculative and leveraged transactions through derivatives totaled 15 times the world economic output of about €30 trillion. Bad debt and toxic assets were securitized and sold to unsuspecting investors around the world. Financial decisions privileged the very short term at a cost to healthy companies and healthy economies.

Recognizing the need to manage the monumental risks posed by sustainability pressures, it was business that took up the call to action. In November 2008, General Electric CEO Jeffrey Immelt called for a "total re-set,"[129] arguing that the economic crisis only adds urgency to the pursuit of sustainability,[130] while Walmart CEO Mike Duke made a similar argument[131] to his employees in 2009. In 2010, Renault/Nissan's CEO Carlos Ghosn made the business case[132] for investing $6 billion in electric cars because of climate change and energy security considerations. In the United States, the Obama administration's framing of "green" in terms of economic growth and jobs added further appeal in the mainstream business community. Not surprisingly, the mantra of "total re-set" was echoed by ecologists concerned about the biosphere itself.

And so you have it, a brief history of value, re-enacted. We have been to the desert and back, through divorce and reconciliation, emerging at the other end of the journey with a renewed vision of sustainable business in a more sustainable world:

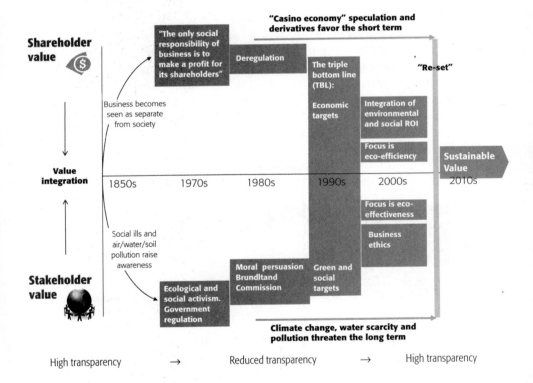

The vision of *sustainable value* offers a compelling challenge to business. There is no question that the big three trends of declining resources, radical transparency, and increasing expectation will continue to reinvent the rules of business. Yet it is equally clear that the principles that have guided corporations for centuries need to be respected and followed.

And so we are left with the question: what exactly is sustainable value and how is it different from the shareholder value perspective and the stakeholder value view of the firm? Is it some sort of compromise – a balancing of interests – or is it something else entirely?

The meaning of sustainable value

Sustainable value – which we defined previously[133] as a dynamic state that occurs when a company creates ongoing value for its shareholders and stakeholders – is a natural outcome of the new external environment. Responding profitably to the diverse needs of such groups as employees, local communities, nonprofits, customers, and others who have a 'stake' in the destiny of the company offers a vision of business in society that is new but not unprecedented in history. More importantly for managers, it is fast becoming indispensable to achieving and maintaining competitive advantage.

A good way to understand sustainable value is to think about it visually. We first pictured sustainable value nearly ten years ago, as shown here. (Every consultant worth his salt has a 2 × 2 matrix in his repertoire, so you will not be surprised to see us with one.)

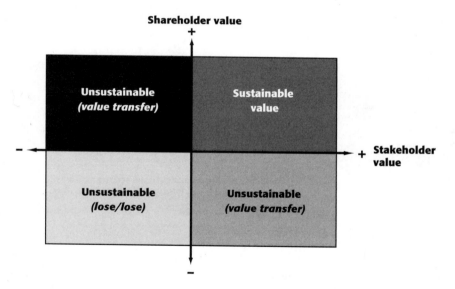

From *The Sustainable Company* (Figure 11-3), by Chris Laszlo. Copyright © 2003 Chris Laszlo. Reproduced by permission of Island Press, Washington, D.C.

Managing in two – rather than one – dimensions represents a fundamental shift in how managers think about value. In a nutshell, companies that deliver value to shareholders while destroying value for stakeholders are building a precarious house of cards, just like those who attempt to "do good" for society and the environment without producing an acceptable market rate of return for their owners. Companies that destroy value in both dimensions (bottom left) rapidly cease to exist, and we will not say anything further about them. Those that create value for both shareholders and stakeholders (upper right) are taking advantage of the new external market reality which creates "pay-offs" for companies who know how to respond to rising sustainability pressures. Satisfying demands of both shareholders and stakeholders is driven by innovation, which in turn leads to reducing costs, differentiating products, growing intangible assets, shaping advantageous "rules of the game," and much more. Yet the coveted prize of sustainable value comes with its own set of unusual rules and dynamics. Value migration is the first on the list.

Value migration

Using the four squares of the sustainable value framework, it is easy to locate any product or company and to visualize its trajectory over time. Take a product and try to place it on the grid at different point of times – say 20 years ago versus 10 years ago versus the present moment – and it quickly becomes evident that the big three trends of declining resources, radical transparency, and increasing expectations are "shifting left" products and business units. A profitable baby bottle or insurance policy that is perceived as creating stakeholder value today (the upper right square) might be seen as destroying stakeholder value five years from now (the upper left square), as new information surfaces about its environmental, health, and social impacts, and as expectations rise for its sustainability performance.

IKEA stopped selling incandescent light bulbs in 2010 because these bulbs are energy hogs,[134] compared with new technologies such as CFLs and LEDs. In today's environment, the perception of wasting electricity and of being bad for the environment are what matters, rather than the price of electricity which, although volatile, has not increased enough to make incandescent bulbs uneconomical.[135]

Gas-guzzling SUVs, toxic household cleaners, baby bottles containing the plasticizer bisphenol A (BPA), and plastic shopping bags are further examples of products for which profitable demand still exists but which are now associated with stakeholder value destruction. This, in turn, is leading to shareholder value destruction in a marketplace that no longer tolerates unbridled harm to society and nature. Consider the value path of these five products over the last quarter of a century. Twenty-five years ago these products were all seen as value creating for both business and society (point A).

The 25-year value path of gas-guzzling SUVs, toxic cleaning products, baby bottles with BPA, plastic bags and incandescent bulbs

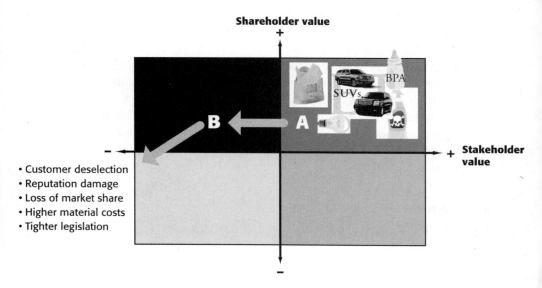

Over this period, all five products came to be seen as harmful to stakeholders (point B) even though the activities of producing, distributing, and using these products had not changed. In fact, in most cases, the products had become less harmful in absolute terms (for example, the category "light trucks" in the U.S. actually improved in terms of fuel economy between 1981 and 2003[136]).

Value transfer (1): Shareholder value +, Stakeholder value −

Carbon dioxide emissions from coal-fired power plants, phthalates in cosmetics, toxic additives in children's toys, volatile organic compounds in carpet adhesives and paints, heavy metals in fabric dyes, and lead solder and brominated flame retardants in consumer electronics are among the many (and growing number) of products that destroy value for stakeholders even while they create value for shareholders. Also in the upper left square are companies that create shareholder value through cost-cutting measures that lead to avoiding overtime pay, under-training on employee safety, or discriminating on the basis of gender and ethnic background. Shareholder value in these cases is created "on the backs" of one or more stakeholder groups, thereby representing a value transfer rather than true value creation.

Value transfer (2): Shareholder value −, Stakeholder value +
When value is transferred from shareholders to stakeholders, the company incurs a fiduciary liability to its shareholders. Actions intended to create stakeholder value that destroy shareholder value put the company's viability into question. Environmentalists often unintentionally pressure companies to take actions in this square without realizing that the pursuit of activities that generate losses is not sustainable either. It is interesting to note that philanthropy, when it is unrelated to business interests and represents pure charity, is also a case of value transfer. Unfocused philanthropy is implicitly a decision to take financial value from the company's shareholders and transfer it to one or more of its stakeholders.[137]

Value creation: Shareholder value +, Stakeholder value +
When value is created for stakeholders as well as shareholders, stakeholders represent an additional potential source of business value. When DuPont designs manufacturing facilities that use less energy, produce zero waste, cost less to build and operate, and are safer, it is creating sustainable value. The new design has a direct impact on the cost base and contributes to the safety of DuPont's staff and to less pollution in the environment. The same is true when Unilever offers liquid detergent concentrates in smaller packaging. Customers prefer them because they are lighter to carry for the same number of washes, while retailers like them because they improve shelf-space utilization, and environmental stakeholders applaud the reduced plastic resin and savings in water and diesel.

Companies are cutting costs by eliminating packaging waste and by right-sizing their products, all in ways that better meet customer needs. They are adding environmental intelligence to their products by making them more recyclable, reusable, biodegradable, less toxic, or otherwise healthier – in many cases at a lower cost as they save on energy and materials. Without any trade-off for the customer or end-user, these products also lead typically to higher sales. Many companies are finding ways to profitably meet unmet societal needs: for example, by providing nutrition, clean water, and communication services to the poor. The key is to provide environmental and social benefits without requiring customers to pay more or accept worse quality in return. Companies that are in the mainstream cannot afford to require their customers to pay the "green premium" that specialty companies have historically charged for such products. Only through process or product redesign and business model innovation can leading companies create new business and societal benefits without consumer trade-offs.

An essential aspect of sustainable value is that, by *doing good* for society and the environment, the company does even better for its customers and shareholders than it otherwise would. Patrick Cescau, the former CEO of Unilever, described his company's journey to creating sustainable value as "no longer just about doing business responsibly; it is about seeing social and sustainability challenges as opportunities for innovation and business development."[138]

Sustainable value and the great debate

Sustainable value takes an integrated perspective on shareholders and stakeholder value. To understand how it is new and different, we look briefly at the prevailing views of value: the first centered on shareholders and the second on stakeholders. While there are other perspectives, what stands out about these two is their dominance in popular opinion (not only among business managers and theorists) and the extent to which they are at odds with each other. In all walks of life you will find people with strong opinions about one view to the exclusion of the other; those who believe that a trade-off is the only possibility.

Unfortunately, an "either–or" approach misses two crucial points. First, the leading management thinkers who first advocated the shareholder perspective were not saying that stakeholder value is unimportant, just that it is a means rather than an end in itself. Leading proponents of the stakeholder perspective were also not saying that shareholder value is unimportant, just that the interests of shareholders and stakeholders must be balanced for business to remain healthy.

Second, the question of validity changes over time as the external environment changes. The three big trends of declining resources, radical transparency, and increasing expectations are revolutionizing the debate: shareholder value and stakeholder value are now blended in the marketplace. And with that, it is no longer useful to give precedence to one over the other.

The shareholder perspective

The shareholder perspective holds that the corporation exists to serve its owners. It is a venture whose only obligation (besides observing the laws of the land) is to create economic value on behalf of those who invested their hard-earned money. By the mid-1980s, one leading management scholar could say with confidence,

> the idea that business strategies should be judged by the economic
> value they create for shareholders is well accepted in the business

community. After all, to suggest that companies be operated in the best interests of their owners is hardly controversial.[139]

During the 1980s, the main change was from accounting measures (such as earnings per share or return on equity) to free cash flow[140] metrics – a change that may seem benign but in fact contributed to the behaviors and practices that led to short-term shareholder value extremism.

In earlier periods the emphasis on shareholder value did not automatically mean a disregard for the needs of stakeholders. "On the contrary, most exponents of this view argue that it is in the interest of shareholders to carry out a 'stakeholder analysis' and even to actively manage stakeholder relations."[141] The key in the strategy process is paying attention to stakeholders for expediency reasons rather than because of any moral responsibility.

Translated into practice, here is how one corporation, the UK-based ICI, stated its value creation goals in the mid-1980s:

> ICI aims to be the world's leading chemical company, serving customers internationally through the innovative and responsible application of chemistry and related science. Through achievement of our aim, we will enhance the wealth and well-being of our shareholders, our employees, our customers and the communities which we serve and in which we operate (ICI Annual Report 1987).[142]

Problems arose when the shareholder value perspective was taken to an extreme, and attention to stakeholder value was all but forgotten. The practice of distributing share option schemes tying managerial motivation to share performance provided huge incentives to managers to do everything they could to push stock prices higher in the short term. Perhaps not surprisingly, here is how ICI reformulated its value creation goals seven years later.

> Our objective is to maximize value for our shareholders by focusing on businesses where we have market leadership, a technological edge and a world competitive cost base (ICI Annual Report 1994).

Critics of the shareholder perspective began to argue that it "is making managers pre-occupied with finance. It diverts them from their job of value creation. It is typically not successful, not even on its own terms, and it undermines the legitimacy of free markets and free enterprise."[143] Events soon appeared to confirm these suspicions. The early 2000s saw the implosion of Enron, WorldCom and Parmalat, while the global financial crisis of 2007 was triggered in part by the actions of firms such as Lehman Brothers, Bear Stearns, and AIG.

By the spring of 2009, the *Financial Times* carried a series of articles highly critical of the shareholder perspective. It boldly announced that, "A palace revolution in the realm of business is toppling the dictatorship of shareholder value maximization as the sole guiding principle of corporate action." Jack Welch, former CEO of GE and one of shareholder value's most ardent supporters, was quoted by the *Financial Times* as saying, "shareholder value is the dumbest idea in the world."[144] The award-winning documentary film *The Corporation* went even further, portraying big business as a psychopath:

> Like all psychopaths, the firm is singularly self-interested: its purpose is to create wealth for shareholders. And, like all psychopaths, the firm is irresponsible, because it puts others at risk to satisfy its profit-maximization goal, harming employees and customers and damaging the environment.[145]

However it is worth remembering that such unfettered pursuit of shareholder value – one that leads to destructive greed – misses the whole point. The actions taken by the management of companies like Enron and AIG were clearly not in the interest of their shareholders. They did not pursue successful shareholder value strategies.

The stakeholder perspective

Followers of the stakeholder perspective argue that the corporation has an obligation to account for, and to balance the needs of, all its stakeholders. The inclusion of stakeholder theory in business strategy dates back to Edward Freeman's work in the early 1980s.[146] The first recorded use of the term "stakeholder" in a business context was in a 1963 internal memorandum of the Stanford Research Institute, referring to "those groups without whose support the organization would cease to exist."[147] Notions of business serving society and balancing various interests date back even further, to at least the 1930s.[148]

Although nuanced in the early literature,[149] the stakeholder view quickly devolved into two schools of thought that we will call respectively the "moralist" and the "pragmatist" variants.

Pragmatists focused on the role of stakeholders in the strategic planning process. As far back as 1965, the strategist Igor Ansoff rejected the view that business objectives should be derived by "balancing" the conflicting claims of stakeholders. He argued that a firm might have economic *and* social objectives, but that the latter were "a secondary modifying and constraining influence" on the former.[150] In the 1970s, the Harvard Business School undertook a project on "corporate social responsiveness" which, as the name implies, emphasized responsiveness to stakeholders rather than moral responsibility.

It linked the analysis of social issues to strategy and organization. A similar project was undertaken by the Wharton School in 1977, seeking to develop a theory of management based on the inclusion of stakeholders.

In the **moralist** variant, "managing stakeholder demands is not merely a pragmatic means of running a profitable business – serving stakeholders is an end in itself."[151] Spurred in part by the social movement of the 1960s and 1970s that sought to promote civil rights and environmental protection, it advanced the idea that companies have a moral responsibility to their constituents – not only those in the economic value chain such as suppliers and labor unions but also in a wider sense to society and nature.[152] Key to this view is the idea of balancing interests, and therefore of implicitly accepting a trade-off between value for business and value for society.

The moralist variant is sometimes referred to as the stakeholder values perspective (with an 's' on the word "value") to underscore the ethical dimension. "The purpose of business" wrote one leading advocate "is not to make a profit, full stop. It is to make a profit so that the business can do something more or better . . . It is a moral issue."[153] In this view, companies are intended to balance competing interests through a process of negotiation and compromise, taking into account the legitimacy and moral claims of each party.

Just as the shareholder value perspective taken too far is not in the interest of shareholders, so the stakeholder perspective taken to its moral conclusion is not in the interest of stakeholders. No less a thinker than Peter Drucker summed it up perfectly:

> Economic profit performance is the base without which business cannot discharge any other responsibilities . . . we know that society will increasingly look to major organizations, for-profit and non-profit alike, to tackle major social ills. And that is where we had better be watchful, because good intentions are not always socially responsible. It is irresponsible for an organization to accept – let alone pursue – responsibilities that would impede its capacity to perform its main task and mission or to act where it has no competence.

So, what changed? Has the Great Debate become meaningless?

The great debate assumes that only one right answer exists in terms of value perspective, and that the competitive environment is static with respect to both sets of arguments. But consider that 30 years ago, stakeholders had a very different role in business than they do today. Back then Freeman naturally grouped stakeholders[154] into two categories: those who exercise economic power, such as customers and suppliers; and those with political power, by which he meant government and single-issue nonprofits including environmental NGOs (such as the Sierra Club) and social activists (at the time, Nader's Raiders). "By *economic power* we mean 'the ability to influence due to marketplace decisions' and by *political power* we mean 'the ability to influence due to use of the political process.' "[155]

By 2010, the big three trends had rendered moot this distinction between economic and political power. Today the demands of civil society are being internalized in the marketplace to such an extent that all stakeholders hold economic sway over corporations. An armchair blogger with damaging information about a company's products or activities in one part of the world can instantly and globally affect its financial worth.

Reflecting the reality of the early 1980s, Freeman went on to say that "public relations and public affairs managers and lobbyists learn to deal in the political arena." That is how NGOs and social activists (Freeman referred to them as "kibitzers") were to be handled by managers.[156] By comparison, today, it would be folly for any firm to delegate stakeholder relations to the PR department. Why are C-suite executives and line managers being made accountable for stakeholder issues? Because stakeholder value increasingly drives economic value at the heart of business strategy.

In 2010, James S. Wallace argued that the two perspectives "are really far more complementary than they are at odds with each other." He cites Peter Drucker, who said it best when he summed it all up in 2003 shortly before his death, offering the following integrated value perspective:

> We no longer need to theorize about how to define performance and results in the large enterprise. We have successful examples . . . They do not "balance" anything. They maximize. But they do not attempt to maximize shareholder value or the short-term interest of any one of the enterprise's "stakeholders." Rather, they maximize the wealth-producing capacity of the enterprise. It is the objective that integrates the short-term and long-term results and that ties the operational dimensions of business performance – market standing, innovation, productivity, and people and their development – with the financial needs and financial results. It is also this objective on which all the constituencies – whether shareholders, customers, or employees – depend for the satisfaction of their expectations and objectives.[157]

In summary

In recent years, rising social and ecological pressures have been redefining the way business creates value. Yet this shift is not new – throughout history, the relationship between business and the rest of the world has gone through turbulent and multifaceted phases. At the center of this relationship is the concept of value: what is it and how do we create more of it?

While it might be tempting to look at value through the single lens of shareholder returns, in reality a solid value model is built on the delivery of tangible end benefits for your customers, employees, and other stakeholders. When these end benefits are consistently delivered via your solutions, products, services, and processes, shareholder value follows. As new needs emerge, new solutions follow, assuring future profitability. In other words, the three dimensions of value (financial, tangible solution, and end benefits) are deeply interrelated and interdependent.

The big three trends are reshaping the end benefits expected from your business – and it is no longer only customers and investors who have a direct say in what those end benefits should be, but everyone with a stake in the future of your company. With new demands on hand, the entire value model has to be adjusted. Yet the good news is that it is no longer necessary to create a painful compromise between delivering value to shareholders and creating value for the stakeholders. Indeed, pursuing both – shareholder and stakeholder needs – creates sustainable value well beyond the expected images of compromise, balance, and trade-off.

With sustainable value as the new frontier of successful business venture, the question is: how do you get it done? How do you respond to the new pressures of social and environmental performance? What is business to do?

In Part II, we turn our attention to these very questions, exploring the full range of options available to business. The field of strategy is at the center of our attention, offering advice and input into the best available strategic response to the new market reality.

Part II

WHAT IT MEANS FOR BUSINESS STRATEGY

The tree of profit
Introduction to Part II

The big three trends – declining resources, radical transparency, and increasing expectations – have been quietly reshaping the very landscape of business. No longer is it possible to keep going with the same old mantra of profit at any cost to society. Goldman Sachs discovered this the hard way when its Abacus hedge fund was accused of unfairly profiting from the collapse in the U.S. housing market.[158] When you include its loss in market capitalization, BP's oil spill disaster in the Gulf of Mexico had cost it over $100 billion before it even capped the well.

Yet the reverse – a business mission to "save the whales" as the *responsible* thing to do even if it means sacrificing profit – is proving equally problematic. A few companies, from Icebreaker to Seventh Generation, are succeeding by putting an environmental or social mission above everything else. But for the vast majority of ventures, pursuing such a mission is just as irresponsible as making money at the expense of the little guy. Shareholder value earned "on the backs" of stakeholders *or* stakeholder value created to the detriment of shareholders is a false choice between remaining a limited niche business and going bust in a world that no longer tolerates unbridled harm.

We are entering an era of *sustainable value* – creating value for shareholders *and* stakeholders simply because it's a smarter way to do business. As shown by the early successes of global leaders, those who know how to create sustainable value are finding an exciting route to creating even more value for their customers and shareholders than they otherwise would.

Time to break out some champagne? Well, let us hold the celebrations for a moment longer, and take you back to the journey we made together in Part I. In it, we made the case that three trends are changing the rules of business. Of all the possible alternatives, sustainable value now represents the most promising business path forward. Yet the trip from point A to point B – in which the three big trends are transformed from threat to business opportunity – is proving to be much more challenging than originally anticipated, with many businesses failing to reach their promised destination of *doing well by doing good*. Managers need to be equipped with more relevant and effective concepts – and it is with some urgency that they are asking for these along with the practical tools for getting it done.

In Part II, we look at the challenge of embedding sustainability through the lens of business strategy, framing *green* and *social responsibility* as factors of competitive advantage. A first objective is to make the new insights accessible for busy managers who want to get the story of sustainability without the dryness of a textbook. A second objective is conceptual rigor in developing sustainability as a business strategy. Too many managers tell us that they are overwhelmed by anecdotal evidence ("Acme Corp makes the business case for green!") Readers want methodological rigor but they want it without having to wade through academic tomes.

Part II is organized into three chapters. The first offers an overview of the field of strategy to enable the reader to see how sustainability is seen as contributing to competitive advantage. Our inquiry looks at whether we really need new answers – hasn't all that needs to be said already been said? By examining the way in which past strategy theories incorporate green and social responsibility, we can show under what conditions embedded sustainability creates business value – and how it strengthens or transforms a company's existing business strategy.

The second chapter introduces three strategy theories and their application to embedded sustainability. Michael Porter and the positioning school represent perhaps the best-known and most widely used framework not only for corporate strategy but also for incorporating environmental and social issues. Kim and Mauborgne's **Blue Ocean Strategy** is equally widely used and offers some uniquely well-suited features for thinking about sustainability, but – we ask tongue-in-cheek – will it really help us keep the oceans blue? Clayton Christensen's **Disruptive Innovation** provides a framework for addressing global challenges that call for transformation rather than incremental change.

We conclude Part II with **Embedded Sustainability**: our strategy framework and set of principles to integrate sustainability into the company and its whole business system. At its core are a set of new profit drivers: the internalization of externalities, rising customer demand for environmental and social performance, and a market redefinition of what it means to achieve competitive advantage.

The good news is that champions of embedded sustainability need only depend on the essential profit-making purpose of business. Embedded sustainability does not require a new moral purpose or, for that matter, new ecological beliefs – you don't have to believe in the science of climate change. Companies who successfully embed sustainability will be better positioned to succeed in markets in which green and social responsibility are everyone's job, invisible yet inspiring, driving both greater profits and the greater good.

3
What would a strategist do?

If declining resources, radical transparency, and increasing expectations are changing the rules of business, shouldn't companies of every stripe be searching – at this very moment – for new courses of action? Continuing only with what worked in the past would be like putting new wine in old bottles, which in ancient times ruined both the wine and its rawhide flask.

But how *can* managers respond in ways that best support their business goals?

Naturally, the field of strategy is the place to start our search for answers. A complex and beloved topic of management (just ask any MBA student), the art and science of business strategy is all about finding the best way for an organization to achieve its vision and objectives. Whatever its larger mission, a company must be able to develop its own uniquely defensible path to creating value for its customers and shareholders. To understand what sustainability means for business advantage, there can be no better guide than the business strategist.

Our journey takes us through the field's main generic responses to sustainability pressures. We attempt to go beyond the usual anecdotal evidence to show the theory behind the business case for sustainability. In spite of solid evidence that ecological and social demands can be sources of competitive advantage, managers on every continent continue to hold the contrary view that they are problems to be minimized, rather than opportunities to be seized. We compare and contrast these two opposing views, which coexist in every industry and increasingly separate winners from losers.

We begin our voyage with a look at the field itself.

The landscape of strategy

Before discovering what a strategist would do, let us consider who that is. A term widely used to mean someone "of importance" or "of great consequence" to an organization, we soon encounter strategic janitorial services. But what does the term "strategy" actually mean? What are its main schools of thought and how have they changed over time? If you are one of the revered "strategy junkies" – thoroughly versed in the topic – you may want to skip to the next section. For everyone else, here is a quick recap of the ever-expanding landscape of strategy.

The pioneers – Alfred Chandler,[159] Igor Ansoff,[160] and E.P. Learned *et al.*[161] – produced their now classic works in the early 1960s, coincidentally around the same time that Rachel Carson imagined Earth without birdsong in *Silent Spring*. They saw strategy as the process of setting a company's direction (where it is going) and aligning its operational processes to that chosen future (how it will get there).

Strategy soon came to be seen as an *externally oriented* concept of how business achieves its objectives.[162] Michael Porter captured it perfectly: "The essence of formulating competitive strategy is relating a company to its environment."[163] It is not to be confused with a company's mission or objectives; neither is it an analysis of internal strengths or weaknesses.

With a half-century of concepts and frameworks behind us, what follows is one way to map the terrain in order to provide a common ground for our exploration of the available responses to sustainability pressures as potential sources of profit.

Strategy = Plan

Alfred Chandler defined strategy as "the determination of the basic long-term goals and objectives of the enterprise, and the adoption of courses of action and the allocation of resources necessary for carrying out these goals."[164] If we look at the world through Chandler's eyes, strategy is all about planning and administration. In essence, for the early thinkers, strategy was a deliberate effort to draw up a multi-year line-of-attack using hard data. The result: detailed objectives, budgets, programs, and operating directives . . . sounds familiar, right? With a detailed analytical plan at its core, naturally such an approach to strategy depended on a world in which the main drivers of change – population growth, income per person, and technology – were relatively stable and predictable.

Strategy = Position

Two decades later, strategy became widely seen in terms of competitive *positioning* – performing different activities than competitors or performing similar activities in different ways. Fans of this approach argued that it is the external environment that drives market opportunities, and that companies must position themselves relative to customer needs and other external forces to pursue strategies distinct from those of their rivals. We are all familiar with the most popular positioning strategies: cost leadership (selling at a lower price but with even lower costs), differentiation (offering premium features at a premium price), and focus[165] (serving the needs of a narrow group of customers). Other examples of positioning include market or product leadership,[166] customer intimacy, and operational excellence.[167]

Strategy = Flexibility

As the rates of external change sped up, fueled by rapid technological innovation and globalization, strategy became more concerned with flexibility and nimbleness. In a world of *hypercompetition*,[168] in which the rules of the game were continuously changing, strategy became a tool for turning chaos into structure.[169] By 1996, leading thinkers were proposing that we look at strategy as "a unique and viable posture based on . . . anticipated changes in the environment and contingent moves by intelligent opponents."[170] Planning no longer occupied center stage: it was the continuous creation of advantage and continuous disruption of the opponent's advantage that ruled the day.[171] By the turn of the century, the strategy giant Clayton Christensen[172] offered companies the ultimate extreme change model: a theory of disruptive innovation that invites businesses to catalyze – and take advantage of – revolutionary changes in their markets.[173]

Strategy = . . . ?

Recent decades witnessed the emergence of strategy management as an academic discipline in its own right. Business managers found themselves stuck in a less than comfortable spot somewhere between strategy as an analytic planning exercise and strategy as structured chaos. To meet the demand for more comfortable alternatives, an explosion of frameworks and approaches followed.[174] In addition to **plan, position**, and **flexibility**, strategy came to be viewed as **pattern** – a consistent and characteristic set of actions; as **perspective** – the unique outlook of a company and its fundamental way of doing things (as in "The Coca-Cola Way"); and as **ploy** – the specific maneuvers of a company to outwit its competitors.[175]

We will not go into the Design, Entrepreneurial, Cognitive, Learning, Cultural, and Political schools of strategy thought.[176] There are many routes to competitive advantage and no one approach can be considered "best" without first taking into account the company's specific circumstances. Yet – and despite the dangers of trying to reduce strategy to a single formula – given today's highly complex and turbulent markets, one particular view fits well the challenge of embedded sustainability:

"strategy = learning process"[177]

And so, with our map of the evolving field of strategy in hand, we are now ready to tackle the next question: What does the field as a whole say about what sustainability means for business value creation?

Generic strategy responses to sustainability

Study the major schools of strategy across the last two decades, and you will find a recurring set of responses to ecological and social factors. Among them, the first concerns business value destruction: it frames sustainability in terms of a trade-off or added cost. All the others address value creation. One such value-creating response – sustainability as a driver of innovation – is a complex composite that cuts across and enables the other value-creating responses.

What follows are snapshots of each of the eight responses we uncovered – they are "generic" in that they apply to business generally and do not attempt to take into account the specifics of particular cases. At first blush, it may seem that the responses are fragmentary and even contradictory. **Added cost** is the opposite of greater **efficiency opportunity**. **Mitigating risk** is usually thought to be about avoiding costs, which is very different from **radical innovation**, with its spirit of competitive advantage. Dig a little deeper, however, and you quickly find that each is valid, but only under certain conditions. Taken together, they represent a rich canvas for thinking about sustainability-driven business value.[178]

Value destruction: It's an added cost

The earliest response was to consider green and social responsibility as an added cost – an inevitable trade-off with profits. A piece in the *Journal of Economic Perspectives* argues that tougher environmental regulation must, by its very nature, reduce profits.[179] This widespread belief is captured here:

> The idea that a business could ever "do well by doing good" . . .
> seems to violate economic logic . . . any business that tried to
> provide or preserve more environmental quality than is lawfully
> required would incur higher costs than its competitors, and its cus-
> tomers would abandon it in search of lower prices.[180]

In short, if it is better for society and the environment, it must cost more for business.

One reason for the widespread trade-off assumption can be attributed to the initial dominance of awareness-raising efforts such as Rachel Carson's *Silent Spring*, Ralph Nader's *Unsafe at Any Speed* and Thomas Berry's *The Dream of the Earth* – each of them powerful works built on the pioneering legacy of Aldo Leopold, dating back to the 1940s.

> Early models discussing the integration of the natural environment
> into organizational decision-making and strategy were primar-
> ily derived from the deep ecology literature. Rather than address-
> ing the issue of competitive advantage, they presented a conflict
> between the economy and ecology and thus between financial and
> environmental performance.[181]

In just one of many examples, a 1994 *Harvard Business Review* article suggests that there is a necessary trade-off between profit and environmental improvement. "Ambitious environmental goals have real economics costs. As a society, we may rightly choose those goals despite their costs, but we must do so knowingly,"[182] say the McKinsey authors.

The message: sustainability can only come with a hefty price tag.

Value creation #1: It's risk mitigation

Managing sustainability-related business risks is not so much about value creation as it is about avoiding its destruction. There are two levels of risk to be managed: the negative sustainability impact and the negative business consequence that follows it. Both must be managed effectively to reduce potential losses. An environmental risk such as an oil spill can be minimized with operational procedures to avoid the spill in the first place. But once it happens, the oil company needs to take actions not only to limit the environmental damage but also to clean it up, compensate the parties that were injured, manage reputational harm, avoid customer and employee rejection, and limit punitive regulation – all of which are business risks distinct from the risk of damage to the environment.

Environmental strategist Andrew Hoffman lists four areas in which mitigating environmental risks can help a firm avoid significant business costs.[183] These are: (1) the reduced costs of environmental response by being proactive in preparing for disasters such as accidents, spills, and releases; (2) reduced remediation costs by proactively managing remediation projects and closing them out ahead of schedule; (3) reduced product liability costs by addressing potential adverse impacts at the design stage; and (4) reduced insurance premiums by limiting environmental risk exposures for employees, contractors, and customers. Sustainability scholar Marc Epstein makes the interesting point that sustainability-driven innovation strategies can be a critical component of mitigating risk.[184] He also notes that sustainability-related business risks are becoming broader and more varied than previously thought, from social issues such as child labor practices to political risks related to corruption. Another sustainability-driven business risk is individual claims against directors and officers resulting from knowingly breaching environmental and social laws.

The presumption: sustainability is about managing potentially costly liabilities.

Value creation #2: It's an efficiency opportunity

Rather than viewing sustainability as added cost, improving efficiency is primarily about cutting the quantity and intensity of energy, waste, and materials. Pollution prevention (reducing pollution at the input stage) is less costly than end-of-pipe treatment and remediation of effluents. In describing the economic value of pollution prevention, environmental strategist Alfred Marcus notes that "by increasing throughput, lowering rework rates and scrap, and using less material and energy per unit of production, a company can save money, enhance efficiency and become more competitive."[185] Business strategists Michael Porter and Claas van der Linde make a compelling argument in favor of this view: "the costs of addressing environmental regulations can be minimized, if not eliminated, through innovation that delivers other competitive benefits."[186] Environmental and social harm is a sign of inefficiencies that offer a creative opportunity for cost reduction across the larger set of business processes. Environmental impacts such as air emissions and materials waste are indications of economic costs that can be driven out of the system in a win–win for business and society.

Over a period of ten years or more, companies such as 3M, Chevron, and DuPont have each reportedly saved billions of dollars from environmental cost-cutting initiatives.[187] Walmart estimates that its sustainable packaging initiative launched in October 2005 will globally save $3.4 billion by 2013 – through the elimination of only 5 per cent of packaging materials in its supply chains. Many companies are finding that sustainability pressures are helping them find new savings in the areas of energy consumption, waste flows, and materials intensity. Whether it is one-shot gains or longer-term and more persistent savings that require changes in capital stock, firms in every sector are finding exciting new cost-cutting opportunities.

The moral: sustainability is an (eco-)efficiency engine.

Value creation #3: It's a factor of differentiation

The next value creating response has been to see environmental and social attributes as a way to differentiate products and services. With this response, the definition of quality or performance is simply expanded to include a sustainability dimension. Companies are still confronted with the same positioning choices relative to their rivals. Only now green and social components become an additional weapon in the competitive arsenal.

Strategy scholars Bob De Wit and Ron Meyer illustrate the point:

> An ice cream manufacturer can introduce a new flavor and more chunky texture, a motorcycle producer can design a special "low rider" model for women, a pay TV company can develop special channels for dog owners and science fiction addicts, and a utility company can offer environmentally friendly electricity.[188]

Just one among many other features, green electricity becomes a product attribute that helps differentiate the utility from its competitors who sell electricity from traditional "dirty" fuel sources such as coal.

Of course customers must be willing to pay proportionately more for the environmental attribute than its cost, and the company must be able to establish credible information about that attribute.[189] Once these conditions are satisfied, companies can expect to profit from adding new environmental attributes even if doing so incurs additional costs.

"Of the possible ways to reconcile their need to deliver shareholder value with intensifying demands for improved environmental performance," says Harvard strategist Forest Reinhardt, "perhaps the most straightforward is to provide environmentally preferable products and then capture the extra costs from consumers."[190] The not-so-hidden assumption here is that green and social responsibility necessarily cost more.

The take-away: sustainability is a product differentiator (but be sure to charge extra for it).

Value creation #4: It's a pathway to new markets

Sustainability pressures create new market opportunities when businesses and consumers demand solutions for their environmental and social problems. At one end are opportunities to help individuals and companies *reduce harm* or *do less bad*, such as end-of-pipe pollution control equipment. In 2010, air pollution control equipment in China alone was a $5 billion market growing at 18 per cent per year.[191] At the other end are opportunities to profitably provide social and ecological *solutions* such as life insurance and banking services to previously uninsurable and unbankable customers (Aviva, Erste Group Bank); a corporate mission to "bring health through food to as many people as possible" (Danone); and the growing number of clean energy and clean water options (for water: P&G, Siemens, 3M, ITT and upstarts such as Filterboxx Water and Environmental[192]).

One of the biggest new markets is meeting the needs of the world's poorest 4 billion people living on less than $4 per day – the so-called base of the pyramid.[193] The World Resources Institute[194] estimates the size of this consumer market at $5 trillion (by comparison, Canada's economy is about $1.5 trillion). Unilever's Indian subsidiary Hindustan Lever Limited (HLL) developed Project Shakti as a way to profitably reach India's poor rural population with products such as shampoos and soaps as well as iodized salt. By leveraging the thousands of rural women's self-help groups established by the Indian government to facilitate local development, the company built a powerful new distributed sales and marketing system. The women are not only selling products and promoting the brands. They provide demonstration services in sanitation and hand washing that help reduce the incidence of diarrheal diseases.[195] They are helping to reduce iodine deficiency, creating significant health benefits in their neglected communities. As entrepreneurs, they contribute to local wealth creation. And for Unilever – HLL's parent company – Project Shakti provides access to a huge and growing market in what the company's director of new ventures calls a great win–win.[196]

Companies enter these new markets either by adapting existing know-how to new needs or through radical innovation, which we explore in the seventh value-creating response. Examples of adapting existing know-how include Vodafone's wireless business in sub-Saharan Africa (one of its most profitable markets), GE's expertise in turbines that enabled it to become a world leader in wind power generation, and Celanese Corporation's expertise in plastic polymers that led to the development of high-temperature membrane electrode assembly (MEA) for fuel cells in cars.[197]

The conclusion: Growing ecological and social needs are creating huge new markets.

Value creation #5: It's a way to protect and enhance the brand

Companies in a variety of sectors are finding that their brand name and corporate image are increasingly based on perceived environmental and social performance. Being seen as above average in this space helps to draw talent, secure loyal customers, become supplier-of-choice, and attract investors.[198] It can also ease negotiations with government regulators concerned about company or industry harm to society and the environment. Companies such as GE and P&G have shown that it can contribute to their overall image as an innovation leader.

Economists argue that corporate value (or "market capitalization" in the case of publicly traded companies) is increasingly tied to intangible assets such as reputation, goodwill, employee know-how, and stakeholder trust. A century ago, a company's stock price was 70 per cent a function of the value of tangible assets such as plant, property, and equipment. Remarkably, today it is intangibles that account for over 70 per cent of the value.[199] With rising expectations for green and socially responsible business, intangible value is increasingly driven by perceived sustainability performance. The financial consequence for BP of its Gulf oil disaster is a case in point: within two months of the accident, the financial cost to BP of fixing and cleaning up the problem was assessed at fewer than $2 billion,[200] but BP's stock price had fallen by over 50 per cent, effectively wiping out nearly $90 billion of its market value.[201]

Of course, in a world of radical transparency, companies cannot *enduringly* make claims that are untrue and unverifiable. Someone, somewhere, at some point in time will discover the fib – and will Tweet it to the world. Renault and British Airways both recently faced charges of misleading sustainability claims, according to the Advertising Standards Authority, a UK watchdog.[202] Such charges – repeated in blogs and spread across social networks – can quickly undermine a company's overall image.

The cautionary tale: Companies can gain or lose significant market value based on stakeholder *perceptions* of environmental, health, and social impacts.

Value creation #6: It's about influencing industry standards

Companies can try to shape government regulations or private industry standards in ways that favor them over the competition. It is the strategic use of government regulation or self-policing industry practices to raise the bar for competitors.[203] When DuPont and a handful of other corporations lobbied the U.S. government for strong national legislation to require significant reductions of greenhouse gas emissions, including a cap-and-trade scheme,[204] it was relying on its industry leadership in low-carbon technologies to eventually yield competitive benefits. DuPont was making the bet that its competitors would incur disproportionately higher costs as carbon emissions become regulated or priced in the marketplace.[205]

The Forest Stewardship Council (FSC) and the American Forest & Paper Association's Sustainable Forest Initiative (SFI) – both founded in the early-mid-1990s – are two voluntary global certification systems established for forests and forest products. They directly or indirectly address issues such as illegal logging, deforestation, loss of wildlife habitat, and climate change. Lumber and paper companies that cannot meet their standards lose membership and/or the right to carry the certification logo. In the case of SFI, in the years following its establishment, "a few companies decided not to commit to the SFI, and subsequently resigned their membership . . . and 15 company memberships were terminated after the companies failed to commit to the SFI."[206] Such voluntary industry standards help raise industry-wide practices and differentiate – through certification schemes – those companies capable of meeting the new expectations of consumers, investors, and other stakeholders.

Another example is the Registration, Evaluation, Authorization and restriction of Chemicals (REACH) legislation, which requires companies to register the chemical substances in their products sold in Europe. The registration process itself and having to declare "substances of very high concern" (SVHC) can be disproportionately costly for competitors from outside the Euro zone, for example in emerging markets.[207]

The lesson learned: Environmental regulations can create desirable barriers to entry (especially if they help keep out low-cost imports).

Value creation #7: It's a driver of radical innovation

Strategists have long seen the potential for environmental and social performance to drive deep innovation. "By thinking creatively about the fundamental nature of their business, executives in certain firms have been able to find ways to reconfigure the whole system by which they create value and deliver it to customers."[208] Consider the case of Tennant, a Minneapolis-based maker of walk-behind floor scrubbers for use in commercial buildings, sports stadiums and other large indoor and outdoor surfaces. While its competitors were busy working to reduce the harshness of their cleaning chemicals, Tennant simply eliminated the use of its chemicals altogether. The company's flagship product, the ec-H2O, electrically converts plain tap water to perform like a powerful detergent. It uses 70 per cent less water than traditional cleaning methods (you can work longer with the same tank fill); it leaves behind no slippery detergent residue on the floor; and it releases no used detergent discharge into water systems. Best of all, the ec-H2O gives its customers the lowest possible total cost of ownership. With several top awards including the European Business Award for innovation, this small company now has a visibility and reputation far exceeding its size.

Nissan is preparing to move beyond fossil fuel engines, investing $6 billion into electric cars at a time when most of the industry is focused on improving fuel efficiency. Monsanto and Bayer Crop Sciences are in the crop protection business, developing plants able to resist pests and increasing drought resistance where water is scarce. Californian company Calera is developing a cement manufacturing process that captures and stores CO_2, while the rest of the industry is aiming to reduce CO_2 emissions.[209] Amazon Kindle and Sony are questioning whether you need a paper book to read, instead of focusing on recycling or sourcing from sustainably managed forests.

The insight: Looking at your business through the lens of sustainability can be a source of tremendous creativity, helping to fundamentally rethink the nature of your business venture.

Put all eight generic responses together, and here is how a strategist might look at ecological and social factors in relation to the business value created:[210]

1 + 7 generic strategy responses

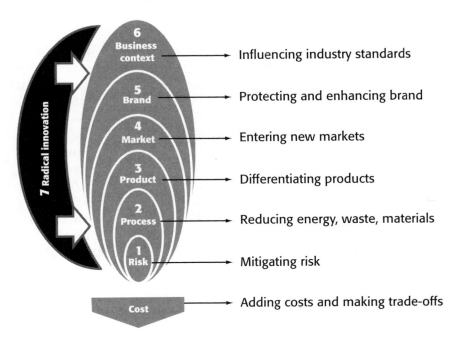

From *The Sustainable Company* (Figure 11-8), by Chris Laszlo. Copyright © 2003 Chris Laszlo. Reproduced by permission of Island Press, Washington, D.C.

The seventh value-creating response – radical innovation – is a complex composite. It touches on the nature of change in business models, product designs, processes, and technologies. It cuts across and enables the other value-creating responses (for example, companies use radical innovation to simultaneously lower costs, differentiate their products, and enter entirely new markets). Radical innovation is also at the heart of the link between sustainability and profit, which is at the core of the sustainable value concept.

To understand how companies develop the *capacity* for sustainability-driven radical innovation, we dig deeper into what underlies strategy as a learning process. We turn to an indirect, multilayered theory – known as the **resource-based view** of competitive advantage[211] – that helps to shed light on how shareholder value is created from superior environmental and social performance.

The deep link between sustainability and profit

Early strategy research did not systematically address the link between sustainability and financial performance. Much of the work was exploratory and lacked rigor.[212] Rather than searching for comprehensive answers, it focused on narrow topics such as the costs of pollution.[213] For anyone grinding through the texts of that era, it would be hard to disagree that "some of this literature is trivial and amounts to little more than the provision of green window dressing to disguise the activities of companies where the environmental impact day to day of operations remains unchanged."[214] Or that some of the writing was based on "simple moralistic exhortation or guilt inducing rhetoric." Even management articles such as Michael Porter's 1991 one-pager in *Scientific American*,[215] which argued persuasively that tougher environmental regulation would lead firms to improve efficiency and competitiveness, were anecdotal and conceptual rather than systematic and empirical.

From about 1995 onward, the field got much more serious about trying to uncover the mechanisms by which environmental and social strategy contributes to financial performance. New theoretical propositions and frameworks were introduced to help managers understand *under what conditions* it "pays to be green."

In many instances, it is not sustainability in itself that increases profitability – hardly a surprising conclusion! Instead, environmental and social strategies force companies to acquire *constituent capabilities* which in turn allow them to develop new *competencies* that lead to competitive as well as sustainability advantages. A subtle distinction but bear with us: the logic and proof – up to now well hidden in scholarly journals – are very convincing indeed.

What we mean by constituent capabilities are the "building-block" skills – both individual and organizational – such as pollution prevention, full cost analysis, design for environment (DfE), social auditing, community outreach, and stakeholder collaboration.[216] These capabilities tie together, over time, to create new competencies such as process innovation, continuous improvement, cross-functional management, and the ability to develop a widely shared strategy vision.

In other words, getting good at managing environmental and social performance leads to new organizational competencies that apply broadly to every aspect of business management. In just one of many such examples, an analysis of the Canadian oil industry found that proactive environmental management leads to three organizational competencies – continuous high-order learning, continuous innovation, and stakeholder integration – that have broadly positive effects on corporate financial performance.[217] Other studies reached similar conclusions for the chemical, pulp and paper, and food industries.[218]

Several studies showed that sustainability strategies require not only new environmental and social capabilities, but also complementary ones. For example, total quality management is not a sustainability capability in itself, but it helps for it to be present for sustainability to pay.[219]

Confused by the distinction between capability and competence? Strategists C.K. Prahalad and Gary Hamel first clarified the distinction in a way that is crucial to understanding how sustainability creates competitive advantage. According to them, capabilities are the building blocks that aggregate into competencies.[220] Companies can have many capabilities – 30 or more – but relatively few competencies – less than five or six.[221] You can think of capabilities as separate skills sets that are only potentially of value to a firm, while competencies configure these capabilities into unique advantages.

Competitive advantage comes from tying together complementary capabilities in a way that profitably serves customers better than competitors serve their customers. Since competencies involve a complex harmonization of capabilities, they are hard to imitate. The more complex the integration of capabilities, the harder it is to imitate the competencies and the easier it will be for a company to maintain its competitive advantage.

This last point is of particular interest because environmental and social capabilities are relatively complex and imply bold disruptive change. Eliminating toxic chemicals, producing zero waste, and profitably serving $4/day-income consumers are all capabilities that lie outside the usual purview of business. For many companies, they require what *Green to Gold* author

Andrew Winston calls "heresy": a sea change in performance to meet customer needs with radically lower use of resources, zero waste, low- or no-carbon emissions, and in ways that actually restore social equity and the environment.[222] Every company has its own heresy capable of driving disruptive, rather than incremental, innovation.

In complexity terms, sustainability capabilities have scientific, technological, organizational, and social dimensions. Developing and tying them together in a unique set of competencies can help establish a valuable competitive position that is hard for competitors to imitate. As one scholar put it,

> Competence in environmental management is composed of many constituent elements built up over time . . . The more complex the relations among the separate elements, the harder it is to copy or duplicate the competence the firm has acquired, and the more valuable it may be in providing competitive advantage.[223]

The strategist's view in a nutshell

Of the eight responses, only one speaks about social and environmental performance in terms of value destruction. Sustainability as an added cost is a minor footnote in the strategist's repertoire, however prevalent it is in mainstream business thinking. The strategist is far more interested in *under what conditions* sustainability becomes a source of value creation. The strategist wants to know *which* of the levels of value creation are available to the company.

With the seven value-creating responses, the field of strategy already covers many bases and begins to point the way forward for companies confronted with ecological and social pressures. Opportunities exist for risk mitigation, improved efficiency, product revenue differentiation, new market entry, better regulatory rules of the game, enhanced intangible value, and radical innovation. These responses reveal a wide range of potential sources of business value.

There is no question that recent strategy studies have helped managers to understand better how ecological and social pressures enter the calculus of business. Yet, in our experience, business practitioners continue to hold beliefs about sustainability that prevent them from fully benefiting from its inherent value-creating opportunities. These contrasting views are widespread in every sector of the economy and increasingly separate winners from losers. The former pursue sustainability strictly where it contributes to competitive advantage, while the latter undertake CSR-type strategies that end up adding costs and that fail to seize the ample opportunities for value creation.

Old beliefs versus best practice

Many business practitioners continue to frame sustainability in terms of environmental protection and social responsibility. Profitably moving to zero harm and to restorative solutions to global problems remains exceptional. Massive market needs waiting to be catered to, such as climate stability or customers at the base of economic pyramid, are largely ignored. As a result, it is still rare to find products that offer solutions to health and social problems, such as the LifeStraw,[224] a personal water filter that costs one fourth of a cent per liter of use, allowing low-income populations to safely drink water that would otherwise be dangerously contaminated.

Compare the following two views of sustainability. In the table below, it is the sum total of the differences between the two columns that calls for a true paradigm shift in business strategy. What we are saying is: many companies are stuck in the left-hand column, while sustainability leaders are de facto approaching sustainability as described in the right-hand column.

PREVALENT VIEW Cost	BEST PRACTICE VIEW Opportunity
Ecological and social factors are treated primarily . . .	
. . . **defensively**. They are negatives to be avoided and sources of blame that must be mitigated	. . . **offensively**. They are business opportunities to be pursued proactively as a way to get in front of the competition
. . . **in isolation**. They lead to a subset of activities producing a particular feature or to a single green product	. . . **systemically**. They are incorporated into every business decision at every point in the life cycle of every product
. . . **in terms of harm reduction**. Goals revolve around concepts such as waste minimization, emissions reductions, energy conservation, and environmental protection	. . . **in terms of zero harm and positive benefits**. Goals revolve around zero waste and clean renewable energy as well as positive benefits such as environmental restoration and meeting the unmet needs of the poor

PREVALENT VIEW Cost	BEST PRACTICE VIEW Opportunity
Ecological and social factors are treated primarily . . .	
. . . **as a niche**. Green products serve a subset of customers or market needs. Mainstream companies offering a green product (such as environmentally friendly electricity) are seen as serving a subset of the total market[225]	. . . **as mainstream**. Environmental and social responsibility is incorporated into the life cycle of products and services, for customers across a wide range of sectors, socioeconomic groups, and geographic markets
. . . **through trade-offs (win–lose)**. Environmental and social attributes cost more or lead to quality and performance trade-offs, as in the earliest hybrid car models.[226] Reinhardt states that "If a business can . . . improve environmental performance while keeping its production costs constant, then obviously it should do so . . . But such opportunities tend to be rare"[227]	. . . **through innovation (win–win)**. Innovation is what allows businesses to embed sustainability without trade-off in cost or quality.[228] Examples are Walmart packaging initiatives, Tennant's floor cleaners, Nissan's Leaf electric car, Calera's CO_2-absorbing cement, and the Kindle/iPad. All are innovations that are better for business and for society in a dynamic of win–win
. . . **as if they require social or green price premiums**. It is assumed that customers must be willing to accept a higher price. Under environmental product differentiation, Reinhardt notes that "changes in the products or the production costs . . . raise the business's costs, but they also enable it to command a price premium in the marketplace"[229]	. . . **as if they must be competitively priced** – and in some cases lower priced. Customers now expect a competitively priced product that embeds sustainability with no trade-offs. This is especially true when the total cost of ownership is considered instead of only the "optical" price, as in comparing LEDs to incandescent light bulbs
. . . **in light of incremental change**. Sure, in some cases entire classes of products had to be replaced, such as CFCs, but for the most part, past corporate environmental efforts sought incremental improvements in performance. A 5 per cent reduction in CO_2 emissions relative to 2010 levels represents an incremental change	. . . **in light of disruptive change**. Massive challenges and monumental global needs require creative solutions that disrupt existing industries and offer radical innovation. An 85 per cent reduction in CO_2 emissions relative to 2010 anticipates a future in which such low levels may be required by law and expected by customers and end-users

PREVALENT VIEW Cost	BEST PRACTICE VIEW Opportunity
Ecological and social factors are treated primarily ...	
... as a subset of existing customer needs. Eco-efficiencies and reduced harm are often pursued without changing the essential parameters of a product's performance	**... as an entirely new class of buyer needs**. Consumers, employees, and investors expect business solutions to global challenges. Demand exists for products and services that remediate social and ecological imbalances and that contribute to the common good

It is hard to imagine that, as recently as 2000, ecological and social factors were still widely treated defensively in a dominant perspective of liability containment and added costs.[230] Corporations sought to ward off environmentalist attacks by groups that were seen as extremist, as in the well-known Brent Spar incident which pitted Greenpeace against Shell.[231]

When mainstream companies did pursue environmentally friendly products and services, it was often symbolic and at the fringe of their business activity. Remember BP's "Beyond Petroleum" campaign, launched in 2000, at a time when its renewable energy investments represented less than 1 per cent of capital expenditures? How irrelevant that campaign has now become after its series of environmental mishaps culminating in the Gulf oil disaster of 2010.

But the tables have now turned, and the extent and magnitude of sustainability pressures and opportunities are revolutionizing market expectations. A handful of leading companies are now turning ecological and social demands into thriving business opportunity. The boundaries between corporations, customers, the media, and government are blurring via partnership-based solutions, with no blame game necessary. Defensive PR efforts are turned into offensive strategies. We are amidst a transformation to an entirely new basis of competition, with new pathways to victory. Could it be that it is time for your company's strategy to catch up with best practice?

In summary

The strategy field as a whole offers a number of ways to address sustainability-driven changes in the competitive environment. We believe that the eight responses are useful but not sufficient for practitioners seeking new ways to address sustainability for competitive advantage. They help make the business case for one-off sustainability actions but they do not provide much guidance for what it means for strategy at the level of the business unit.

For the most part, business practitioners continue to believe that they must choose between shareholder and stakeholder value – much like automakers a few decades ago were forced to choose between low price and high quality. Just as the Japanese automobile industry demonstrated decades ago, an *either–or* perspective is a poor paradigm to be imprisoned by. What the field of strategy makes clear is that sustainability can become a *both–and* proposition, fueled by innovation to create less costly *and* more desirable products that profitably offer environmental and social benefits. Unfortunately, the widespread belief continues to exist that such win–win initiatives must be rare and that they seem to "violate the economists' truism that there is no free lunch; they even seem to imply that there are lunches one gets paid to eat."[232]

We now dig deeper into the field by examining three well-known strategy frameworks through the lens of sustainability. We discover their principles, assumptions, and conclusions to help practitioners deal more proactively with sustainability as business opportunity rather than as cost or moral obligation.

4
Cool strategies for a heated world

If social and environmental pressures are best managed as opportunity, what frameworks, concepts, and approaches can help managers make sense of the ways sustainability creates business value? How exactly does it strengthen a company's existing business strategy or offer it pathways to new ones?

In this chapter, we review three strategy frameworks to help managers clarify and organize conceptually their sustainability-related business risks and opportunities:

1. Michael Porter's **Generic Strategies** – perhaps best known and most widely used not only for business strategy but also for incorporating environmental and social issues

2. Kim and Mauborgne's **Blue Ocean Strategy**, which offers unique advantages for companies pursuing new market opportunities based on ecological and social drivers

3. Clayton Christensen's **Disruptive Innovation**, providing a framework for addressing global challenges that call for radical rather than incremental change

Our choice of theories is guided by several factors. First, we wanted concepts that apply at the level of the business unit rather than at the level of functions such as marketing or at the corporate portfolio level. Second, we privileged outside-in approaches. Theories that take the external environment as the organizing factor are built on the idea that "firms should not be self-centered, but should continuously take their environment as the starting point when determining their strategy"[233] – an idea that is highly relevant given the profound changes to the external environment occasioned by declining resources, radical transparency, and rising expectations. In contrast, strategy theories based on an inside-out perspective that "strategies should not be built around external opportunities, but around a company's strengths"[234] are less appealing to the task we have on our hands. Third, we wanted to include a dimension of disruptive innovation that reflects the magnitude of sustainability challenges such as climate stability, food security, social justice, and universal access to clean water, none of which can be met by simply tweaking the status quo.

For those of you familiar and comfortable with all three frameworks, we invite you to head straight to Chapter 5. For the rest of us, Michael Porter is the first stop.

Michael Porter and the positioning school

Michael Porter is a leading proponent of management thinking that views strategy as "position," what Henry Mintzberg refers to as locating an organization in its environment.[235] In this optic, strategy is the mediating force – or "match" – between the organization and its environment.

Strategic positioning is about performing different activities from those of rivals or performing similar activities *differently*. It is not to be confused with operational efficiency, which is about performing similar activities *better* than competitors. Why is this distinction important? Because eco-efficiency and many other sustainability efforts are often geared to operational improvement which, while value-creating, do not represent a strategic move. In contrast, Porter's framework offers insights into understanding under what conditions sustainability contributes to strategic advantage.

In *Competitive Strategy: Techniques for Analyzing Industries and Competitors*,[236] Porter proposes three generic strategies – cost leadership, differentiation, and market segmentation (or focus) – which lead to distinct positions through which companies achieve competitive advantage. While Porter has been attacked for being too simplistic,[237] the fact of forcing a position is beneficial where companies try to do everything well and be all things to all people. As Porter noted in 1996,

> Continuous improvement has been etched on managers' brains. But its tools unwittingly draw companies toward imitation and homogeneity. Gradually, managers have let operational effectiveness supplant strategy. The result is zero-sum competition, static or declining prices, and pressures on costs that compromise companies' ability to invest in the business for the long term.[238]

Strategic competition is about finding new positions that profitably draw customers away from established positions or bring new customers into the market.

This is a key point for managers contemplating sustainability. At a time when competitors can easily benchmark each other to eliminate inefficiencies, improve customer satisfaction, and achieve operational best practices, many industries are experiencing what Porter calls competitive convergence.

> The more benchmarking that companies do, the more they look alike . . . As rivals imitate one another's improvements in quality, cycle times, or supplier partnerships, strategies converge and competition becomes a series of races down identical paths that no one can win.[239]

The question is, can sustainability provide a new and relatively untrammeled source of strategic advantage? In Porter's terms, can ecological and social factors enable a company to perform different activities from those of rivals, or to perform similar activities differently? The answer will vary by industry as sustainability performance matures over time. But the very slow pace at which companies in most sectors are adopting sustainability thinking, combined with continued growth in the underlying sustainability challenges themselves, almost guarantees a large source of strategic advantage for the foreseeable future.

Sustainability performance will ultimately disappear as a source of competitive advantage, when all firms shift to clean energy and zero waste, eliminate toxic chemicals and meet other market expectations for ecologically and socially attuned business practices. But if recent trends are any indication, it will be several more decades before that happens. Undoing ecological idiocies (such as the incandescent light bulb which converts 90 per cent of incoming electricity into heat when the goal is light) of the past two centuries is no small task. Until it is accomplished, companies at the forefront of sustainability performance will stand to gain significant advantage.

The three generic strategies

The three generic strategies are part of a larger set of frameworks including Porter's well-known Five Forces (to assess industry attractiveness) and value chain analysis (to implement the strategies). Here we consider only the first one with an eye on sustainability: how do ecological and social factors strengthen or change a company's business strategy?

The three generic strategies are defined along two dimensions: scope (the size and composition of the market) and strategic strength (or competency relative to competitors). The alternatives – low cost, differentiation, and focus – emphasize the need to choose between incompatible positions and to avoid being caught in inherent contradictions such as being simultaneously the low-cost player in an industry and its most differentiated.

The three generic strategies

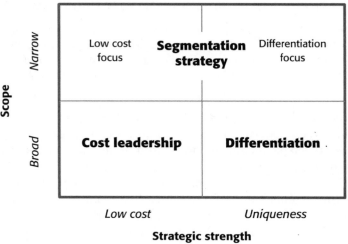

The airline industry offers a perfect illustration of the framework as a whole and the specific risks of being "caught in the middle." High-end, full-service operators, such as United Airlines or Continental, with extensive routes and maximum comfort are broad-scope differentiators. Southwest Airlines is pursuing cost-based segmentation by competing on price with cars over point-to-point routes with limited services and only basic comfort levels.

When Continental launched its CALite operations in an effort to emulate Southwest, it effectively straddled two positions: by simultaneously trying to cut costs to compete with Southwest and to differentiate based on Continental's full-service approach, it did neither well and ultimately closed shop. CALite is an example of being caught in the middle by being unwilling to make trade-offs and hard strategic choices. While Southwest had only one type of aircraft (the Boeing 737), Continental had 16 different types of plane. While Southwest flew from low-cost, secondary airports near big cities, Continental's hubs were all based in major city airports or smaller airports with not much demand. Southwest had localized maintenance, Continental kept its maintenance facilities at its main hubs. For all these reasons, CALite was unable to deliver the quick turnarounds at the lowest cost needed to compete with Southwest, while of course Continental's regular passengers became increasingly disenchanted with what they saw as poor-quality service.[240]

Sustainability as a source of cost leadership

Companies choosing to compete on cost appeal to price-sensitive customers. When pursuing this strategy, you must have lower prices than rivals and, in order to achieve above average profitability, even lower costs. Mathematically, the cost reduction must be proportionately greater than the price reduction in order to achieve above average margins. There are several ways to achieve cost leadership, which many of us are using on a daily basis, including high asset turnover, low operating costs, and superior control over supply chain procurement.

Sustainability can be a fantastic driver for a company seeking cost leadership because it leads to fewer materials, less energy, zero waste, and the redesign of its products and business model with fewer negative (and potentially costly) externalities. Furthermore, social and environmental performance can make a virtue of such cost savings by promoting the resulting products and services as greener and more socially attuned in a market that increasingly expects it.

Walmart is an obvious example of cost leadership with a broad scope. Seen through the lens of Porter's framework, it becomes immediately clear how the retailer's sustainability objectives to improve truck and store efficiency (two of the near-term objectives for achieving 100 per cent renewable energy) and to reduce waste (on its way to achieving zero waste) contribute to its strategic advantage. Within three years, embedded sustainability led it to improve truck fleet fuel efficiency by 30 per cent and store energy efficiency by 45 per cent.[241] The focus on eliminating 5 per cent of packaging materials is expected to yield $3.4 billion in savings by 2013.

And what about Walmart's third sustainability goal: to "sell products that sustain our resources and the environment?" Rather than see the move to sustainable products as a differentiation strategy, there is a case to be made that it reinforces its cost leadership. Without attention to sustainability attributes in its products and supply chains, Walmart risks losing its license to operate (in the intangible sense of societal approval) as well as increased difficulty with opening new stores in new markets and alienating an increasing number of consumers for whom environmental attributes matter.

Sustainability as a source of differentiation

Differentiation is all about creating unique (and, to customers, uniquely valued) attributes for which your company can charge a price premium proportionately greater than the costs they incur. These attributes can be based on performance, quality, aesthetics, dealer channel, availability, brand image, customer service, and many other factors. Nike athletic shoes and BMW cars come to mind as examples of broad-scope differentiation strategies.

A differentiation strategy is possible when customers have very specific needs and companies possess unique capabilities to satisfy those needs in ways that cannot be easily imitated by their rivals (think Apple's design skills and Pixar's animation know-how). In some cases, unique brand management capabilities lead companies to differentiate products that are otherwise difficult to distinguish from competitor products, as in the case of Chiquita bananas or Starbucks coffee.

Green and social performance attributes can reinforce product, process, and brand uniqueness. In cosmetics, natural and organic ingredients contribute to the luxury image of brands such as Sanoflore and Dr.Hauschka, both owned by L'Oréal. At a recent management seminar, a L'Oréal senior executive perceptively remarked that, some time in the future, nature itself will be the ultimate luxury.

In cars, the top-of-the-line Lexus LS600h, priced at over $100,000, bills itself as an ultra-luxurious vehicle that delivers a "formerly contradictory combination of jaw dropping engine performance, fuel efficiency, and low emissions."[242] The quietness and cleanness of the electric engine are obvious differentiators in the luxury segment but more surprising is the recent announcement of upcoming electric vehicles from performance car manufacturers. Speaking to a group of children, Norbert Reithofer, CEO of BMW, said that "When you get your drivers' licenses in 10 years you will drive an electric BMW."[243] Added Adrian van Hooydonk, director of BMW Group Design: "It will celebrate the good life over the fast life."[244]

Companies as diverse as Johnson Controls, Danone, Siemens, Henkel, and BT are all pursuing differentiation strategies with sustainability performance in their core activities. Sustainability contributes to their ability to differentiate in one of two ways. At the most basic level, it simply adds a new product attribute, such as Fairtrade certification. Customers purchase fair-trade coffee at Starbucks for its image, flavor, availability, store ambience, and because it promises equitable payment practices to its coffee producers. Fair trade does not require Starbucks to be green and socially responsible in other aspects of its business. In the second case, sustainability performance contributes to differentiation along many existing attributes of differentiation: it redefines quality, aesthetics, image, and stakeholder relations. In the embedded sustainability model, a product or service that embodies sustainability does not compromise on functionality or price. There are no trade-offs in usability, reliability, or durability. However, the product – whether a light bulb, household cleaner, bank loan, or car – will look and feel very different from its conventional counterpart.

Utilizing sustainability for market segmentation (focus)

Companies with strategic focus target specific market segments and have limited product lines. When competing via focus, you select a subset of customers within the industry and tailor your strategy to serving them to the exclusion of others. Two variants exist: cost focus and differentiation focus. The former seeks cost advantage in its selected segments while the latter exploits special needs. In both cases, there is an underlying assumption that the targeted segments are poorly served by broad-scope competitors. "The focuser can thus achieve competitive advantage by dedicating itself to the segments exclusively."[245]

The small but growing number of consumers who demand environmentally friendly, nontoxic, socially equitable, and otherwise sustainable products and services offer an ideal segmentation opportunity for green and socially attuned companies. "Small businesses have barely scratched their potential," sustainability guru Joel Makower says. "In every market now, there's a retailer, dry cleaner, auto mechanic, coffee shop with a green consciousness."[246] The rapid growth of environmentally aware consumer groups such as the True Blue Greens,[247] LOHAS,[248] and Cultural Creatives[249] favors (but does not guarantee) niche profit opportunities for small and mid-size companies who use sustainability to strengthen focus strategies.

Here is a sample set of focused sustainability differentiators and their broad-scope counterparts.

Focused differentiator	Broad-scope differentiator
Chesapeake Biofuels, LLC	DuPont
Pangea Organics	L'Oréal (selected brands)
Seventh Generation	Clorox Green Works
Patagonia	Nike Considered (line of apparel)
Triodos Bank	Westpac Banking Corporation
Ecowork LLC	Herman Miller
Tom's of Maine	Procter & Gamble
Taylor Companies	Herman Miller

In almost every case, the focused differentiator is able to charge a price premium that the broad-scope counterpart is not. Often, this is because a focused differentiator can be seen to be 100 per cent green and socially attuned (Patagonia) while bigger companies have business units that are seen as unsustainable (Nike outside its Considered line). There is always a subset of sustainability customers who are willing to pay more for a specialized company's products because of its uncompromised image and ability to "live its values."

What sustainability means for strategic positioning

No matter which of the three generic strategies a company is pursuing, social and environmental performance can strengthen (or weaken if done inappropriately) strategic positioning. It can drive a company to perform existing activities differently (for example, recycling water used in manufacturing instead of discharging it as waste) and to perform a different set of activities (for example, providing a service to recycle a customer's waste water stream). Sustainability-driven initiatives to reduce costs, differentiate products, enter new markets, and enhance reputation should be seen in the context of reinforcing the company's existing strategy and business priorities.

What happens when the goal is not to strengthen the company's existing strategy but to change it? How can sustainability help a business migrate to a new strategy – one that is more profitable and defensible in a sustainability-hungry marketplace? In the next section, we turn to another framework, Blue Ocean Strategy, to help managers answer these questions.

Blue Ocean Strategy

The underlying idea of Kim and Mauborgne's Blue Ocean Strategy is simple and appealing. The business universe is made up of . . .

> . . . two distinct kinds of space, which we think of as red and blue oceans. Red oceans represent all the industries in existence today – the known market space [in which] increasing competition turns the water bloody. Blue oceans denote all the industries not in existence today – the unknown market space [in which] demand is created rather than fought over.[250]

Existing market space turns into red oceans when supply exceeds demand and when industries experience competitive convergence. "A variety of product and service categories have become more and more alike. And as brands become more similar, people increasingly base purchase choices on price."[251] Slowing global growth combined with a fall in trade barriers and the technologically fueled ability to rapidly imitate competitor moves are bloodying the waters and causing niche markets and monopoly havens to disappear.

The cornerstone concept of Blue Ocean Strategy is **value innovation**, which says that the best approach to strategy is not to focus on benchmarking competitors but to create "a leap in value for buyers and your company, thereby opening up new and uncontested market space."[252] Rather than trying to beat the competition, creators of blue oceans make the competition irrelevant. Rather than making products either cheaper or more unique than competitor products, they focus on creating unique customer value.

With value innovation, Kim and Mauborgne are able to go beyond Porter-type trade-offs between cost and differentiation. Their point is that value without innovation keeps companies trapped in existing paradigms, making incremental changes that are not sufficient to make them stand out in the marketplace. On the other hand, innovation without value tends to be technology-driven and pioneering, going beyond what mainstream customers are willing to accept and pay for. Only by combining innovation and value can companies favorably affect their cost structures *and* their value proposition to buyers. "Value innovation occurs only when companies align innovation with utility, price and cost positions."[253]

The value innovation concept provides an excellent framing for sustainability-driven business strategy. Ecological and social issues facing businesses often lead their managers to make only incremental changes inside the existing paradigm – such as Nestlé's eco-water bottle with less plastic and greater compressibility – when the real challenge is moving beyond plastic water bottles altogether. Ecological and social issues also lead managers to envision products that the market is not ready to accept, from bamboo-paneled computers to solar shingles and fake trees[254] that scrub CO_2 from the air. At the time of this writing, such products failed to achieve any measure of mainstream market penetration. Only by aligning innovation with utility and price will sustainability lead to products and services that have market acceptance, and only by aligning cost with utility and price will the company be able to capture a portion of the value created.

For those companies able to take a value innovation approach to sustainability, blue oceans await, as market expectations and buying behaviors grow to incorporate social and environmental attributes. The need to reduce reliance on fossil fuels, eliminate waste, bypass toxic chemicals, and restore the health and integrity of communities create new markets for those companies who can align their innovation efforts with sustainability-framed definitions of utility, price, and cost. Some have criticized Blue Oceans Strategy for leading mainly to "blue ponds"[255] rather than oceans in terms of market size.

When applied to challenges such as climate stability, water and food security, and biodiversity, it quickly becomes apparent that the potential for sustainability-driven value innovation is as vast as the biggest oceans.

There is no question that the majority of today's ecological and social challenges call for system-level change. The electric car will not succeed without a new fueling infrastructure; clean energy will likely involve changes in the distribution and transmission of electricity; and cellulosic plastic will require innovations in recycling technologies and disposal practices. Value innovation is well suited for such challenges as it is inherently whole-system in nature.

> Because buyer value comes from the utility and price that the company offers to buyers and because the value to the company is generated from price and its cost structure, value innovation is achieved only when the whole system of the company's utility, price and cost activities is properly aligned.[256]

In contrast, eco-efficiency initiatives that conserve energy and cut waste – no matter how huge the savings – do not create blue oceans because they leave the utility proposition unaffected. Eco-efficiency can contribute to the cost-leadership strategies described in the previous section, just as bolt-on sustainability attributes can contribute to product differentiation, but neither provides the whole system transformation required for blue oceans.

"In this sense," conclude Kim and Mauborgne, "value innovation is more than innovation. It is about strategy that embraces the entire system of a company's activities . . . achieving a *leap* in value for both buyers *and* themselves." What a perfect framing for embedded sustainability! It challenges companies to move away from incremental change and mere tweaks to existing product designs, business models, and technologies. For example, holding CO_2 emissions constant at 2010 levels or even reducing them 30 per cent by historic standards may turn out to be vastly insufficient in the electric utility, steel, aluminum, cement, oil and gas, and automobile sectors.

What is the size of opportunity in terms of business value creation? In a study of the business launches of 108 companies, Kim and Mauborgne found that 86 per cent of the launches were line extensions, meaning incremental improvements within the red oceans of existing market space, and the remaining 14 per cent were launches aimed at creating blue oceans. Yet the line extensions accounted for only 39 per cent of total profits while blue oceans generated 61 per cent of total profits. The authors conclude: "Given that business launches included the total investments made for creating red and blue oceans (regardless of their subsequent revenue and profit consequences, including failures), the performance benefits of creating blue waters are evident."[257]

Companies that are first in their industry to launch sustainability-driven blue oceans can expect significant and lasting strategic advantage. First movers who *value innovate* alternatives to fossil fuels, distributed electricity generation, cellulosic plastic, and *in vitro* meat substitutes have the possibility to create new, profitable, and uncontested market space for years to come.

Blue Ocean Strategy tools, frameworks, and principles

Kim and Mauborgne offer easy-to-use and highly visual tools. Among them, the strategy canvas visually captures the key success factors in the known market space. It enables us to see where the competition is currently investing, the factors the industry currently competes on, and what customers receive from the existing competitive offerings on the market.

Take a look at the strategic canvas for wines shown below. A new competitor, Yellow Tail,[258] took an industry with two segments (fine wines and table wines) and turned it on its head by making its new wine offering "easy to drink", "easy to select," and "fun." It eliminated the wine complexity, daunting range, and enological terminology of fine wines and it raised the retail store involvement relative to table wines, thereby drawing in many non-wine drinkers including those who previously favored beer and ready-to-drink cocktails.

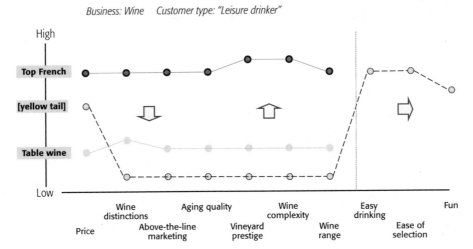

Strategic profile: current vs. [yellow tail]

Business: Wine   Customer type: "Leisure drinker"

Source: W. Chan Kim and Renée Mauborgne, *Blue Ocean Strategy: How to Create Uncontested Market Space and Make the Competition Irrelevant* (Harvard Business Press, 2005); used with permission from Jens Meyer, Adjunct Professor, INSEAD/Cedep.

Like Yellow Tail, sustainability leaders can reduce or eliminate factors that other companies in their industry have long competed on – fancy packaging, sourcing long distances, high energy intensity, chemically potent, serving only the richest consumers – and introduce entirely new factors such as fair trade, drought resistance, and biodegradability.

What would the strategy canvas look like for Tennant's ec-H2O described in the previous chapter? By eliminating cleaning chemicals altogether, it offers comparable cleaning performance with fewer water dumps and refills, along with fewer health and environmental risks to employees using the product, allowing commercial customers to integrate chemical-free cleaning into their green building operations.

To draw a new strategy canvas, Kim and Mauborgne offer a four-actions framework that lends itself to sustainability thinking:

1. Which of the factors in the strategy canvas should be reduced well below the industry's standard?

2. Which factors that the industry takes for granted should be eliminated?

3. Which factors should be raised well above the industry's standard?

4. Which factors should be created that the industry has never offered?

Asking these four questions through the lens of ecological and social sustainability yields a rich palate of opportunities in every sector.

Seeing differently

In *The Da Vinci Code*, author Dan Brown reveals to the reader that, in Leonardo da Vinci's painting of *The Last Supper*, there is a woman at the table – Mary Magdalene – contradicting what everyone knows: the 12 apostles are all men and the apostle to Jesus' right is John. If you are like many of us, after reading the book or seeing the movie, you rushed to your computer to Google the image of *The Last Supper*, only to be hugely mystified by what appears to be the image of a woman. How is it that we had never seen her before? Who was this woman? Was she in fact Jesus' wife?

In a similar spirit, Kim and Mauborgne's framework is designed to help managers see opportunities that exist but that may not be immediately visible. They do this by broadening the scope of thinking, pushing us to reach beyond current core customers to customers that are "on the fence" and even non-customers who reject the existing industry offering.

> Instead of looking within [red ocean] boundaries, managers need to look systematically across them to create blue oceans. They need to look across alternative industries, across strategic groups, across buyer groups, across complementary product and service offerings, across the functional-emotional orientation of an industry, and even across time.[259]

As a driver of blue ocean opportunity, sustainability broadens the available scope of value to include stakeholder value (not just customers), environmental, health, and social dimensions (not just the economic one), and the life cycle value chain (not just the company's own operations). It provides an additional lens through which innovation opportunities are identified and developed.

Cemex, the third largest cement company in the world, discovered a new and profitable blue ocean while creating societal value in its home market. Its Patrimonio Hoy program, launched in 1998, supports home building among Mexico's poor by extending micro-credit to small groups of customers who commit jointly to repay the debt. The program has enabled 75,000 families to build houses one room at a time in a third of the time at a third less cost. According to the program's general manager, by 2002 Patrimonio Hoy was generating positive cash flow from operations of over 2 million pesos per month.[260] "Whereas Cemex's competitors sold bags of cement, Cemex was selling a dream, with a business model involving innovative financing and construction know-how."[261] The previously untapped market of relatively poor do-it-yourselfers turned into a $650 million a year opportunity, with Cemex achieving 15 per cent *monthly* growth rates. According to Kim and Mauborgne, Cemex had created a blue ocean of emotional cement that achieved differentiation at a low cost.

Yet, while Blue Ocean Strategy lends itself to the business challenge of sustainability, Kim and Mauborgne seemed to have missed the full extent of the opportunity in this space. Their primary reference to sustainability (in the ecological and social sense) is an isolated product attribute (or customer utility factor) which they term "environmental friendliness."[262] Environmental friendliness is treated as one of many factors on a par with "customer productivity," "simplicity," "convenience," "risk," and "fun." In a personal communication with one of us (Chris Laszlo), Renée Mauborgne acknowledged that Blue Ocean Strategy has huge – and still unexploited or underexploited – applications to sustainability-driven business strategy.[263]

The notion of creating entirely new market spaces is appealing to sustainability champions, but how can they be sure that they are aiming high enough? To answer this question, we turn to a powerful framework for thinking about disruptive innovation. Clayton Christensen offers us the third and final framework needed to understand how sustainability creates strategic advantage.

Clayton Christensen's disruptive innovation

Clayton Christensen developed his theory of disruptive innovation to help companies "handling or initiating revolutionary changes in their markets."[264] As such, it is particularly relevant to the many sustainability challenges that require radical, not incremental, business solutions. Take, for example, the case of climate change. The Intergovernmental Panel on Climate Change (IPCC) Fourth Assessment report calls for 80–95 per cent reductions in global human-induced CO_2 emissions by 2050 relative to 1990 levels – a huge reduction given that over this period the world's population will increase by about a third while affluence (measured by mean global incomes) is also expected to increase.[265] How will business respond to such a challenge?

A useful distinction is made by Christensen between what he calls sustaining technologies and those that are disruptive. *Sustaining* technologies improve the performance of established products "along the dimensions of performance that mainstream customers in major markets have historically valued." In Christensen's framework, sustaining technologies can be discontinuous or incremental. In either case they offer customers better performance than what existed before. By contrast, *disruptive* technologies usually result in worse product performance, at least in the near term. They appeal to nontraditional markets that uniquely value the innovation, despite limitations that make it unattractive to the mainstream.

Industry leaders tend to "overshoot" customer needs simply because technology allows them to – remember all the gadgets and features of your cell phone that you never touched? Pursuing "hot" new features, industry leaders compare new technologies with existing ones, when instead they should be comparing them with market demand for performance.

The concept of disruptive technological change is key to what Christensen calls the innovator's dilemma. In the face of disruptive change, industry leaders are often handicapped by the very factors that lead to their success; managing the change calls for a different set of management principles and strategy approaches than those that incumbents typically use to preserve their acquired advantage.

The question here is whether disruptive change adequately describes sustainability challenges such as climate change and global poverty that call for radical innovation in production process and product design. These challenges require not only reduced harm but also solutions that help restore imbalances in society and nature. To answer this question, let's turn to, perhaps, the most famous case in the Christensen repertoire.

The disk drive industry

The most detailed Christensen case study of disruptive innovation is that of computer disk drives. It showcases the evolution of hard disk drives beginning with the 14 inch drive technology introduced by IBM in the 1950s and ending with the 2.5 inch drive technology that became standard in notebooks in the 1990s.

After the initial introduction of the 14 inch disk drives, sustaining innovations improved their capacity at an average rate of 35 per cent per year.[266] When 8 inch drives were introduced, they initially did not appeal to mainframe computer users because of their limited capacity, but they found a niche position with manufacturers of minicomputers. Sustaining innovations increased the capacity of these drives until the 5.25 inch drive was introduced, which once again failed to interest the existing market because of limited storage capacity (10 MB instead of 60 MB for the 8 inch drives available in 1981) but found a market with emerging personal computer (PC) makers. With the advent of PCs, competition shifted from differentiation based on storage capacity to differentiation based on size.

The next disruptive innovation came with the 3.5 inch drives, similarly offering size benefits. Once again existing customers of mainstream products, such as the IBM XT and AT, appeared to be looking for higher-capacity drives at a lower cost per megabyte, rather than smaller size. Incumbent manufacturers of the 5.25 inch drive decided against investing in the 3.5 inch technology arguing that it could never be built at a lower cost per megabyte than the 5.25 inch drives. As Christensen points out with great clarity, it was managerial thinking and market analysis, and not technology, that prevented the incumbents from investing in the new format.

After the introduction of the 3.5 inch drive, the basis of competition shifted from reducing size to improving reliability as parts previously handled mechanically were now handled electronically. Further innovations (including the move to 2.5 inch and then 1.8 inch drives) were sustaining innovations that improved performance along criteria that existing customers cared about: weight, ruggedness, and low power consumption as well as smaller physical size. Not surprisingly, given Christensen's thesis, incumbents were able to seamlessly make the shift to the new formats because existing mainstream customers now valued the new technologies' attributes. Market research and customer demand supported the 2.5 and 1.8 inch drives right from the start.

The lessons from the disk drive industry are that disruptive innovations are typically missed by leading manufacturers, because they result in a product that is not immediately appealing to their mainstream customers. Incumbents are focused on established trajectories of higher performance and higher margins. The firms that lead the industry in adopting disruptive technologies are in every instance new entrants to the industry, not its incumbent leaders. The irony is that industry leaders are toppled precisely because they listen to their customers and invest in new technologies that provide them with the kinds of performance improvement that these customers are asking for. Ironically, careful study of market trends and the detailed assessment of customer needs become strategic liabilities.

Established industry leaders appear to develop a kind of deafness to new emerging market realities. Could it be that such disregard for disruptive change explains why many industry leaders fail to fully onboard sustainability challenges in their core business activities?

The electric car

In the automobile market, the electric car technology of the 1990s – GM's EV1 – was a classic example of disruptive technology that failed to get support by the senior management of incumbent firms. The EV1 had too short a range, too poor acceleration, and appealed to too small a niche market to interest them. As a technology, electric cars had as late as 2009 attracted only new entrants – 30 companies in all[267] – not a single one an existing automobile player. Even the best known among them, such as Tesla and Fisker Automotive, had succeeded in serving only niche markets.

But what about the 2010 entry of the big car companies into plug-in electric vehicles, such as the GM Volt and Nissan Leaf? Is the next generation electric car a case of disruptive innovation or is it a radical but sustaining one? Using the disk drive analogy, do electric cars today parallel the shift from 8 inch drive technology to 5.25 inch drives, or is it the case of the shift from 3.5 inch drives to 2.5 inch drives?

Christensen's view of the electric car

In *The Innovator's Dilemma*, published in 1997, Christensen presents a future-oriented case study, "using a personal voice, to suggest how I, as a hypothetical employee of a major automaker, might manage a program to develop and commercialize one of the most vexing innovations of our day: the electric vehicle."[268] A review of his forward-looking analysis 14 years ago and comparing it to what exists today provides a fascinating opportunity to test his framework.

Christensen asks two questions. First, does the electric car pose a legitimate disruptive threat to companies making gasoline-powered automobiles? Second, does it constitute an opportunity for profitable growth?

To answer his first question, he graphs the trajectories of performance improvement demanded in the market versus the performance improvement supplied by the technology. Recall that for a disruptive technology to succeed, its technological performance must eventually exceed market expectations.

In the visual overleaf, his original 1997 trajectories for electric car technology performance versus market demand are shown as straight and dotted lines ending in the late 1990s. The technology performance of three electric cars in 2011 are superimposed: the Chevrolet Volt (a plug-in hybrid electric that uses a gasoline-powered engine to extend the range of the electric battery), the Nissan Leaf, and the Tesla Model S.

The three graphs make it pretty clear at a glance that the electric car is a disruptive technology and that it is a threat to the big gas-powered car makers.

Electric car performance vs. market demand

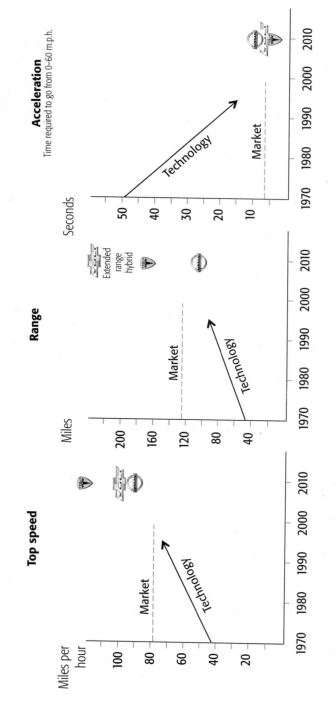

Source: drawn from Clayton M. Christensen, *The Innovator's Dilemma* (Collins Business Essentials, 1997), p. 238, based on data from Dr. Paul J. Miller, Senior Energy Fellow, W. Alton Jones Foundation. Data for the Chevy Volt, Nissan Leaf, and Tesla Model S are drawn from company websites.

The technology performance of electrics is catching up – and now exceeding – market demand for performance along key criteria. So what else can we learn by comparing the 1997 forecast with the 2011 reality? Christensen's trajectories for "top speed" and "acceleration" appear to have been pretty much bang on. As regards the limited range capability of electrics, there are several ways car companies can approach the problem. They can choose to focus on market segments such as city commuters who do not need long-range capabilities. They can develop technological solutions for longer ranges (Tesla currently offers a battery pack option with a 300 mile range while the Chevy Volt uses a hybrid drivetrain to extend the range up to 600 miles). Or they can convince consumers that recharging frequently is easy and convenient (the projected Nissan approach).

Of the three 2011 models, two are from incumbent firms and one (the Tesla Model S) is from a new entrant. Prices are still higher than conventional gas-powered equivalents: $49,900 for the Tesla S, $41,000 for the Chevy Volt, and $32,500 for the Nissan Leaf.[269] The higher-priced Tesla is clearly the performance leader and exceeds market demand requirements in all aspects. Recently Toyota formalized a partnership with Tesla to manufacture the Model S (and, in 2012, the all-electric RAV4). Toyota will not only be investing $50 million of capital into Tesla but will also provide engineering and production systems for the development of electric vehicles.

Given the above analysis, will incumbent firms such as GM and Nissan (and Toyota) succeed to become leaders in the new technology? Recall that Christensen's findings show that incumbents almost never succeed in doing anything more than defending their market share. Will new entrants such as Tesla gain significant market share or can we expect new (and lower-priced) players to emerge?

In order to understand why industry leaders have the cards stacked against them in dealing with disruptive technological change, Christensen proposes the concept of a value network.

The value network: why successful industry leaders fail

A value network is the *context* within which a company makes decisions such as how to respond to customers' needs and what resources to allocate to potential projects. Within a given value network, a company is conditioned to perceive the economic value of a new technology through the value lens of its existing technologies. According to Christensen, "in established firms, expected rewards ... drive the allocation of resources toward sustaining innovations and away from disruptive ones."[270] Remember the blinders used to limit and guide a horse's vision? That, to a degree, can be the consequence of our entrenched value networks.

The way in which value is measured differs across networks, leading to a unique rank ordering of product performance attributes. Mainframe computer manufacturers perceive value in terms of disk capacity, speed, and reliability. These attributes define the boundary, for disk drives, of their value network. In contrast, PC manufacturers perceive value in terms of disk size, ruggedness, and low power consumption. It is therefore unsurprising, given their relative value networks, that mainframe players failed to value the shift from 8 inch to 5.25 inch drives.

Product attributes are not the only defining factors of value networks. The organizational mind-set and culture also evolve in incumbent firms to support sustaining innovations of existing technologies.

When it comes to sustainability pressures, many companies fail to recognize business opportunities because they are limited by the existing value networks. Corporations are designed to close ranks against outsiders such as activists perceived to have social or environmental agendas. The prevailing mind-set is to lobby against government regulations that are seen as impeding their freedom of action. Most of all, every fiber of the corporation exists to privilege quarterly shareholder earnings. Creating social and ecological value, however relevant to business success, is simply not in the DNA of today's corporation.

Andrew Hoffman talks about the need for organizational transformation as companies go from environmental management to integrating environmental issues in the core of their business strategies.

> A shift from environmental management to environmental strategy requires a concurrent and supporting shift in organizational culture, structure, reward systems and job responsibilities. Managers must focus on developing an organizational culture that will encourage a merger of environmental and economic interests in the decision making of its employees.[271]

In the case of the electric car, customers value its quietness, reliability, and torque. (Electric cars reach peak torque at 0 rpm and keep it through 6,000 rpm, while gasoline engines begin with low torque and peak in a narrow range before falling off again. The result is much faster acceleration for electrics without the need to change gears.) In addition, customers value the independence from oil, which recent history has shown to be price-volatile and a source of geopolitical conflict. Finally, customers value the "environmentally friendly" attribute of electrics. The reduced mile-per-gallon equivalency and the possibility of charging the cars using electricity from clean energy sources provide perceived societal benefits.

In many ways, the electric car in 2011 is benefiting from the overshooting of customer needs by conventional gasoline-powered car manufacturers. In the face of existing traffic laws and increased congestion on the roads, cars with massive horsepower ratings, top speeds above 80 miles an hour, and ranges above 120 miles exceed the market demand for performance. The huge number of luxury options at the high end, from massaging seats to private TV stations for rear-seat passengers, is also creating an umbrella for electrics that focus on the new performance criteria.

Christensen's pattern of managerial decision making

Christensen suggests a characteristic pattern of decision making across every industry. The pattern is reflected across the six steps shown below. What happens if we apply each of the steps to the evolution of the automobile industry's electric car technology from the 1990s to 2010? Christensen could only guess at how the electric car story would play out. As the table below shows, he was right on the money with the majority of the steps.

	Description of the step	The electric car 1990s–2010
Step 1: Disruptive technologies were first developed within established firms	Although disruptive technologies are most often commercialized by new entrants, "their development was often the work of engineers at established firms, using bootlegged resources"	**True**. The EV1 was developed by GM in the 1990s
Step 2: Marketing personnel then sought reactions from their lead customers	The marketing organizations in incumbent firms show the disruptive technology to lead customers of the existing product line, asking for an evaluation. Finding little interest, marketers drew up pessimistic sales forecasts. The prototype technology is then rejected by management	**True**. Electric cars were downplayed and even outright rejected by the marketing departments of GM and Chrysler who compared their performance with existing gasoline-powered cars and found these early electrics wholly unattractive
Step 3: Established firms step up the pace of sustaining technological development	In response to the needs of current customers, the marketing managers focus instead on "faster, better, cheaper" sustaining innovations	**True**. Instead of electric cars, GM and other car companies turned to SUVs, bigger-horsepower cars, and sustaining fuel-efficiency improvements of the 100-year-old gasoline-based internal combustion engine

	Description of the step	The electric car 1990s–2010
Step 4: New companies were formed, and markets for the disruptive technologies were found by trial and error	New companies, often with frustrated engineers from incumbent firms, are formed to develop the disruptive technology	**True**. By 2009, some 30 electric car companies – all new entrants to the automobile industry – have been formed. They include Tesla, Miles, Think, Aptera and Fisker Automotive
Step 5: The entrants moved upmarket	Once the start-ups get a hook in the market, they make sustaining improvements to the technology to move into higher performance categories	**True**. The all-electric Venturi Fetish sells for over $400,000. The Tesla Motor Roadster goes for $100,000. The Fisker Karma has a projected price of $80,000
Step 6: Established firms belatedly jumped on the bandwagon to defend their customer base	When the new entrants begin to invade established market segments, incumbents introduce the new technology to defend their customer base in their own market	**True**. The GM/Chevy Volt and Nissan Leaf are introduced in 2010. Other plug-in electrics from major auto companies are coming in 2011 and beyond

The story of the electric car poses interesting questions about other sustainability-driven innovations. Should major sustainability challenges such as water scarcity and global poverty be approached as opportunities for disruptive technological change – favoring new entrants and initially serving only a small number of new customers – or should they be approached as sustaining innovations (both incremental and radical) that incumbents can undertake as a way to better serve their existing mainstream markets? How should managers of incumbent firms manage sustainability challenges that present disruptive change?

In summary

Among the plethora of strategy theories, three modern classics offer a palette of solutions. Michael Porter and the positioning school suggest that, if managed right, social and environmental performance can reinforce any of the generic strategies. You can use sustainability efforts to strengthen your existing cost leadership, boost differentiation, or discover a better focus. Blue

Ocean Strategy offers practical tools for turning the vast canvas of sustainability pressures and needs into new unexplored and uncontested market territories. Clayton Christensen warns against the blinding effect of existing market success, and offers tools for recognizing disruptive innovation opportunities where some only notice poor performance.

In the next chapter we bring Porter's **Generic Strategies**, Kim and Mauborgne's **Blue Ocean Strategy**, and Clayton Christensen's **Disruptive Innovation** together into a single framework for understanding how sustainability contributes to business strategy. Building on the insights of the strategy field, we come to the heart of our discussion on sustainability and what it means for business – and offer a radically new way to approach it.

5
Embedded sustainability

It might seem as if the following words come straight from the handbook of green business or a sustainability manager's press release:

> Not since the days of the Great Depression has there been such a severe decline of public trust in business and in our economic system – nor has there been a better opportunity to build a new era of business-led excellence and leadership in our industry and beyond. We believe that doing good and doing well go hand in hand and that economic prosperity, environmental stewardship, and empowerment of people can, in an integrated way, become a source of innovation and competitive advantage for the long term.[272]

But, perhaps surprisingly, these words are from a Chief Financial Officer, Jen-niffer Deckard, who in 2011 became President of Fairmount Minerals, a company that operates in an industry – mining – hardly celebrated by the green movement.

Fairmount Minerals, the third largest industrial sands company in the U.S., is not typical of its industry. Since 2005, it took on a complete overhaul of its business strategy and practices with the goal of integrating social and environmental value into every aspect of company life. It developed new processes such as the reuse of its spent sand and the recycling of its bulk bags; new products, such as low-cost water filters for emerging markets; and new relationships, such as external dialogues connecting the needs and desires of over 850 of its stakeholders. Once sustainability became everyone's job – and deeply embedded into the DNA of the company – it also became a way to improve competitive positioning. For an industrial sands company, acquiring mines in close proximity to the end market is a crucial driver of profitability. In light of the low unit value of the product and high transportation costs, location is a key source of competitive advantage.

In 2006, Fairmount Minerals set its eyes on a potential mine in Wisconsin and engaged stakeholders in the community in a discussion about co-planning mine operations. When the Town of Tainter selected it over a competitor seen as less sustainable, the local newspaper wrote a telling story called "The Tale of Two Sand Companies." Going beyond compliance in mining operations made all the difference in getting preferential access to new strategic assets.

From the American Midwest, we travel to Austria, the birthplace of the Erste Group Bank. Founded in 1819 as the first Austrian savings bank, the Group went public in 1997 with a strategy to expand its retail business into Central and Eastern Europe. By 2010, Erste Group's customer base had grown from 600,000 to 17.5 million, with more than 50,000 employees serving clients in over 3,000 branches in eight countries.[273]

By early 2008, as the Central and Eastern European markets settled into a steady but slowing growth, the banking industry's products and services appeared homogenized and indistinguishable to an average customer, while the internal efficiencies of Erste Bank were approaching their maximum potential. The decade ahead raised a new question for the Group: from where should its source of competitive advantage come? In its search for competitive advantage, the Group had a bold new idea: to bet on the Bank's centuries-old history and decade-old ownership structure in which 31 per cent of the Group shares were owned by a nonprofit foundation, thus distinguishing it as a 'good' bank with a socially minded owner.

While initially the integration of social value into the core of the Erste Group Bank identity and strategy was discussed as a source of better positioning through differentiation, in the following years the company discovered that it represented an entirely new way to create and capture value. In addition to connecting sustainability to business priorities in its existing markets, the Group also discovered a new and largely uncontested market space. The good.bee holding, co-founded by the Erste Group Bank and its key shareholder, the Erste Foundation, is an inclusive financial services company built on the principles of microfinance and social entrepreneurship. The holding builds on microfinance – the well-established mechanism that started with the idea of lending very small amounts to foster entrepreneurship and poverty alleviation – to develop a broader range of services. Now operating in Romania, its first test market, good.bee offers micro-credit, micro-payments, micro-savings, and micro-insurance to unbanked and under-banked populations as a financially profitable mechanism of social development. As Sava

Dalbokov, Erste Bank's veteran executive and CEO of good.bee puts it, "good is groovy!"[274]

Fairmount Minerals and the Erste Group Bank are just two of hundreds of companies we studied – and worked with – in an effort to understand how sustainability "done right" can create sustainable value. What unites these companies is a unique response to the environmental, health, and social pressures they face. They pursue sustainability as thriving business opportunity – but not all opportunity is created equal. Unlike the majority of companies that simply *bolt on* sustainability to their existing strategy and processes, like a poorly fitted Band-Aid, these pioneering businesses *embed* sustainability into the very DNA of their businesses, thus deeply transforming their strategy and operations for enduring value creation.

Embedding sustainability

Embedded sustainability is the incorporation of environmental, health, and social value into the company's core business with no trade-off in price or quality (i.e., with no social or green premium). The goal is not green or social responsibility for its own sake. It is meeting new market expectations in ways that strengthen the company's current strategy or help it to develop a better one. At its best, it is invisible, similar to quality, yet still capable of hugely motivating employees and creating loyalty in consumers and supply chain partners.

Embedding sustainability can improve strategic positioning in the Michael Porter sense explored in the previous chapter. Even if a business continues to have negative environmental and social impacts on stakeholders, embedding sustainability can strengthen its cost leadership, product differentiation, or focus. This is the case for Fairmount Minerals described above. Jewelry from the Richline Group – with its supply chain traceability[275] – has helped it achieve preferred status with retail clients such as Walmart. Clorox is gaining market share with its Green Works line of nonallergenic, nontoxic, biodegradable plant-based cleaning products.[276] The China Ocean Shipping Company (COSCO) is streamlining its delivery system, cutting CO_2 emissions by 15 per cent and saving 23 per cent on logistics costs.[277] Stories like these are typically about doing less bad, or becoming eco-efficient.

The Erste Group Bank is an example of embedded sustainability leading to entirely new market opportunities based on "doing good" – a particular kind of Blue Ocean Strategy. Whether it is manufacturing components for wind turbines or recycling customer waste, formerly unsustainable businesses are retreading themselves as profitable providers of sustainability solutions. Such is the case in DuPont's transformation from a carbon-intensive commodity chemicals manufacturer to a leader in sustainable agriculture, green building materials, bio-based packaging, biofuels, and fuel cell components. Also exemplary is Clarke, formerly a provider of synthetic chemical-based mosquito control products, which recently transformed itself into an integrated environmental services company. Its new mission is preventing disease and creating healthy waterways through the use of its natural larvicide, Natular™, for which it won the U.S. Presidential Green Chemistry Award in 2010.[278] Rather than just doing less harm, companies like DuPont and Clarke are learning to become eco-effective.

Companies can strengthen existing strategies with only incremental changes in sustainability performance. Greening its delivery systems won't alter COSCO's underlying shipping model but it can help reinforce cost leadership, just as more energy-efficient stores help Walmart deliver on its promise to customers to save them money. In other cases, existing strategies are strengthened through radical changes in sustainability performance. Tennant's innovation in floor cleaning technology based on ionized tap water instead of cleaning chemicals is a step-jump in reducing environmental impact (from less harmful chemicals to no chemicals).

Similarly, companies that migrate to sustainability-driven Blue Ocean Strategies can do so with incremental or radical change. Ecological and social pressures are introducing new performance parameters such as clean, quiet, and fair that appeal to nontraditional customers who uniquely value them. Among the global industry leaders: GE's migration from manufacturer of gas turbines, appliances, jet engines, and other industrial equipment that notoriously polluted the Hudson River, to its current Ecomagination and Healthymagination product portfolios offering sustainability solutions for individual and business customers, is a prime example of embedding sustainability in pursuit of uncontested blue oceans.

As you ponder the idea of embedded sustainability, consider the story of U.S.-based GOJO Industries, Inc. Founded in 1946 with the first one-step heavy-duty hand cleaner and the 1952 introduction of the first portion-controlled dispenser for tough soils markets, GOJO today is a mid-size private company focused on safeguarding resources and advancing public health for future generations. It helped set industry standards for sustainable skincare in introducing the world's first green certified hand soap and instant hand sanitizers. As a member of the United States Green Building Council (USGBC), GOJO was instrumental in the inclusion of hand hygiene requirements within LEED-EBOM (Existing Buildings: Operations & Maintenance).

Recent advancements include SMART FLEX™ technology, the company's lightweight, recyclable PET refill bottle made with 30 per cent less material. The new bottle offers the same durability as a standard rigid HDPE bottle. Another is the Plastics to Playgrounds program, enabling it to divert more than 50 per cent of its solid waste from landfills through a partnership with a local toy manufacturer, reducing environmental impact while having a positive impact on the lives of children.

In 2010, GOJO declared ambitious long-range sustainability goals as part of its core strategy. The company is striving to "bring well being to 1 billion people every day by 2020" through efforts to improve hand hygiene when soap and water are not available. It is continuing to target reductions in water usage, solid waste, and greenhouse gases. It also sponsors scientific research to advance quality of life and reduce risks to well-being. For example, after a university study[279] revealed the vulnerability of refillable bulk soap dispensers to bacterial contamination, the company is working to educate the industry about unnecessary health risks of bulk hand soap contamination.

With its emphasis on innovation and continuous learning, GOJO is just one more example of an industry leader committed to embedding social and environmental sustainability into its business . . . a company that declares itself "passionate about creating a healthy world by delivering solutions that positively impact people, places and the environment."[280]

Another small/mid-size company example is Bohinj Park Hotel. Envisioned as one of the first "green" hotels in Eastern Europe, Bohinj Park Hotel could hardly bet on price premiums to make its business model viable. Instead of focusing only on marginal but highly visible environmental and social attributes such as soaps, towels, and the usual hotel eco-efficiency practices, the hotel and resort has environmental performance embedded into its very walls. Combining geothermal and co-generation technologies, the hotel produces its own energy for all hotel operations, including the usually heat-demanding workings of an aqua park. Water is continuously recycled throughout the system, with heat collected from the warm shower water before it is reused for toilet flushing. Floor heating ensures a comfortable feeling, while special cool-heat grids with their inaudible and energy effective work, significantly outperform the classic air-conditioning systems. Wall and window insulation is fortified by a one-of-a-kind insulated roof, while LED lighting and wireless room controls allow for optimal room performance independent of particular guest behavior. Socioeconomic development of a remote Bohinj region is also embedded into hotel operations: it is one of the largest local food consumers, employers, and community activists, with all health and wellness amenities open to local residents for free throughout the entire year. It is no surprise that the Bohinj Park Hotel generates 17.22 kg of CO_2 per guest per night, a whopping tenfold difference compared with 174.82 kg produced by "standard" hotels in the region. As for the financial impact, the company managed to move energy expenses from the first to the last of major items in its cost structure, with energy representing only 14 per cent of the overall expenses. The savings are then channeled into other activities of the hotel, such as food and catering, allowing the company to produce superior performance without price premium.

If your head is spinning from all the different ways that sustainability can embed into business strategy, that's because there are many routes to creating sustainable value. What is important is that every company can benefit, no matter what its starting point or where it wants to go. Even dirty industries undertaking incremental change can reap large rewards as they develop the capacity for integrating business and societal benefits.

Bolt-on sustainability and embedded sustainability are two strikingly different approaches to managing social and environmental pressures in pursuit of value creation. It is the ability to recognize the difference between the two that separates winners and losers across industries and continents. To better understand embedded sustainability, let's look next into what it is not.

Just bolt it on!

Many companies "bolt on" sustainability like an afterthought to their core strategies, despite their best intentions. They trumpet green initiatives and social philanthropy that lie at the margins of the business, with symbolic wins that inadvertently highlight the unsustainability of the rest of their activities. If Nike's Considered line of footwear is sustainable, what are its other products? If the 2011 Chevrolet Cruze touts its use of eco-friendly cartridge oil filters,[281] what do GM's other vehicles use? Sustainability becomes programmatic: a headquarters endeavor pinned onto one person or one department charged with finding and communicating those things that the company is doing anyway and that can now be repackaged as sustainability leadership.

A good tip-off that sustainability is bolted on is when it is declared to be a separate strategy, one that is de facto parallel to the company's main business. Another is internal teams working without the close collaboration of suppliers, customers, NGOs, and other stakeholders. A third is viewing corporate responsibility as a balancing act in which economic interests are traded off against social and environmental targets. We can of course point to obvious cases such as Exxon-Mobil's[282] corporate citizenship strategy[283] promoted through its corporate-level sustainability working group. But the reality is that the vast majority of companies pursue bolt-on green and social responsibility projects that are poorly integrated into the rest of their value-added activities.

Ask yourself: Does your company have a separate function or department responsible for sustainability performance with its own dedicated link on the corporate website? Does it have flagship green products – like the Chevy Volt, priced at nearly double its gasoline equivalent – for which customers must pay extra?

We have all heard real-life stories of bolt-on sustainability. You might even find familiar the case of the sustainability manager hired at a telecommunications company. After a year on the job, she produces a glossy sustainability report, largely designed by external consultants, which brilliantly covers topics ranging from ethics to information security. On environmental protection alone, the report highlights double-digit successes in energy conservation across major data centers, paper recycling, and hybrid cars for sales fleets. The problem: business unit heads run the other way when they see her coming, the CEO never mentions sustainability in his quarterly webcasts with analysts, and hardly a single employee believes sustainability is anything other than a public relations exercise. The wireless group fails to address core sustainability issues such as EMF[284] risk to cell phone users; the broadband and fixed-line businesses are only barely compliant with WEEE and RoHS regulations of heavy metals, toxic chemicals, and recycling of electronic equipment. Opportunities to serve the poor in emerging markets are largely ignored, and the company is a laggard on making products available to disabled and aging customers.

Also familiar might be the case of the specialty chemicals supplier's offsite meeting of its top executives. A consultant is asked to brief the top team on sustainability and what it means for the core business. The briefing is followed by a heated discussion about the growing attacks by international NGOs, opinion leaders, government agencies, and consumer groups who increasingly view the company's product portfolio as harmful to human health and the environment. "Our strategy in the core business is hugely profitable," comments the CEO. "Even with declining market shares and growing regulatory pressures, we can continue to make money doing what we've always done." Two years later the company has in place several sustainability initiatives from green packaging and employee well-being programs to a foundation for educating young women in emerging countries. But its core business is increasingly demonized worldwide, sales are down and employee turnover is at an all-time high, even though for the time being profits remain strong.

Stories of bolted-on sustainability are, unfortunately, all too common. They produce self-reinforcing narratives about sustainability and corporate social responsibility being necessary costs rather than profit opportunities. With the bolt-on approach prevailing in practice, it is no surprise that much of today's sustainability efforts bring about cynicism among both corporate managers and social activists, with little value created for either party. Yet there is a viable alternative – built on radically different theory, principles, and practices – that is increasingly pursued by leading businesses of different sizes and shapes around the globe.

So . . . what are the differences between bolt-on and embedded sustainability?

We know how to meet the demands of shareholder value – and years of thinking about managerial excellence has produced remarkable expertise in this area. We also know how to create stakeholder value: traditional approaches such as CSR and philanthropy that predictably lead to trade-offs and added costs. Now we have bolt-on sustainability efforts producing fragmentary and symbolic wins at the fringes of a company's activities.

What we are still discovering is how to meet both shareholder and stakeholder requirements in the core business – without mediocrity and without compromise – creating value for the company that cannot be disentangled from the value it creates for society and the environment. Companies like Fairmount Minerals and the Erste Group Bank are showing us how embedding sustainability in the core business can create enduring value for shareholders and stakeholders in a win–win for business and society.

Here is one way to think about bolt-on versus embedded sustainability as two strikingly different ways to manage social and environmental pressures for business opportunity:

	Bolt-on sustainability	Embedded sustainability
Goal	Pursue shareholder value	Pursue sustainable value
Scope	Add symbolic wins at the margins	Transform core business activities
Customer	Offer "green" and "socially responsible" products at premium prices or with diminished quality	Offer "smarter" solutions with no trade-off in quality and no social or green premium
Value capture	Focus on risk mitigation and improved efficiencies	Reach across all seven levels of sustainable value creation
Value chain	Manage company's own activities	Manage across the product or service life cycle value chain

	Bolt-on sustainability	Embedded sustainability
Relationships	Leverage transactional relationship. Stakeholders such as customers, employees, and suppliers are resources to be managed and sources of input	Build transformative relationships. Co-develop solutions with all key stakeholders including NGOs and regulators to build system-level change
Competitor	Operate only in win–lose mode in which any gain is competitor's loss	Add cooperation with competitors as potential source of gain
Organization	Create a "scapegoat" department of sustainability	Make sustainability everyone's job
Competencies	Focus on data analysis, planning, and project management skills	Add new competencies in design, inquiry, appreciation, and wholeness
Visibility	Make green and social responsibility highly visible and try to manage the resulting skepticism and confusion	Make sustainability performance largely invisible but capable of aligning and motivating everyone

It might all seem rather obvious, but what does it mean to systematically and pervasively embed sustainability into a business, without trade-offs in quality, performance, or aesthetics and without a price premium? How can it create value for the company, no matter where its business is today or where it wants to go?

To answer these questions, we offer a framework to guide managers who want to integrate sustainability into the DNA of their companies. Informally, we have been using the methodology for close to a decade in our consulting and executive education. The resulting distillation owes much to the managers who have applied it in their organizations and provided us with feedback and suggestions along the way.

The *ES Cloud*

At this point, you may ask, why do we need a framework? What is its purpose? Renowned business educator Derek Abell argues that what he calls "currently useful generalizations" are important tools of competent managers. They are a way of entering the debate, and opening up questions, rather than providing a watertight result.[285] In a similar vein, effective frameworks help managers to discover new ways of looking at a situation. They push managers to ask the right questions, rather than necessarily give the right answers.

The embedded sustainability framework – which we name the *ES Cloud* – is offered in this spirit.

A key goal of the *ES Cloud* is to help managers think about what embedded sustainability means for their business. The framework is not a new strategy concept as much as a new way to mull, and to use, existing strategy concepts. It draws on Michael Porter's positioning theory, Kim and Mauborgne's Blue Ocean Strategy, and Christensen's disruptive innovation to show how embedded sustainability can enhance a company's business strategy. It offers a way for managers to think about using embedded sustainability to migrate from one type of strategy to another.

The *ES Cloud* also provides fresh insights into sustainable value creation. The sustainable value matrix, discussed in Chapter 2, is a way to reframe sustainability as a source of value creation. By rethinking their business through the lens of shareholder *and* stakeholder value, managers use the matrix to discover business opportunities that might otherwise remain obscured. The *ES Cloud* goes a step further, making clear *how* sustainable value supports business strategy.

Welcome to the Cloud

To explore it, managers ask two questions. The first is "How green and socially attuned is your business?" along a spectrum from ecologically and

How green and socially attuned is your business? (now and in the future)

socially harmful (left extreme) to leadership in solving global problems (right extreme.) The second is "what kind of change do you want?" with options ranging from incremental (bottom of vertical axis) to radical (top of vertical axis.)

Depending on where they see their business on the map and where they want to go with what kind of change, embedded sustainability will produce different strategy outcomes.

Where is your business today?

Begin by assessing where your business is today in terms of sustainability performance. First, in sustainability terms, is your *industry* part of the problem or part of the solution? The carpet industry, no matter how green and socially attuned it becomes, will always be part of the problem – even if it asymptotically moves towards Ray Anderson's vision of a zero footprint. Visually, it will always be on the left-hand side of the *ES Cloud*. On the other hand, if you are in the business of providing clean water, renewable energy, or nutritional products to the poor – as do units within Unilever, GE, and DuPont – then you are helping to solve global sustainability challenges. Second, is your *company* more or less sustainable than other companies within the industry? General Motors is less green than the average car company while Honda is relatively more so, as measured by the average fuel economy of their fleets in comparable categories (passenger cars, 2WD light trucks . . .) and their funded commitments to clean fuel technologies.

Based on the nature of your industry and the performance of your company relative to its competitors, you can decide where the business maps on the horizontal axis. One important disclosure: many managers who are too bought-in to their company's internal narrative will assume that their business is clean, green, and socially responsible – even in cases where it has a large negative footprint. To test initial assumptions, you need to ask whether your industry meets established principles of sustainability such as those of The Natural Step or Cradle-to-Cradle. You also need to inquire into how your company is *perceived* externally. Confronting external stakeholder perceptions and internal technical data can be eye-opening, as in the case of food and beverage companies who package their products in containers that use the plasticizer bisphenol A (BPA) or wireless companies who deny the existence of cell phone radiation risk. In both cases, the internal corporate view – supported by technical and scientific data – is very different from external stakeholder views supported by another set of data.

Where will your business be in the future?

What is your vision for the business in 5, 10, or 15 years? Will it continue with the same underlying strategy in the same industry with better positioning? Or will embedded sustainability offer an opportunity for it to change business strategies? In the language of Blue Ocean Strategy, if your existing business is turning into a red ocean of destructive competition, then pursuing new uncontested market space may be the way out of certain death – and embedding sustainability may provide one (though not the only) path forward.

If today you are in the lower left of the *ES Cloud*, embedded sustainability can either lead to better positioning (staying with the same underlying strategy in the same industry but being greener and more socially attuned) or it can lead to a new strategy that has solving global problems at its core. These alternatives are shown below. Remember that no position or path on the map is "better" than any other, and companies can create business value in a wide variety of situations.

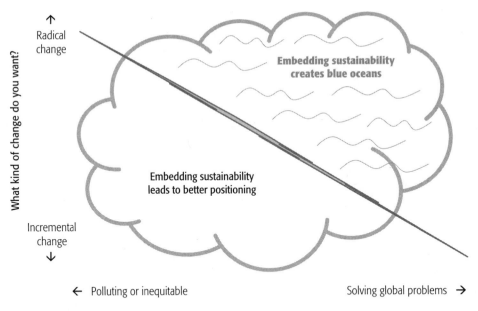

How green and socially attuned is your business? (now and in the future)

In staring at the boundary between "better positioning" and "blue oceans," you may begin to wonder about the kind of sustainability change you should undertake. That is what we turn to next.

What kind of change do you want?

It is not enough to know where you are and where you want to go. You also need to know what kind of change will get you from here to there. There are three types of change to consider: incremental, radical, and disruptive. Following Clayton Christensen's terminology, sustaining change can be incremental or radical – the key is that it improves product performance "along the dimensions of performance that mainstream customers in major markets have historically valued."[286] Disruptive innovation is always radical and introduces a new set of performance parameters that are uniquely valued by nontraditional customers. The case of the electric car described in the previous chapter illustrates disruptive change in the case of sustainability-driven innovation.

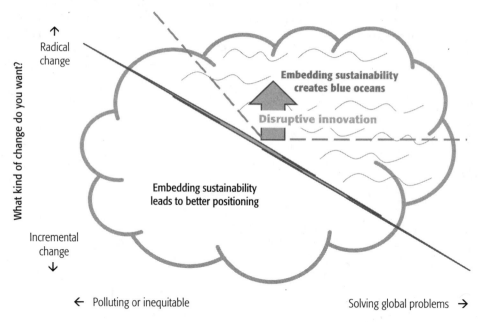

How green and socially attuned is your business? (now and in the future)

For an unsustainable business that wishes to remain in its existing market space, changes in sustainability performance typically lead to improving its strategic positioning through eco-efficiencies. Blue oceans await those that dare to use embedded sustainability to transform their businesses into providers of solutions to environmental and social problems.

In the following section, we invite you to play around with the Cloud. The many examples serve as our version of Lego® blocks to build and mold different business cases and pathways. And don't forget to add your own examples, both real and imagined.

Exploring the Cloud

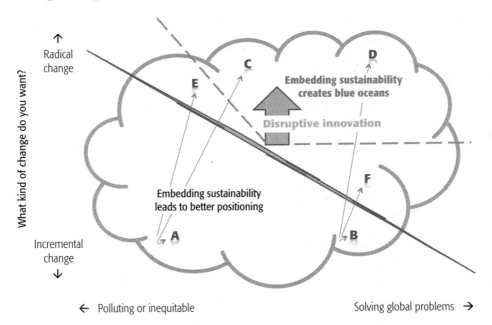

How green and socially attuned is your business? (now and in the future)

So, what are the different starting points and pathways possible?

In case A, a business has negative impacts on society or the environment and is on a trajectory of incremental change. Embedding sustainability will not help such a business be seen as green or socially responsible, but it can improve its competitive positioning, for example by lowering costs through further energy conservation or waste reduction.

Case B is for a company already in the business of providing ecological or social solutions to the market. It is also on a path of incremental change to its sustainability performance. Here, embedded sustainability reinforces its core strategy of being a sustainable company.

In cases C and D, embedding sustainability becomes the driver for Blue Ocean Strategies. Radical change in sustainability performance is a way to create uncontested market space – whether starting from a point of being "dirty" (C) or "green" (D).

Points E and F are interesting special cases. A "dirty" industry can pursue radical change in sustainability performance without necessarily creating blue oceans. This is the case in the dry cleaning industry as some players choose to switch from perchloroethylene to liquid CO_2 technology. Although dramatically less toxic, liquid CO_2 technology serves the same customers based on the same performance attributes. Equally, a "green" business (F) can create uncontested market space with only small changes in sustainability performance. Cell phones that connect individuals and communities in developed markets can, with minor adaptations, serve low-income populations in emerging markets, giving them access to information and job opportunities that would not otherwise be available to them.

Managers can map their businesses on the *ES Cloud* to determine the strategy framework (Porter, Blue Ocean Strategies, and disruptive innovation) that best applies to them. Here are some illustrations:

1. Most mainstream automobile companies map to point A. They are relatively polluting and serve relatively high-income consumers using nonrenewable resources such as oil. Embedding sustainability can help them improve their strategy positioning by further lowering costs (for example, new OEM paint systems that reduce spray waste to nearly zero) or helping them to further differentiate their products (for example, the hybrid Ford Fusion with its high fuel efficiency)

2. Nissan/Renault's $6 billion investment in plug-in electric vehicles and its decision to launch the all-electric Nissan Leaf in December 2010 maps it to point C. The company is undertaking disruptive innovation with a technology that currently undershoots mainstream market needs. It is co-serving a new customer – governments that are anxious to get the strategic transportation sector off oil dependence – in a classic case of Blue Ocean Strategy

3. IBM's Smarter Planet is a business that in some parts maps to point B. It is aimed at helping customers reduce energy dependence and climate change while increasing the livability of cities. "Smart grids" are an example of incremental change in sustainability performance – reducing electricity use but not changing the fuel source of the electricity generated

4. Emerging businesses such as those in biotechnology (Novozymes), clean energy providers (Vestas Wind Systems A/S), and those serving customers with incomes of less than $3 per day (Bharti Airtel has figured out a way to profitably sell a wireless minute for under 1 cent,

allowing it to reach poor households in rural India[287]) map to point D. They are the quintessential example of using sustainability pressures to create uncontested market space through disruptive innovation. Growing markets for water desalination, drought-resistant crops, and soy-based nutritional products for the base of the pyramid exist because of sustainability pressures

The *ES Cloud* allows any business – no matter what its level or trajectory of sustainability performance – to embed sustainability into its business strategy to improve its competitive positioning, to pursue new Blue Ocean Strategies, and to search for additional disruptive innovation opportunities.

How about dirty red oceans?

While many options and pathways exist, the biggest opportunity by far is to migrate from an existing red ocean of a polluting or inequitable business to a blue ocean of providing solutions to global problems. Because of the scale and magnitude of global sustainability challenges, such a migration in business strategy typically requires disruptive innovation (see point G [overleaf]). To take two obvious cases, America's oil dependence will not be resolved by raising the fuel efficiency of its cars by 25 or even 50 per cent; and meeting the needs of the 4 billion people who are largely excluded from global markets cannot be done with only minor modifications to existing business models.

Formerly unsustainable businesses that "crack the nut" of clean and socially equitable solutions to global problems will find a growing and largely uncontested market space in the years ahead.

Consider the case of the Burlington Chemical Company.[288] Founded in the 1950s, Burlington began as a producer of chemicals and dyes for the U.S. textile industry. When government regulations of effluent water quality tightened in the 1980s, Burlington attempted to help its customers by producing more environmentally friendly chemicals and dyes. But with the textile industry in continuous decline and many companies going overseas to take advantage of lower labor costs, Burlington was unable to avoid disaster: it soon found itself in a red ocean of destructive competition in the face of continuously declining market demand. Between 1995 and 2000, both its revenues and average selling price fell by half.

In the 2000–2004 period, Burlington successfully restructured – in part because it was able to leverage its clean textile dye technology. More importantly, during this period it developed a new bio-based business – based on sustainable chemistry – for the manufacturing and service industries. The

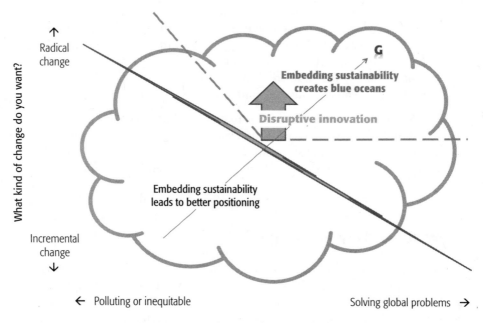

How green and socially attuned is your business? (now and in the future)

new products used vegetable oils, soy-based fabric softeners, and new green cleaning systems.

Burlington migrated from purveyor of textile chemicals and dyes to provider of bio-based sustainable chemistry solutions for a variety of industries. At two critical points, the company faced survival threats that were resolved by embedding sustainability into its core business. In the 1980s it improved its positioning in the red ocean of textile chemicals and dyes by developing products that were low in toxicity and more energy-efficient than competitor products. In the 2000s, it made a radical change in its portfolio when it sold its chemical business and reinvested in biotechnology-based products. This time, embedding sustainability through disruptive innovations led it to relatively uncontested market spaces providing sustainability solutions to other companies. For example, it developed a line of biodegradable surfactants that can be used by customers in registered formulations for approval by Green Seal, the EPA's Design for the Environment (DfE), and Canada's EcoLogo programs.

By 2004, the company had realized a positive cash flow for the first time in six years and an improving balance sheet.[289] Today it is a relatively small company with 32 employees, billing itself as a "total solution provider" and manufacturer of "environmentally friendly chemicals for a greener tomorrow."[290] Here is a way to make sense of Burlington's strategy migration:

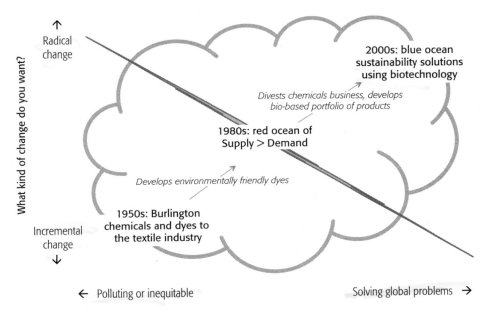

How green and socially attuned is your business? (now and in the future)

So, what are the foundational assumptions and principles that guide embedding sustainability into the very DNA of your company? Here is a starter list of imperatives to direct your efforts to deeply integrate social and environmental performance into existing business strategies and to explore opportunities for migrating to new strategies based on providing sustainability solutions.

The ES principles

The principles of embedded sustainability are simple yet – taken as a whole – capable of shifting companies from a cost-based paradigm to the opportunity-driven best practice of today's sustainable value leaders. They capture the essence of what it means to embed sustainability into a company's core business without trade-offs or price premiums.

Value creation principles

1. Maximize sustainable value, not shareholder value *or* stakeholder value (and not a balance or compromise of the two)

2. Focus on meeting customer *and* stakeholder needs. Look at every business decision through an outside-in perspective of stakeholder issues, interests, and frustrations

3. Expand the scope of action from the organization's own boundaries to each of its product's life cycle value chains

4. Go beyond risk mitigation and cost cutting to sustainability-driven product differentiation, brand respectability, regulatory influence, and radical innovation

5. Integrate sustainability performance into the core business, not only at the fringe (hybrid cars for the sales force!) or symbolically (a green product line)

Relationship principles

6. Engage and integrate a diverse set of stakeholders, including those who represent social and ecological interests that prima facie are opposed to the company's interests. Co-develop business solutions with those external partners who can provide access to specialized knowledge about environmental and social issues and increase buy-in and market acceptability of the company's activities and products

7. Build relationships that are *transformative* rather than *transactional.* They should instill commitment and responsibility, embed business in the community, and create a sense of co-ownership for business solutions. Avoid the perception that people and nature are simply viewed as production resources to contractually benefit the company

8. Compete cooperatively as well as adversarially. Cooperating with competitors can create differential business value when complexity is high or when the industry benefits from new regulatory standards. In these cases, companies with superior sustainability performance benefit more than the industry average

Capabilities development principles

9. Learn creative and empathetic "right-brain" skills such as design thinking and generative engagement in addition to traditional "left-brain" skills such as data analysis and project management. Rather than only analyzing fragmented problems in order to take actions that are planned by insular teams seeking to control outcomes, managers learn to co-create solutions through collaboration with stakeholders who, taken together, give voice to the entire business system

10. Ask heretical questions about what sustainability pressures mean for the business. Rather than only exploring less harm, consider what zero harm and positive benefits look like for core business activities. Consider the magnitude of global challenges such as climate change and global poverty when designing business solutions. Learn to unlearn existing routines, assumptions, and frames of reference

11. Make sustainability everyone's job, rather than managing it through a scapegoat department or function. Abolish the title of "Sustainability Manager"

12. Become indigenous. Acquire "native capability" for "co-inventing contextualized solutions that leverage local knowledge."[291] In global markets, corporations develop local understanding, build local capacity, and encourage flexible market development through local partnerships

While the principles might appear rigid and nearly dogmatic in nature, we invite you to think of them as starting precepts for business conduct in today's marketplace. By no means are they the only principles or intended to be a complete set. On the contrary, we invite you to add your own by joining our community at www.EmbeddedSustainability.com.

Before we conclude this exploration of the essence of embedded sustainability, let us revisit three cornerstones of business strategy: **competitive advantage**, **activity analysis**, and **externalities**. Through the lens of embedded sustainability, the meaning of these three concepts changes substantially. For managers who want to embed sustainability into their businesses, grasping these concepts becomes paramount in today's world.

Competitive advantage

It is nearly impossible to explore the field of strategy without immediately stumbling on the concept of competitive advantage. Competitive advantage has been defined as the ability of a company to achieve above-average indus-try returns.[292] Examine this definition in depth, and it becomes patently clear that the emphasis is on financial gain rather than on a broader definition of value that includes – in addition to money – individual well-being, soci-etal good, and ecological sustainability. To achieve competitive advantage, companies are urged to pursue one goal above all others and with single-minded determination: create superior value for their clients in ways that translate into the highest possible cash returns on invested capital.[293] With an overweening attention paid to clients, the traditional understanding of competitive advantage cannot account for the existence of multiple stake-holders, those diverse constituents along the value chain who, as the term implies, have something at stake relative to the company, be it their employ-ment, their health, or their community. Superior value is also assumed to be only economic and technical in nature. Strategy texts typically define the dimensions of client value in terms of price, performance features, qual-ity, availability, image, and ease of use.[294] Yet competitive advantage today encompasses many new opportunities to achieve superior value through *stakeholder* value creation.

Value-added activity analysis

To the notion of competitive advantage we add another concept crucial for embedding sustainability: the *way* in which companies create superior buyer value. Perhaps the best-known and most widely used concept here is that of value-added activities. Collectively, all the value-added activities of a product or service are represented by the value chain of the company. Primary activi-ties typically include R&D, production, logistics, marketing and sales, and service. Support activities include functions such as HR and infrastructure management. Michael Porter popularized this model of the generic value chain.

At a first glance – and in light of the big three sustainability trends – it is striking that, in Porter's framework, no activities are specifically designated to address the environmental or social impacts (negative or positive) on diverse stakeholders along the value chain. Equally absent are upstream activities such as raw material extraction and downstream activities such as product end-of-life. But if we take a minute to think about it, none of this is surpris-ing given the external environment in 1985 that was not yet characterized by radical transparency or by consumer expectations for sustainable products (though the bell of declining resources was already ringing loudly[295]).

Value-added activities today extend horizontally from cradle to grave, or cradle to cradle in the case of products that can be reused in one way

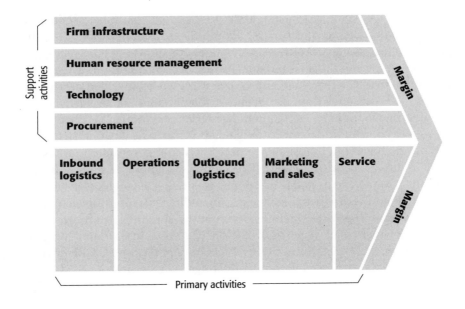

or another, and vertically to include a diverse set of stakeholders who are impacted by activities at each stage of the life cycle.

Externalities

Open a typical MBA economics textbook, and you will see externalities defined as the "direct effects, independent of any price changes, that the actions of some households or firms have on the utility of other households or on the output of other firms, none of whom have invited these effects."[296] In other words, externalities are the benefits (or costs) that economic actors impose on others without being paid (or without paying the price) for their actions. When a manufacturer provides technical training in a community to increase its local pool of skilled labor, it often improves the general level of education and welfare in the community – a value it does not fully capture. The training provides a positive externality for the community. On the other hand, the chemical wastes in a river produced by a paper and pulp factory, when the ecological, social, health, and economic costs of the waste are borne by society and not by the company, is an example of a negative externality.

Since Arthur C. Pigou's work in the early 20th century, it was assumed that the government, through taxes and subsidies, would maximize total societal welfare by eliminating any divergence between marginal private benefits and marginal costs to society. Marginal private benefits are reflected in the value of a product or service at market prices. Marginal costs to society are the aggregate value to society of all the resources used, whether or not that value is reflected in market prices. Remember our story of Takeharu Jinguji in Chapter 1? You can think of marginal private benefits as the market price of his caught fish. The marginal cost to society includes the added destruction to marine ecosystems from his longline fishing – externalities such as snaring albatross in his baited hooks and the marine pollution of his boat (and of course his contribution to overfishing bluefin tuna to near extinction).

With the benefit of hindsight, we now know that government has largely failed to take the necessary corrective actions to achieve a balance between present private benefits and future public well-being. Pigou himself was concerned about the ability to balance private utility with future social welfare. "The social enthusiasm which revolts from the sordidness of mean streets and the joylessness of withered lives is the beginning of economic science," he wrote in the 1920 edition of *The Economics of Welfare*. "[T]he environment of one generation can produce a lasting result, because it can affect the environment of future generations. Environments, in short, as well as people, have children."[297]

Now a cornerstone of economic theory, the very existence of externalities as an acceptable business principle is being challenged by the new market reality. Laws and regulations play an important role in context setting and will continue to do so in the future. But increasingly it is the *internalization* of externalities – the privatization of public costs and benefits – that is forcing marginal social benefits and marginal social costs to balance. Take, for example, the recent report by the World Resources Institute and A.T. Kearney focused specifically on fast moving consumer goods (FMCG). A comprehensive analysis of trends in sustainability, the study offers the following mind-boggling statistic:

> Based on our scenario of more stringent climate change regulations, enhanced and enforceable forest policies, growing water scarcity in key agricultural regions, informed biofuel policies, and a greater consumer demand for green products, we estimated a reduction of 13 to 31 percent in earnings before interest and taxes (EBIT) by 2013 and 19 to 47 percent in 2018 for FMCG companies that do not develop strategies to mitigate the risks posed by environmental pressures.[298]

In other words, if you are a FMCG company and you are not internalizing the externalities proactively in the present, you will be dragged into action by downward pressure to the bottom line.

In summary

Embedded sustainability is a new response to a new business reality. Unlike trumpeted CSR initiatives that create stakeholder value at the expense of shareholders, or bolt-on efforts to tag on social and environmental issues at the margins, embedded sustainability offers pathways to enduring profits in the core business.

The foundations and principles of embedded sustainability are strikingly different from most environmental and social endeavors permeating business today. That is why for most managers, embedding sustainability is the road less traveled. The good news is that there are many pathways to the coveted destination. Whether it is strengthening your existing market positioning or discovering new uncontested market space, the *ES Cloud* offers you a way to map where you are, envision where you want to go, and to design a pathway that makes sense for your company and its broad context.

Embedding sustainability demands a deep rethink of business. It also requires the development of new competencies, processes, and practices adequate for the challenge of sustainable value creation. Now that we have looked into the "what" of embedded sustainability, it is time to explore the "how" and to discover what it takes to get it done.

Part III
GETTING IT DONE

The roots of change
Introduction to Part III

Don't get us wrong: we have nothing against the "sweetheart companies" designed first and foremost to be green and socially responsible, the Patagonias and Whole Foods of the world. These enterprises are built from the very start on the foundation of sustainability values and principles. Yet, with all due respect, they have it almost easy, while the traditional players have to struggle to transform themselves into more sustainable versions of their former selves. Of course, it is an immense task to build the world's best vacuum cleaner, but just imagine what it would take to transform that working vacuum cleaner into the world's best TV set – without unplugging it or slowing down its performance!

So, if you are considering this seemingly impossible task, how do you get it done? How do you go well beyond the limits of CSR and the often symbolic results of bolt-on strategies, to embed sustainability into the very DNA of your business? How do you make it work?

To answer this question, we turn our attention to the emerging stories of mainstream companies embedding sustainability into their core business. While most of these examples around the world are at a very early stage, we can find no better way to ground our explorations of strategy execution than to draw on real-life examples of mainstream companies we have worked with or studied closely.

Surely, for a part of the book focused on the "how" of embedded sustainability, you have a right to expect great clarity, precision, and logical sequential to-dos. Indeed, that was our own vision as we began the comprehensive study of emerging best practices in creating sustainable value. That was our expectation: after what was to be due time to systemize the knowledge and experience of cutting-edge companies we would have a tight and easy-to-follow methodology. As we jumped into the task, we had images of tool kits, simple rules, and 12 easy steps fueling our enthusiasm.

Yet it should come as no surprise that, for a challenge as complex and demanding as embedding sustainability into the business core, no simple recipes are possible. No matter how tempting it is to spell out a few catchy bullet points for you, in reality, much of the sustainability journey is messy, nonlinear, and repetitive. Simplifying and negating this reality will only damage your ability to play with and design a truly masterful embedded sustainability business strategy.

In the following chapters, we invite you to join us through the journey. Part III is imagined as a reference point for a diverse set of topics, which, when interwoven, create a fabric for the practice of embedded sustainability. We hope that the threads and the patches offered will give you concrete and tangible resources for making your own efforts impactful.

We start Part III by exploring a few unexpected capabilities that emerged as essential for the task at hand. While traditional business skills remain vital when embedding sustainability into the DNA of your company, they must be complemented by competencies rarely valued in the corporate world: design, inquiry, appreciation, wholeness. These are the starter "muscles" we want you to build before jumping into the game.

From competencies we move on to processes, and look into the four broad elements of change management relevant to embedding sustainability. In a somewhat artificial division, we put aside issues of strategy content, and focus solely on the many dimensions of the change process, beginning with the question we are asked most often: "How do we start?"

Finally, we get back to the issues of content and look into the key conversations needed to embark on a solid embedded sustainability pathway. In the last chapter of Part III we recap the key concepts and then lay out the steps and corresponding questions to ask when designing your own road map.

While the "how" of embedded sustainability may not come packaged as polished steps or concise bullet points, we hope that the pages ahead offer you a meaningful, real, and relevant platform for making your own organizational transformation work – with competencies as our first stop.

6
Hot competencies for a cool world

In a sunlit room around a huge conference table, nine senior managers are hard at work. At first glance, the intense discussions and passionate engagement might appear to be those of a typical strategy meeting: formulating the problem, analyzing options, arguing positions, and deciding possible courses of action. You can almost see what comes next: the final verdict, a recommendation followed by drafts of the "strategic document," and then off to meet with the deployment teams. Internal communication processes that cascade through the company; action planning meetings built around key performance indicators . . . We've all been there, right?

Now take a second look. The meeting briefs, scattered around the table, offer little more than a set of forceful questions. The well-stacked PowerPoints and reams of data have given way to Post-it notes, markers, and giant flip charts. The table in front of you is one of 40 such tables in a giant convention room hosting well over 300 people for a strategy meeting. Intense roundtable discussions are interrupted by skits and other creative presentations to the entire community. And if that is not shocking enough, you just recognized suppliers, customers, academics, NGO activists, and policy workers playing it cool at every turn.

What is unfolding in front of you is not a product of a change guru's imagination gone wild. In China and the U.S., Brazil and Singapore, managers come together to make – and implement – strategic solutions for the new challenges facing business. The challenges in question offer entirely new levels of complexity and demand entirely new ways of addressing them: in the era of declining resources, radical transparency, and increasing expectations, no cookie-cutter recipe will do. The changes are drastic, fast, and furious. The answers lie way outside of traditional organizational boundaries. The know-how is in the hands of mortal enemies. The solutions cannot be compart-mentalized. Welcome to the end of business-as-usual.

While a 300-people strategy dialogue is one of the more extreme examples of how companies respond to today's complex business reality, it does speak pointedly to the demand for new competencies needed to drive social and environmental value into the very DNA of business. Yes, the trusted aptitudes of the corporate world, often referred to as left-brain capabilities,[299] are still in the game: we continue to need solid analysis, precise measurement, and clear planning. Yet alone these staples of business success are simply not enough. A new set of competencies, more often associated with the right-brain world of artists, inventors, and Cultural Creatives,[300] is required for the unexpected, complex, and messy challenges of sustainable value creation. Here, we will speak about four of them.

Design, inquiry, appreciation, wholeness. A surprising set, no question about it – perhaps straight from the pages of a new-age, self-help book? Not to worry. By now, these new business aptitudes have been around for more than a few years, and companies big and small have experimented with them and succeeded in creating sustainable business value.

Design

Ask any business leader – whether Indian, American, Russian, or Swiss – what is the job of a good manager, and the answer will surprise you by its remark-able consistency. Management is all about decision making. In fact, the idea of decision making as the main task separating a manager from the rest of the organization has become deeply ingrained in our thinking.[301]

Decision making, according to popular wisdom, boils down to a "selection of a course of action among several alternatives."[302] As systems thinkers Rich-ard Boland and Fred Collopy point out,[303] this involves a particular attitude or approach to problem solving, one which tends to dominate management practice and education. This decision attitude is built on the assumption that it is relatively easy to come up with alternatives to consider, but rather diffi-cult to choose among them.[304] Complex analytical tools and reasoning tech-niques are necessary to overcome the central difficulty of choice.

So far so good? Indeed, the decision mind-set has served us well, and much of business strategy and implementation is built on the ability to analyze, assess, and choose the right course of action. Yet, when it comes to the task of embedding sustainability into the core business without compromising

> We should not underestimate the crucial importance of leadership and design joining forces. Our global future depends on it. We will either design our way through the deadly challenges of this century, or we won't make it. For our institutions — in truth, for our civilization — to survive and prosper, we must solve extremely complex problems and cope with many bewildering dilemmas. We cannot assume that, following our present path, we will simply evolve toward a better world. But we can design that better world.
>
> **Richard Farson**
> Psychologist and author

on price and quality, one thing becomes obvious: we have nothing to choose from.

Go back in time only few years and put yourself in the shoes of Walmart managers aspiring to create the first examples of sustainable value. In October of 2005, Walmart CEO Lee Scott made a startling announcement broadcast to all 1.6 million employees and communicated to some 60,000 suppliers around the globe.[305] Walmart was initiating a far-reaching "business sustainability strategy," whereby environmental value was to be embedded into the current pillars of the company's competitiveness: big box stores, world-class distribution and outstanding supply-chain management. Three clear goals were selected as part of its vision of sustainability integration: "To be supplied 100 percent by renewable energy; to create zero waste; and to sell products that sustain our resources and the environment."[306] Only one minor problem: nobody knew how to get it done.[307]

Imagine yourself at those early meetings dedicated to turning these goals into reality. As you ponder the enormity of the goals set forth by the company's top management, it becomes obvious that all the skills and aptitudes that brought about success in the past are no longer enough. Yes, great analytical techniques in support of great decision making are still important. But for a manager ready to choose the best alternative to create sustainable value, one thing is missing: the choices have to exist first. And this is where design comes into play.

Forget fashionable clothing and fancy kitchen utensils, and consider design as an attitude, a mind-set, or a mode of thinking. At the core of such an attitude is

> Engineering, medicine, business, architecture and painting are concerned not with the necessary but with the contingent — not with how things are but with how they might be — in short, with design.
>
> **Herbert Simon**
> Economist and Nobel Memorial Prize recipient

an assumption strikingly different than that of the decision attitude. If decision is all about making a hard choice between easy-to-identify alternatives, design attitude assumes an easy choice between difficult-to-create alternatives.[308] Unlike bolted-on sustainability that requires little change in products and processes and thus relies heavily on what already exists, embedding social and environmental value into the core business creates a whole different ball game. Tim Brown, CEO and President of IDEO, ranked among the ten most innovative companies in the world, illustrates this new reality in the following way:

> a management philosophy based only on selecting from existing strategies is likely to be overwhelmed by new developments at home and abroad. What we need are new choices – new products that balance the needs of individuals and of society as a whole; new ideas that tackle the global challenges of health, poverty and education; new strategies that result in differences that matter and a sense of purpose that engages everyone affected by them. What we need is an approach to innovation that is powerful, effective and broadly accessible. Design thinking . . . offers just such an approach.[309]

Now, if design thinking represents a crucial competence to be acquired as a complement to good decision making, how do we develop it? What are the elements and characteristics of good design that a company should consider?

Tim Brown makes a useful distinction in his thought provoking *Change by Design*. To generate great choices and to come to meaningful solutions, a team has to attend to three overlapping spaces: an **inspiration** space, where insights and inputs are made; an **ideation** space, where insights are translated into ideas; and an **implementation** space, where the best ideas are brought forth into reality.[310] While you, as a reader, might appreciate a defined sequence in our presentation of the three spaces, in reality a team might move in and out of the spaces through multiple iterations and with no clear boundaries between them. Each of the spaces, however, offers unique benefits and challenges.

Inspiration

Some years ago, in conversation with professors and students at the Cleveland Institute of Art, we heard a story of a surprising experiment. A group of students received an assignment to design a comfortable, light, multifunction backpack. With designs submitted mid-way through the course, the second part of the assignment was distributed: to take the same demands and limitations, and add one more to it. With a vision to minimize waste, students were asked to make sure the backpack required the least number of parts possible. With only one additional design requirement, the change in the final products was staggering. Not only were the new designs less wasteful and often more elegant; the anticipated cost of production went down significantly across the board.

"Design is the first signal of human intention,"[311] says Bill McDonough, the controversial architect-designer and half of the author team behind the sustainability bestseller, *Cradle to Cradle*. What the backpack story illustrates is the central task of the inspiration space in the process of design: to develop a clear intent and to translate it into specific requirements and constraints for the project.

Dan Pink, an author who did much to popularize design thinking and other right-brain capacities as essential for business, suggested two fundamental constraints for each good design: utility enhanced by significance. "A graphic designer must whip up a brochure that is easy to read. That's utility. But at its most effective, her brochure must also transmit ideas or emotions that the words themselves cannot convey. That's significance."[312]

Tim Brown and his IDEO team speak about three key constraints for every solution: "feasibility (what is functionally possible within the foreseeable future); viability (what is likely to become part of a sustainable business model); and desirability (what makes sense to people and for people)."[313]

Bill McDonough and his partners bring the following poetic constraints to every sustainable solution they sink their teeth into: "Our goal is a delightfully diverse, safe, healthy and just world, with clean air, water, soil and power – economically, equitably, ecologically and elegantly enjoyed."[314] The world's largest green roof, 10.4 acres of a plant-covered space atop Ford Motor Company's Dearborn Truck Plant,[315] is one of McDonough's projects developed in line with his extraordinary design principles – delivering outstanding environmental value while saving the company $35,000,000 upon installation.[316]

Whether it is simplicity or poetics that attracts you the most, when it comes to the task of embedded sustainability, the role of clear intent is essential. The concept of embedded sustainability challenges the very assumptions, the design principles of business as a whole. We know how to meet the demands of shareholder value. We also know how to create stakeholder value. What we are still discovering is how to meet both requirements at once without mediocrity and without compromise. Clearly, we have a design problem on our hands.

Of the many companies that are successfully inventing new design requirements for embedding sustainability into their core businesses, the global nutrition, health and wellness giant Nestlé comes to mind – despite its controversial past surrounding infant formula marketing practices.[317] In 2007, Nestlé introduced its first *Shared Value* report, spotting specific "design requirements" for its products and operations. Each set of requirements featured clear shareholder and stakeholder value components to be balanced and harmonized. Here are a few examples: "Reducing our environmental footprint and reducing operational costs," "Improving workers' earning capacity and creating a skilled workforce," "Helping farmers improve earnings and assuring our supply of quality raw materials," as well as "Expanding lower income segment's access to nutrition and broadening our customer base."[318] By creating requirements that align social and environmental goals with the existing business priorities with no trade-offs, the company created conditions for successful innovation.

If intent – manifested through clear constraints and requirements – represents the goal of the ideation stage of design, then engagement with your stakeholders represents its primary method. To create meaningful and impactful requirements, it is crucial to be deeply engaged with all parties who have value at stake. Whether it is your own company's employees, customers, suppliers, or other stakeholders, understanding their needs at a nearly visceral level becomes crucial. Here is how designer and author Jane Fulton Suri speaks about this principle of good design:[319]

> Directly witnessing and experiencing aspects of behavior in the real world is a proven way of inspiring and informing [new] ideas. The insights that emerge from careful observation of people's behavior . . . uncover all kinds of opportunities that were not previously evident.

Applied to the task of embedding sustainability, first-hand observation and insight into the needs and realities of the plethora of stakeholders becomes the best source of ideas for products, services, and processes to be reimagined. And since sustainability needs – and solutions – developed by nonprofits, suppliers, end consumers, activists, and regulators are rarely the focus of business attention, engagement becomes a muscle worth exercising.

Ideation

While the inspiration space offers insight and guidelines for the future, ideation space is there to translate insights into ideas worth exploring. But unlike the celebrated rapid-fire brainstorming sessions typical of mainstream business, idea generation within a design mind-set is a take-your-time, hands-on, deliberate and iterative process.

In the words of a design veteran,

Design thinking is inherently a prototyping process. Once you spot a promising idea, you build it. The prototype is typically a drawing, model, or film that describes a product, system, or service. We build these models very quickly; they're rough, ready, and not at all elegant, but they work. The goal isn't to create a close approximation of the finished product or process; the goal is to elicit feedback that helps us work through the problem we're trying to solve. In a sense, we build to think.[320]

Playing with different ways of embedding sustainability into a process or product becomes a part of strategy development. When you take time to build your ideas from the ground up, you have a better chance of a tight fit between social and environmental efforts and existing company priorities. While it may look like you are wasting valuable time sketching and experimenting with things that might not see the light of day, investing into ideas allows you to test earlier, make mistakes faster, and get to solid solutions sooner. For the remarkably complex challenge of creating sustainable value, prototyping offers a way to explore uncharted territories with minimal risk.

GE, the global diversified technology, media, and financial services company, has showcased the value of rapid collaborative prototyping with its celebrated Treasure Hunts. Designed as focused, three-day multistakeholder sessions, the Treasure Hunts offer an in-depth audit of energy or water use, generate viable improvement options, and set the foundation for implementation.[321] Originally developed by Toyota, the Treasure Hunt usually starts on a Sunday afternoon to minimize disruption of operations. A cross-functional group of GE employees, suppliers, contractors, and representatives of other companies are split into small teams and trained to identify opportunities in the facility where energy and resources are needlessly in use. An actual hands-on audit follows, and by the next morning each team generates the first leads for possible improvement. Monday is the time to connect with the operations professionals and technical experts to prototype the ideas and test their viability – this process also builds buy-in at the facility. And through the iterative process of prototyping, testing, and discussing, by Tuesday afternoon each team has at least ten ideas with cost saving assessments already in place. The impacts of the GE Treasure Hunts are far-reaching. As Gretchen Hancock of GE reports,

> While efficiency projects are the direct outcome of the hunt, GE has trained more than 3,500 of its employees globally to think about wasted energy and water in a different and powerful way. Those individuals have identified more than 5,000 projects that have the opportunity to drive energy efficiency, eliminate 700,000 metric tons of greenhouse gas emissions – and $111 million in operational cost.[322]

Implementation

While inspiration brings about insight, and ideation turns the insight into viable alternatives, implementation is all about creating conditions for success. As the GE example illustrates, the three spaces overlap and interact: the sustainability audit might provide inspiration; the engagement with the facility managers produces ideas and fosters buy-in; and the buy-in becomes the first step to implementation. Of course, successful implementation of any kind of change depends on a number of factors. One factor stemming from design thinking is particularly relevant to the challenge of embedded sustainability: participation.

In the UK, The Co-operative Bank asks customers to lead the ongoing development of its Ethical Policy, which determines where the bank does and does not invest.[323] U.S.-headquartered retailer Walmart supports its employees in the development of voluntary Personal Sustainability Projects, for which commitments such as recycling or exercising serve as a mechanism for embracing a company-wide commitment to sustainability as a business philosophy.[324] In South Africa, the cell phone banking company WIZZIT bets on its customers to sell its unique services to unbanked and under-banked people in poor areas of the country. Since the company focuses on making banking affordable and accessible to the country's poor, the 1,300 independent sales agents – called Wizzkids – also have to serve as educators, advancing financial literacy among those who may never have had a bank account. Becoming a Wizzkid also offers a valuable source of income for the underprivileged.[325] In the meantime, throughout the globe, GE is promoting $200 million for the Ecomagination Challenge, an open innovation initiative that allows anyone –and everyone – to contribute to GE's product development.[326]

What connects all of these examples is a new collaborative approach to getting things done. For customers, mere consumption is increasingly insufficient. For employees, mindless execution is less and less acceptable. For civil society, monitoring and reporting alone is hardly satisfying. Yes, good products, processes, and policies are still the necessary minimum – but they alone are not enough to compete. Jonas Ridderstråle and Kjelle Nordström argue this point well in their bestselling book *Funky Business*: "The surplus society has a surplus of similar companies, employing similar people, with similar educational backgrounds, working in similar jobs, coming up with similar ideas, producing similar things, with similar prices, warranties, and qualities."[327] In a world of abundance and surplus, what we increasingly need is meaningful experience.[328] Giving the stakeholders a chance to truly participate – and co-create – the new reality of business is the best way to design such an experience.

Whether it is products, services, processes, or procedures into which you strive to embed sustainability, design is a competence essential to your success. In the absence of ready-made solutions and formulaic practices, we cannot analyze ourselves into a sustainable future. Rather, we have to create one. And when it comes to creation, design has a pretty good track record.

Yet design alone is not enough. In fact, the following capability is essential to mastering design thinking. Ask yourself now, what might it be? Yes, we are talking about inquiry.

Inquiry

Think of the last business meeting you sat in where the objective was to come up with a particular solution. With a clear agenda set well in advance, and background materials distributed in preparation, you are now gathered and ready to tackle the challenge. Close your eyes and imagine yourself right at the start of the meeting. Really try it. What were you thinking? What did you pay attention to?

Chances are, you came prepared with a list of proposals ready to be offered along with well-developed arguments. Indeed, as managers, we are expected to provide answers – not knowing is hardly an acceptable position. Yet, if recent research is any indication, predefined answers may not be the best route to high performance.

In 2004, scholars Marcial Losada and Emily Heaphy published a study focused on what makes business teams effective.[329] Among the dimensions explored, the researchers studied the relationship between performance and the way conversations are structured. In particular, they focused on how many answers or solutions are generated during corporate meetings compared with how many open-ended questions were asked. They called this relationship the inquiry/advocacy ratio – referring to deep explorative questions as "inquiry" and to strong points and suggestions as "advocacy." (For the record, it might be worth mentioning that "Do you agree with me?" does not constitute an inquiry within this terminology.) To make sure performance is measured adequately, the researchers looked at profitability (SBU profit and loss statements), customer satisfaction, and 360-degree evaluations that offered assessments of the team members by superiors, peers, and subordinates. What Losada and Heaphy discovered is a striking difference between high-performing and low-performing teams when it comes to the use of questions and answers in daily work. High-performing teams balanced inquiry and advocacy, offering on average 1.143 questions for every answer rendered.

Medium-performing teams used about one inquiry for every two advocacies. But when it came to low-performing teams, the ratio was immensely unbalanced: barely one question was asked for every 20(!) points, arguments, solutions, and proposals.[330] Other scholars, including Chris Argyris and Donald Schön[331] as well as Peter Senge,[332] offer similar insight into the importance of this balancing task.

> If I had an hour to solve a problem and my life depended on the solution, I would spend the first 55 minutes determining the proper question to ask, for once I know the proper question, I could solve the problem in less than five minutes.
>
> **Albert Einstein**
> Physicist and Nobel laureate

What the data suggests is that, while answers are important, it is questions that we need to pay attention to if high performance is our goal. And when it comes to the uncharted territory of embedded sustainability, questions have a crucial role to play.

What are the key activities and impacts of the product's life cycle – from the very earliest (such as service planning or raw material extraction) to its end-of-life? Who has a stake in your company and what matters to these stakeholders? What risks do we face along the value chain – upstream and downstream – and how can these risks be translated into opportunities? In cascading levels of detail, what would our services look like if sustainability was embedded without compromise in quality and with no green or social premium? The art of the question becomes essential if sustainable value is the final destination. As few proven solutions exist, and rushed decisions are dangerous, inquiry – rather than advocacy – becomes the best vehicle for value creation, the best shaper of what is possible and the best tool for co-creation.

In the late 1990s, the Weatherhead School of Management – with which the two of us have the good fortune of being connected – made a commitment to building a new home for itself. The world-renowned architect Frank O. Gehry and his firm, Gehry Partners, became collaborators in the design and construction of the new Peter B. Lewis Building. In the process of design, the team started with surprisingly simple questions: "What is teaching?" "What is learning?" "What is an office?" "What is a faculty?"[333]

In ways similar to architecture, embedded sustainability calls for inquiry into fundamentals. Remember the story of Lush solid shampoo we shared in Chapter 1? When developing this product, the company went back to very basic questions. What is a shampoo? What does a great clean hair experience look like? How can we deliver the same end benefits to the users – but offer much better environmental and social value? Embedded sustainability is the ultimate exploration territory. Inquiry becomes a mechanism for meaningful exploration; sustainability becomes a new lens through which to rediscover – and redesign – your business.

If balancing inquiry and advocacy is of crucial importance to the task of embedded sustainability, how can we learn this delicate act? What options do we have to consider and adopt?

In his 1990 groundbreaking work *The Fifth Discipline: The Art and Science of the Learning Organization*, Peter Senge offered a colorful palette of skills available for balancing inquiry and advocacy. While some of the skills are less effective for our purpose (including politicking, interrogating, dictating, or withdrawing), most of them have an important role to play in organizational development. Developing the essentials of these skills will serve you well in the task of sustainable value creation while, at the same time, supporting business priorities as a whole. Opposite is the menu of options adopted from Senge's *The Fifth Discipline*.[334]

It is clear that organizational life creates a need for each of the four aspects of the balancing act – observing, telling, asking, and generating. You might find some of the options on the menu more appealing than others; but it is remarkable what happens to a meeting once your repertoire expands. So, as you continue to build your inquiry muscle, here are a few simple ways to check if you are conquering the art of the question:

1. **An open end**. Good questions are open-ended. How do you know that your question is a real inquiry? If you can answer with "yes" or "no," or provide any other "correct" answer, you probably just fell off the tracks of true inquiry. "How might we . . ." or "What would it look like to . . ." are among the best ways to question your way into embedded sustainability

2. **Generative power**. Good questions create. Period. If you are spotting a wave of excitement, inspiration, and desire to co-create as a result of the question asked, chances are you are amidst a generative inquiry. And since much social and environmental challenges offer highly contested, touchy, and daunting issues to resolve, designing generative questions is an insurance policy against deadlock, energy drain, and withdrawal

3. **Masterful assumptions**. Nearly all questions we pose have built-in assumptions. "How should we create a department of sustainability in our company?" assumes that there is an agreement around the need for such a department. Skillfully managing assumptions – being aware of them, choosing carefully, and aligning assumptions

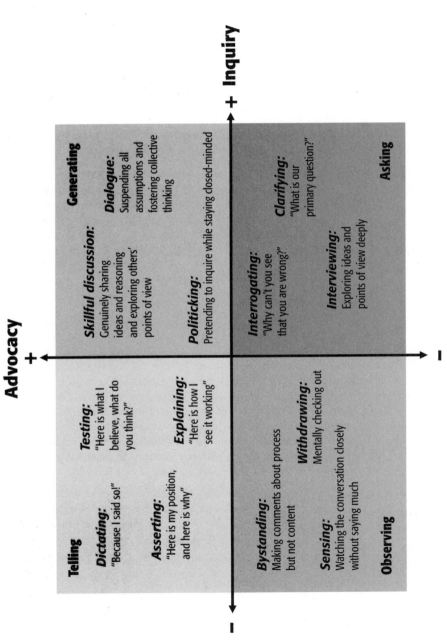

masterfully – is crucial for the entire trajectory of your embedded sustainability effort

Eric Vogt, Juanita Brown, and David Isaacs offer a perfect illustration of the power of open-ended, well-designed generative questions in their 2003 exploration of *The Art of Powerful Questions.*

> The director of HP Labs wondered why the organization was not considered the best industrial research laboratory in the world. He charged Barbara Waugh, a key staff member, with coordinating the effort to respond to the question, "What does being the best industrial research lab in the world mean?" To that end, Waugh initiated a global network of conversations around that question, using the company's technology infrastructure along with face-to-face gatherings to support the dialogues. Just by exploring the practical implications of the question in a disciplined way, the Lab began to see productivity gains. But one day, an HP Lab engineer came into Barbara's office and said, "That question is okay, but what would really energize me and get me up in the morning would be asking, 'How can we be the best industrial research lab *for* the world?' "
>
> That one small shift changed the entire game by scaling up meaning and shifting the assumptions embedded in the original question. It profoundly altered the context of the inquiry – to become the best *for* the world as the larger context for becoming the best in the world. This question obviously "traveled well" – it was no longer just the Lab's question, but something that many others at HP began to ask themselves.
>
> Employees at HP Labs and throughout the whole company responded to this new focus with a tremendous surge of collective energy. HP's E-Inclusion effort, a major project to enable the world's poor to enter the new economy while providing critical medical and other information to communities in the developing world, stemmed in large measure from the HP for the World exploration.[335]

The Hewlett-Packard story illustrates the power of questions to shift from one mind-set or paradigm into another. The company started its exploration within the traditional mind-set of shareholder value as the primary objective of the company. The new question allowed entrance to a new paradigm, where shareholder value is not abandoned, but extended and reimagined within the context of sustainable value.

> A paradigm shift occurs when a question is asked inside the current paradigm that can only be answered from outside of it.
>
> **Marilee Goldberg**
> Author

All in all, inquiry is a competence desirable for a vast array of business challenges. When it comes to embedded sustainability, however, inquiry is not merely desirable, it is essential. But are all questions created equal? To search for the answer, it is time for us to turn our attention to the next competence vital in an age of environmental and social demands: appreciation.

Appreciation

On a minimalist yet provocative stage at the 2010 TED conference, Chip Conley shares a story of a maid who had been a friend and employee at the hotel he owns for 23 years. (TED is a magical community built around breakthrough ideas, so if you have not checked them out yet, we guarantee you a new addiction.) In the story, Chip speaks about a question he posed for himself and his company, which was inspired by his friendship: how can somebody find joy in toilet cleaning?

Perhaps an unusual question for a leader in search of better business results, but for Chip the inquiry was a matter of survival. In the wake of the dot-com crash followed by the September 11th terrorist attacks, San Francisco Bay area hotels went through the largest percentage of revenue decline in the history of American hotels. Conley's company was the largest hotel operator in the area, and finding a way to weather the storm was the name of the game.

In search of possible solutions, Chip accidentally stumbled on a familiar but neglected concept: Maslow's hierarchy of needs. Pondering the pyramid that covers needs such as shelter, food, water, safety, love, esteem, and self-actualization, he wondered how his company addressed the higher categories of needs of its customers and employees. Building on this interest, the company started to systematically inquire into its employees' sense of meaning and its customers' sense of emotional connection with the organization. Miraculously, the more attention the company paid to meaning and connection, the more meaning and connection seemed to be created. Customer loyalty went through the roof; employee turnover dropped to one-third of the industry average; and the company tripled in size during the five-year market downturn.[336]

The story of Chip Conley and his Joie de Vivre Hotels speaks pointedly to the question of what makes up a good inquiry. When it comes to generating positive change, all questions are not created equal. What we inquire into counts. In fact, questions can often determine the very destiny of a company.

Hardly anyone has contributed more to our understanding of the power of good questions than organizational behavior scholars David Cooperrider, Ron Fry, and Suresh Srivastva, the co-originators of appreciative inquiry. Appreciative inquiry (or AI) is a change management philosophy often celebrated as the most important innovation in organizational development of the past decades. Just like any traditional change management approach, appreciative inquiry takes on a challenging area of company performance – whether it is productivity, customer satisfaction, cost efficiency, or any other domain. But unlike traditional problem solving, AI looks for answers in less than obvious places. Instead of analyzing past *failures and gaps* in an attempt to improve performance, through the process of appreciative inquiry, managers systematically search for and analyze *successes* – and mainstream companies from Ernst & Young to Walmart are buying in.

So, what does this shift look like, exactly?

When a major airline experiences excessive baggage loss, it is tempting to focus on specific instances of failure in trying to understand what went wrong. Appreciative inquiry shifts the focus of analysis from the extraordinary baggage loss towards extraordinary arrival experiences – systematically finding and analyzing situations when a passenger had an exemplar arrival even when all circumstances, from weather to air traffic control, worked against the company.

For a car service company striving for 100 per cent customer satisfaction, it is normal to look into each lost or dissatisfied customer, searching for reasons for failure. Appreciative inquiry challenges the company to deeply understand reasons behind each loyal and satisfied client, assuring that there is a compelling reason for every customer to stay with the company in the future.

For a specialty coffee company going through rapid growth, costs are the name of the game. Instead of focusing on inefficiencies, appreciative inquiry invites the company to find the best but underutilized practices throughout all major practices, and assures that such cost-saving practices become the norm, rather than an exception.

Whether it is manufacturing or services, small or large, for all organizations AI discoveries differ dramatically from traditional strategic change efforts. When we focus on what we are doing wrong, we become experts in repeating our own mistakes. The analysis depicts to the last little detail how to fail, but tells us little about how to succeed. When we address the issue on hand by bypassing the many cases of past failures, and focusing on examples where similar issues were resolved successfully, not only do we find surprising answers, but we also energize employees, foster creativity, and avoid blame games among our team, thus assuring successful turnaround in the change process.

And what about results? For an approach traditionally perceived as "soft," appreciative inquiry has a remarkable track record.[337] For Hunter Douglas's Window Fashions Division, using appreciative inquiry in a business process improvement initiative generated savings of $3.5 million in the first year. Green Mountain Coffee Roasters successfully achieved the "25¢ Challenge," which allowed for a reduction of operating costs of 25 cents per pound of coffee, approximately a 7 per cent reduction in gross costs. Managers of Santa Ana Star Casino believe that appreciative inquiry was instrumental in driving revenues and achieving profit turnaround of $10 million in 2003. The list goes on.

This is all well and good, you might say, but what does it have to do with the challenge of embedded sustainability?

As it turns out, quite a lot. Among the many things that make AI relevant are two discoveries crucial to embedding sustainability.

First, **inquiry and change are simultaneous**. We used to think that analysis comes first, then recommendations, then decision, and only then implementation. What we are discovering is that questions themselves foster change, long before any formal answers are attained and implemented. As David Cooperrider and Leslie Sekerka put it:

> Inquiry *is* agenda setting, language shaping, affect creating, and knowledge generating. Inquiry is embedded into everything we do as managers, leaders, and agents of change. Because of omnipresence of inquiry, we are often unaware of its presence. Nevertheless, we live in the worlds our inquiries create. Inquiry itself *intervenes.*[338]

Second, **organizations move in the direction of their study**.[339] Not only does the change start immediately with the question posed; but the questions we ask determine the collective trajectory of our organizations. What we fight, fights. What we appreciate, appreciates. Remember Chip Conley's accidental discovery we shared at the beginning of this chapter? Inquiry into meaning and connection led to more meaning and connection – and brought about great financial dividends for his hotel chain along the way.

Put these two discoveries together, and it becomes clear that appreciative inquiry is nearly tailor-made for the challenges of embedded sustainability. Since there are plenty of gaps and weaknesses in this domain, inquiring into everything that is wrong with environmental and social performance in business has produced an abundance of blame, disconnect, and hopelessness. We have all been through countless conferences, briefings, and meetings where everything that is wrong was flashed out to the point of complete exhaustion – with little positive change in sight. What we need now is an ability to appreciate – to grow – everything that is right, inquiring into successes, however small, necessary to embed sustainability into products, processes, and policies. Whether it is cross-boundary collaboration, rapid innovation, or past designs for win–win, every company has experiences and best practices that could serve as a foundation for the new tasks of sustainable value creation. Appreciating such experiences – systematically and diligently – is an essential embedded sustainability skill to master.

Let's do a little experiment. Pull out paper and pen. Got it? Now, think about the many meetings you participated in over the past three months – and choose the one that stands out as the worst meeting of all. Remember that one? Now write down a list of factors that – in your mind – made the meeting so bad. Just list them one by one, no rush.

Chances are, the list in front of you looks a little bit like this:

Worst meeting

- No agenda
- Bad facilitation
- People came unprepared
- Lots of private conversations and email checking
- A few talk all the time and ask lots of irrelevant questions
- No clear agreements by the end of the meeting

Now, flip the page, and write a new list. This time, go back to the very best meeting you had in recent years. Think about everything that made it work. At least a few of the following points probably made your list:

<u>Best</u> <u>meeting</u>

- Clear agenda
- Great facilitation
- Passion and commitment
- Open & honest conversation
- Discussion of things that matter
- Sense of excitement
- Relaxed but focused atmosphere

We have run this experiment with hundreds of managers. Remarkably, every time we compare the two lists one thing jumps out. Do you see it, too? The two lists don't match. Yes, indeed, some points are nearly identical – especially those that touch on "technical" elements of the meeting. But then things get interesting. What we discover, in essence, is that focusing on what does not work and then eliminating those drivers of failure does not produce success. You can have the best agenda, best facilitator, and forbid the use of cell phones, but that does not bring you passion or commitment. The same thing happens for much more complex challenges – whether it is customer loyalty, employee satisfaction, or embedded sustainability, appreciative inquiry will give you answers dramatically different than those of deficit-based inquiry. Removing the bad does not guarantee the good. At best, all you get is "not bad." And for a business striving to generate a profit in the era of declining resources, radical transparency, and increasing expectations, "not bad" is simply not good enough.

Now, one more request. Bring yourself back to the second list and recall that best meeting. What do you feel? Can you see the faces around the room? Can you sense the excitement? Hopefully, for you as for many others, appreciative inquiry evokes positive emotions (otherwise, accept our apologies). A nice add-on, one might think, but hardly essential. Well, a few additional facts might be in order here.

In the past few years, the science of positive emotions has made significant progress. What we now know is that positive emotions bring about a wide array of personal and individual benefits: they generate optimal functioning, expand habitual models of thinking and action, build personal and interpersonal resources, and enable flexible and creative thinking.[340] And when it comes to performance, positive emotions – such as appreciation, validation, and encouragement – are vital. Remember the studies of Marcial Losada and Emily Heaphy[341] we explored earlier in this chapter? In addition to a high inquiry/advocacy ratio, the researchers also focused on the ratio of positive to negative verbal and nonverbal behavior and expressions in teams of different effectiveness levels. What they discovered is that low-performing teams had a ratio of .363, while high-performing teams had a ratio of 5.614 – showing nearly six times more positive than negative behaviors in group interactions. Appreciation matters.

It might matter even more when it comes to the challenge of embedding sustainability into the DNA of business. With piles of contested, difficult, and controversial issues behind us and before us, the ability to generate appreciative inquiry and to focus on shared strengths is a competency worth investing in.

A number of companies are doing exactly that. Green Mountain Coffee Roasters, which made it to number one on the list of *Corporate Responsibility Officer Magazine*'s 100 Best Corporate Citizens in 2006 and 2007, has been using appreciative inquiry for its sustainability needs since 2000.[342] Fairmount Minerals, a relative newcomer to the sustainability world, ran its first whole-company AI summit in 2005, which allowed it to realign its strategy, and led to new product development, core process improvements, and increased employee engagement.[343] In 2008, Walmart used AI with its sustainability efforts, managing a successful multistakeholder process for whole-industry change for Walmart dairy suppliers.[344]

In general, solutions similar to appreciative inquiry leapfrog a company towards an aligned sustainable value strategy, while energizing its employees to follow through on the designed goals and models. But in addition to shifting the "what" of strategy and organizational development, appreciative inquiry also changes the "who" and the "how." It builds on a clear understanding that embedding sustainability for mutual value demands an entirely new ability to move from fragmented and local to unified and systemic. It is time for us to look at the final competency on our starter list: wholeness.

Wholeness

In our search for the competencies that are most important for the successful integration of social and environmental value into core business activities, we have looked at design, inquiry, and appreciation. One more capability stands out as essential for the challenge of embedded sustainability. In contrast to the limited and fragmented notions of shareholder value, stakeholder value, and customer value, sustainable value demands an aptitude for wholeness across a range of dimensions:

- **The wholeness of "who."** The creation of sustainable value requires consideration for, and the engagement of, the interests, demands, opinions, and commitments of all parties involved – shareholders, employees, customers, suppliers, local communities, media, government, and society at large

- **The wholeness of "what."** The creation of sustainable value demands deep integration of social and environmental considerations into the entire make up of your company's products or services. Product design, manufacturing process, performance-in-use, and end-of-life are re-envisioned, bringing together consumer value, shareholder value, and value to other key stakeholders

- **The wholeness of "how."** The creation of sustainable value expands the traditional organizational boundaries, commanding a deep understanding and active redesign of the entire value chain, upstream from raw material extraction and downstream all the way to product disposal. Every step of the business and every corresponding process and policy are re-envisioned, creating a whole process for a whole value

- **The wholeness of "why."** Finally, the creation of sustainable value brings back and reaffirms the vital and fundamentally positive role of business in society as an engine of innovation, well-being, and prosperity in the broadest possible terms, giving back what some might consider an intrinsic nobility and purpose to the profession of management

Sustainable value offers a qualitatively different, breakthrough, "in-harmony" alternative to the inefficient, carbon-intensive, stakeholder-alienated, short-term-oriented, throwaway economy of the present. But its appeal is only proportionate to the difficulty of its implementation. In a world where specialization rules, functional silos are celebrated, organizational boundaries are fixed, stakeholders are automatically at odds with shareholders, and outsourcing is a must, the idea of wholeness may appear as the less than obvious choice.

Yet, if sustainable value is our end goal, and embedded sustainability is our primary means, wholeness is no longer optional. The immense challenges of environmental and social prosperity are complex, interdependent, and dynamic. They cut across the entire business system – and beyond – and thus require a systemic approach. Seeing and acting in accordance with the magnitude of the whole is the new skill to master.

For some of us, it comes naturally. Peter Senge and his colleagues behind the organizational learning movement offered this illustration of an aptitude for wholeness at the most fundamental level:

> Farm children learn naturally about the cycles of cause and effect that make up systems. They see the links in the milk the cow gives, the grass the cow eats, and the droppings which fertilize the fields. When a thunderstorm is on the horizon, even a small child knows to turn off the floodgate on a spring-water well, for fear that runoff carried downstream by the rains will foul it. They know that if they forget to turn off the gate, they'll have to boil their water, or carry it by bucket from far away. They easily accept the counterintuitive fact of life: the greatest floods represent the time when you must be *most* careful about conserving water.[345]

For many of us, wholeness is an atrophied muscle, waiting to be rebuilt. For centuries, our science has taught us to break things into pieces and focus on the parts – Newtonian physics being the prime example. Margaret Wheatley, who offered a stunning exploration of the new science of quantum physics, chaos theory, biology, and evolution, and its implications for managers in her *Leadership and the New Science*, speaks about an alternative for us to consider:

One of the first differences between the new science and Newtonianism is a focus on holism rather than parts. Systems are understood as whole systems, and attention is given to *relationships within those networks.* Donella Meadows, an ecologist and visionary author, quotes an ancient Sufi teaching that captures this shift in focus: "You think because you understand *one* you must understand *two,* because one and one makes two. But you must also understand *and.*" When we view systems from this perspective, we enter an entirely new landscape of connections, of phenomena that cannot be reduced to simple cause and effect, or explained by studying the parts in isolation. We move into a land where it becomes critical to sense the constant workings of dynamic processes, and then notice how these processes materialize as visible behaviors and forms.[346]

Whether wholeness is a skill you use daily, or an aptitude rarely applied in your business life, the challenge of embedded sustainability is guaranteed to use it all, and then demand some more. Here are a few exercises you can use to continue building your wholeness muscle:

- **Learn the language of systems thinking.** The discipline of systems thinking has developed a diverse set of tools that allow you to understand the elements of a system and the relationships between them. While "feedback loops" and "system archetypes" may appear complicated at first, these terms for analyzing and depicting the whole come in handy when you are discovering the mechanism behind your product sales, employee turnover, or process innovation. Using this language to understand the relationship between social and environmental pressures and your company's performance will facilitate the process of embedding sustainability

- **Practice life cycle analysis.** Whether it is a product or service that you offer, understanding the entire life cycle, from cradle to grave, from raw material extraction to end-of-life processes, is essential for managing sustainability risks and discovering opportunities to create environmentally and socially driven value

- **Play with stakeholder mapping.** We have said plenty about the crucial importance of understanding and engaging your stakeholders for the goal of sustainable value. Both of these tasks start with a very simple step: knowing who your stakeholders are. Even the smallest business may be surprised by the number of people that have a stake in its future. Mapping out your stakeholders – and relationships between different groups and networks of stakeholders – is a great way to build wholeness reflexes

All in all, the task of any wholeness exercise is to help you develop a particular way of looking at the world around you. Embedding sustainability into your core business demands an ability to see the big picture, and understand the linkages and drivers that make up the system. Like many complexity skills, wholeness cannot be learned by reading about it. The good news is that we have plenty of pressures to start practicing it. Maybe it is time to have a coffee with that activist group you've been avoiding for some time now. After all, like it or not, they are part of your whole, too.

In summary

Unlike the streamlined recipes for bolt-on sustainability, the task of embedding social and environmental value into the DNA of a business demands new thinking and unorthodox solutions. Whether you are pursuing embedded sustainability as a way to strengthen your existing market positioning or to explore uncharted waters, the journey ahead demands a mastery of new competencies. Design, inquiry, appreciation, and wholeness represent only a starting point in the list to be discovered and conquered. Yet companies finding a way to create sustainable value have shown that these four are a good foundation for action.

As the journey of embedding sustainability is long and trying, solid skills are vital in reaching the desired destination. Now that we have gone over these building-block essentials, it is time to turn our eyes to something much more tangible: making change stick.

7
Change management redux

We started our travels into the "how" of embedded sustainability with a bird's-eye view of the competencies and capabilities required to effect change. Yet, as has been said about many other skills, these competencies cannot be developed by reading about them. Rolling up one's sleeves and walking the talk is the best – indeed the only – way forward. So, it is now time to put our feet firmly on the ground and figure out how to get things done. What does it take to create sustainable value? How do you embed sustainability into the very DNA of your business?

To answer these questions, we turn our attention to emerging success stories. While no single company is yet to reach the coveted top of the mountain "higher than Everest," as Ray Anderson, Chairman of the carpet giant Interface puts it, a number of explorers have started the journey from bolt-on to embedded sustainability and enjoyed its early benefits and rewards. Their stories guide our travels.

Now, for a chapter focusing on change management, it would be entirely normal to expect a clear set of tools and steps designed to guide you through the confusing and turbulent corridors of change. Yet our research and data led to a very different story. Following the personal invitation of Henry Mintzberg to "learn our way into strategy," we found that every instance of successful integration of social and environmental value into products and services showed paths that were emerging, iterative, and messy. It turns out you cannot analyze your way into sustainability. You can only learn and innovate your way into it.

As obvious a discovery as that may be, its implications are far-reaching. In essence, embedding sustainability breaks the expected sequence of change management. Traditionally, it is assumed that you first develop the strategy, and then implement it. In fact, the line between strategy and execution has become so sharp that it is taken as a sign of great wisdom to hear business leaders such as Jamie Dimon, now CEO of JPMorgan Chase, assert: "I'd rather have a first-rate execution and second-rate strategy any time than a brilliant idea and mediocre management."[347]

Yet, for most of us who lived through at least one strategic management process, it is rather clear that the line, if it exists at all, is less of a Great Wall of China, and more of a jagged set of dots guiding the ever-changing dance between strategy and execution. Roger Martin, strategy theorist and practicing manager, offered this passionate illustration in his *Harvard Business Review* article:

> If a strategy produces poor results, how can we argue that it is brilliant? It certainly is an odd definition of brilliance. A strategy's purpose is to generate positive results, and the strategy in question doesn't do that, yet it was brilliant? In what other field do we proclaim something to be brilliant that has failed miserably on its only attempt? A "brilliant" Broadway play that closes after one week? A "brilliant" political campaign that results in the other candidate winning? If we think about it, we must accept that the only strategy that can legitimately be called brilliant is one whose results are exemplary. A strategy that fails to produce a great outcome is simply a failure.[348]

Indeed, early successes with embedding sustainability echoed Martin's strong questioning of the illusive line between strategy and execution. But even more so, they challenge the sequence of change itself. Every single company we studied that dared to refuse sustainability as a cost, that ventured into the unknown terrain of sustainable value creation, and that refused to settle for the bolt-on sustainability approach, had to do so in the near dark, each step leading to the next, experimenting and taking action – and producing results – long before a truly comprehensive strategy could be articulated. Long before it became clear what strategic pathways would take one from here to there, companies had to take first steps, reap the first low-hanging fruits, develop the first new capabilities, and survive the first failures. In other words, they had to learn their way into embedded sustainability.

Following the somewhat surprising results of our research, in this chapter we speak about the *process* of embedding sustainability, sharing the key challenges and solutions companies uncover along the way. In the next chapter, we will put all the pieces of the puzzle together, and offer some thoughts on how the *content* of embedded sustainability strategy could be developed to meet the demands and needs of your specific situation.

So, let's roll up our sleeves.

From here to there: walking the talk

Unlike all-too familiar CSR and bolt-on sustainability efforts, embedding sustainability into the core of business without compromises on price or quality requires a comprehensive business makeover. This transformation does not happen overnight. The experience of companies who have already ventured into this territory suggests four interdependent and interconnected lines of action to guide the journey:

- **Getting the right start.** Mobilizing, educating, and acting around specific "low-hanging fruits"

- **Building the buy-in.** Aligning company, value-added activities, and all key stakeholders around the vision of embedded sustainability

- **Moving from incremental to breakthrough.** Developing clear but unorthodox goals, designing the strategy, and capturing value through co-creation and innovation

- **Staying with it.** Managing learning and energy while making sustainability ubiquitous but largely invisible in business practice

While the above list may suggest a possible linear sequence, in reality, much of the sustainability journey is nonlinear, repetitive, and messy. Engagement of one business unit after another demands a "right" start; new action calls for new education, while building true buy-in remains a daily task. Many low-hanging fruit are pursued and harvested before companies are even ready to play with – let alone design – a masterful embedded sustainability business strategy.

In the following pages, we invite you to explore these four broad elements of the process that stand as the cornerstone to integrating social and environmental value into core business activities. Instead of giving you definitive prescriptions, we would like to offer a rich buffet of options, derived from real stories of real managers pursuing tangible outcomes. Picking and choosing your own plateful of dishes may be the best way to create a nutritious meal that is right for you.

Getting the right start

Among the many questions we hear at executive education seminars, conferences, and client meetings, one of the most frequently asked is, "How do we start?" Indeed, the right start is crucial when attempting such a contested and often controversial venture. But there is little magic to the start of this change management process. Just as with any other organizational transformation, embedding sustainability into the core business starts when someone somewhere within the organization decides to take the first step.

Acquiring organizational sponsorship

For most companies, the initial sponsorship comes from senior management. At DuPont, the global chemical company, the current commitment to put "science to work by creating sustainable solutions essential to a better, safer, healthier life for people everywhere" was built on a long-term top executive commitment. Former CEO Dick Heckert (1986–1989) led the decision to phase out fully halogenated chlorofluorocarbons (CFCs) in the late 1980s. Ed Woolard, who led the company from 1989 to 1995 referred to himself as the "Chief Environmental Officer" and set the company on a "goal of zero" – zero injuries, illnesses, incidents, wastes, and emissions. Chad Holliday, the CEO from 1995 to 2009, former chairman of the World Business Council for Sustainable Development, and co-author of the sustainability book *Walking the Talk*, set sustainable growth goals for DuPont which require a full integration of economic, social, and environmental performance. This high level of commitment continues to this day under the current CEO, Ellen Kullman.

At Gorenje, a Slovenia-based home appliance manufacturer, sustainability is managed by the management board, with new businesses initiated and overseen by the company's president and CEO, Franjo Bobinac. Coca-Cola's commander in chief, Muhtar Kent, also considers himself the "chief sustainability officer" of the international beverage giant[349] while Brazilian food company Nutrimental got much of its first push from founder Rodrigo Loures.

Getting senior management commitment and sponsorship creates a springboard for all future action and makes the job of aligning a company's many interests and functions all that much easier. To make sure such sponsorship is bestowed, it is crucial to frame sustainability efforts as a *source* of competitive advantage *in support of existing* business priorities – rather than a new initiative pulling already tight resources in a questionable direction. The words of Lee Scott, Walmart's former CEO who led the company commitment to embedding sustainability since 2005, speak volumes to the power of the right framing of the new effort:

> What's been interesting for me as we've started this journey on sustainability, is really the shallowness of my motivation to start . . . I simply looked and said: where are the exposures that this company faces? What have we learned from the past that we should listen

to? Where are our weaknesses? Where will people attack us? What is it that we need to do better if what we want to do is to be able to stand on the fact that we sell for less and we take care of customers? Because, as you know, in our world today, all of a sudden, it is "Wal-Mart sells for less," but at what cost to society? That was the motivation for getting the first group together . . . what's been amazing to me is that what I thought was going to be a defensive strategy that would cause people to not be able to harm Wal-Mart because we've shored up our defenses, is turning out to be entirely the opposite. This is an offensive strategy. This is a strategy about merchandise. This is a strategy about cost management. This is a strategy about attracting and retaining the best people, the most creative minds, because those are the people . . . who this subject resonates with . . . There is an old saying that even a blind pig stumbles into an acorn once in a while – I feel a little bit that way.[350]

While most successful transformations rely heavily on top-down commitment, a number of companies have succeeded by harvesting the power of line managers to champion and sponsor change. At Herman Miller, a global furniture company, a cross-functional group named the Environmental Quality Action Team (EQAT) has been providing organization-wide sponsorship since 1989. Managing and connecting the dots across diverse challenges such as Design for Environment, Indoor Air, Packaging/Transportation and Environmental Law Impact Process, EQAT was the mechanism for setting zero-landfill as the first clear goal in 1991 and starting the process of embedding sustainability in the strategic core of the company. By 2008, the public company posted net sales of $2.012 billion, while becoming one of only six companies to make it on Fast Company's "Fast 50" Most Innovative, Fortune's "Most Admired," and Fortune's "100 Best Companies to Work For" lists.

For Si.mobil, the first private mobile operator in Slovenia, a journey towards sustainable value also started at the bottom of the organization, when a group of IT specialists decided to try some new ideas suggested by the growing "green IT" movement. As the IT department enjoyed clear financial benefits from these efforts, a voluntary company-wide "green team" was called upon.

Choosing between top-down and bottom-up approaches to initiating change ultimately depends on what fits best for the established company's culture and practices. In either case, building your case for embedded sustainability on the grounds of solid knowledge and insight is crucial. In the fast-changing field of sustainability, educating ourselves on the art of sustainable value becomes an ongoing investment with a rather high rate of return.

Gaining key insights

While rising social and environmental pressures may seem like a momentary fashion trend – the "flavor of the day" – their demands on business have been growing and building momentum for decades. The good news: great resources have been expended and many field-trials developed and tested to help you find your own way forward.

For Weatherchem, a U.S.-based plastic closures company, getting an in-company educational program was the best way to gain foundational knowledge in the field. Globally present Green Mountain Coffee Roasters, Nike, Waste Management and many others draw insight and develop collective knowledge via the Society for Organizational Learning's Sustainability Consortium. The growth of specialty degrees relevant for sustainability in business also means that you can acquire knowledge and resources necessary for the complex multidisciplinary task of embedded sustainability – and the mushrooming of job posting sites tailored to this need means that it is easier to connect supply and demand in the labor market.

A number of excellent books may also come in handy as you build your own understanding of how to create and maximize sustainable value. Several have already made a real difference in managerial thought and action. Stuart Hart's *Capitalism at the Crossroads: Next Generation Business Strategies for a Post-Crisis World*, which came out in an updated third edition in 2010, along with *Green to Gold: How Smart Companies Use Environmental Strategy to Innovate, Create Value, and Build Competitive Advantage* by Daniel Esty and Andrew Winston, frame sustainability issues from the perspective of business strategy and focus on creating advantage for business and society without trade-offs. *Biomimicry: Innovation Inspired by Nature* by Janine Benyus and *Cradle to Cradle: Remaking the Way We Make Things* by William McDonough and Michael Braungart offer a detailed and science-based foundation for sustainability thinking. And for those looking for the big picture on the relationship between the economy and the rest of planet, *The Ecology of Commerce: A Declaration of Sustainability*, a classic by Paul Hawken, an entrepreneur behind the Smith & Hawken gardening supplies empire, is one of the original "great books," as is his co-authored masterpiece with Amory and Hunter Lovins, *Natural Capitalism: Creating the Next Industrial Revolution*. You can also find an updated list of our personal favorites in the "Good finds" section of our website, www.EmbeddedSustainability.com.

While we offer the lists above as a mere starter kit, we invite you to explore and develop your own collection of good finds within the field. Starting your journey by exploring best practices and tried-and-true frameworks might just save you some time and bruised foreheads along the way. Once your own blueprint for sustainable value creation begins to emerge, it is time to get your hands dirty and venture further into the unknown. Scanning your company's (or business unit's) impacts to establish a baseline of sustainability performance is the next step.

Establishing the baseline

It is hard to assess existing sustainable value creation without an in-depth understanding of the environmental, social, and economic impacts of the business's current activities. How is stakeholder value being created or destroyed today? What is the social, health, or environmental value currently embedded in the products and services? Where are we leaking value? Where is financial value being created "on the backs" of key stakeholders?

To gain insight into these questions, the impacts on stakeholders need to be assessed upstream starting from raw materials extraction and downstream to product end-of-life. Life cycle value chains are assessed because, in today's competitive environment, companies from banks to makers of children's toys are being held responsible for the activities of their value chain partners. Fortunately disciplines such as life cycle assessment (LCA) and carbon footprinting are becoming well established – you can start, for example, with *Lifecycle Assessment: Where Is It on Your Sustainability Agenda?* by Deloitte Consulting.[351] That being said, a company-wide LCA often requires a significant effort in terms of management time and resources. You might find it easier to focus on only a few high-impact product lines instead and prioritize stakeholder impacts to make the data collection effort manageable.

In each of the environmental, social, and economic spheres, stakeholder impacts are organized into distinct categories. Typically companies choose not to focus on all categories, and instead select a subset tailored to their business. In the panel overleaf is how one author and sustainability practitioner, Bob Willard, suggests we think about the menu of impact scans.[352]

Tennant, a U.S.-based floor cleaning equipment manufacturer, publishes data on its own energy use and greenhouse gas emissions alongside emissions for the cleaning machines produced by the company. GE, the global infrastructure, finance, and media conglomerate, makes a wide range of data available to public at a dedicated Metrics page. The retailer Walmart takes impact scans to an entirely new level. Within its Sustainability 360 approach, which allows for a more comprehensive view of the business and engagement of more than 100,000 suppliers, more than 2 million associates and millions of customers around the world, the company publishes its own impacts information as a mere appetizer to the goal of measuring (and managing) the impact of its myriad end-to-end supply chains. While the goal is still far from being reached, its July 2009 Sustainability Index initiative is well on its

Environmental footprint

1. **Energy**. What are trends in usage? What is the fuel mix? Where are the greatest energy demands in the supply chain?

2. **Water**. What are water consumption rates? What are current levels of water contamination and waste water reuse? Discharge impacts on local watersheds?

3. **Air**. What is the product's life cycle carbon footprint? Where in the supply chain are CO_2 emissions highest? What are the air emissions of NO_x, SO_x, and particulates?

4. **Waste**. How much waste is landfilled versus recycled? What waste occurs in the supply chain? What happens to obsolete/used products?

5. **Land use**. How does supply chain impact global land use? What are the rates of material sourcing from certified forests, fields, and mines?

6. **Biodiversity**. How are local flora and fauna affected by raw material extraction? How do facilities impact biodiversity? What is the impact of product use and disposal?

Social impacts

1. **Working conditions**. What are the working conditions throughout supply chain? What are total lost workdays and total hours of sick leave as a percentage of total work time?

2. **Product safety**. Are products built, used, and disposed of in a safe manner for all?

3. **Community impacts**. What is the community impact of the company's activities? Is it better off? What is the average commuting distance or the level of car dependence?

4. **Social equity**. Does the company make good-faith efforts to meet the unmet needs of underserved consumers? Are fair wages paid along the life cycle value chain?

Economic impacts

1. **Jobs**. How does the company handle redundancies and outplacements? Is job training geared to the employee's career development or only short-term company needs?

2. **Economic growth**. Is the company contributing to regional economic expansion? Is it investing in the region's competitiveness? Is the company creating a local tax base?

way with the top-tier suppliers engaged in the assessment by 2010. After the supplier assessment, a comprehensive life cycle analysis database developed by a consortium of universities, suppliers, retailers, nongovernmental organizations, and government officials will provide a basis for creating simple tools for customers to make better choices about the products they buy, informed not only by price but also by easy-to-understand sustainability performance based on factors such as embedded carbon content, water use, and waste.[353]

For most companies, managers initially assess stakeholder impacts by drawing on data from internal management systems. But as you can readily see from existing efforts, many of the impacts – and data – lie outside the organization's boundaries. Structured dialogues with stakeholders, such as community advisory panels, add valuable external perspectives. Seeing the world from the perspective of stakeholders is a powerful lens through which to assess sustainability performance. Even more so, research shows that managers who engage stakeholders and proactively address stakeholder perceptions can better anticipate changes in the business environment and avoid being surprised by shifts in societal expectations that can put shareholder value at risk.[354]

Harvesting the low-hanging fruit

While organizational momentum and commitment are being built, with the education and experience of managers, employees, and external partners growing every day, and the impacts scan and life cycle assessment are keeping you busy, it is time to begin experimenting in earnest with real-life sustainable value projects.

Choosing a project to start with is paramount. Companies do best when they focus on the "low-hanging fruit" – small but visible changes that promise rewards.

For Walmart, the international retail giant, cost and supply management stands at the center of its success and long-term strategy, so the sustainable value efforts introduced by the company in mid-2004 were aligned with its traditional operational strengths and strategic priorities. Redesign of packaging and distribution models allowed for significant reduction of paper, plastic, and fuel expenses – all on top of significant environmental benefits. One of Walmart's first experiments in this domain was an effort to "rightsize" the packaging for a children's toy product line, where a few inches were shaved off the packaging box to better fit the actual product. The small – and surprisingly obvious – effort saved 3,425 tons of corrugated paper materials, 1,358 barrels of oil, 5,190 trees, 727 shipping containers, while creating savings of $3.5 million in transportation costs.[355]

For Fairmount Minerals, U.S.-based industrial sands company, packaging was among the first areas it explored. Traditionally, the company employed single-use bulk boxes that held a maximum of 1,400 pounds of resin used to coat the sand. Hundreds of trucks were used to transport the material per year. One of the sustainable development teams worked with the suppliers to come up with a bulk bag that holds 1,850 pounds and reduces the number of trucks needed to haul the material. The bag is reusable up to 11 refills and is recyclable. The bulk boxes used a plastic liner with wooden pallets while the bulk bag has eliminated the pallets altogether. That makes it lighter, and stackable up to three times its height. It also requires less manpower and increases maximum truck loads. Here's how the two packaging options compare:

For Henkel, the German adhesives, detergents, and cosmetics company operating via subsidiaries in 75 countries throughout the world, much of the low-hanging fruit lies in product development and innovation. While some innovations require significant investment, others demand nothing more than a new lens of embedded sustainability. One of the company's best-known products, the world's first glue stick, Pritt, went through a transformation process that continuously increased the sustainable value generated. The original solvent-free glue stick was reformulated in 2000, replacing the traditional oil-derived polyvinylpyrrolidone (PVP) with renewable starch; renewable raw materials now account for 90 per cent of the product's dry weight.[356] But the quick win for the product was a much simpler change: after the research showed that customers often fail to use up the whole stick, leading to large quantities of waste, the company decreased the volume of the product,[357] leading to reduced costs without affecting usability.

In search of low-hanging fruit, GE began engaging employees in all parts of the business to see where energy savings could be found. That might be turning off the lights when a factory is idle, or installing a switch so that lights could be turned off. To make sure that there is enough incentive, managers were being measured on how much energy savings they had achieved. So far GE has saved $100 million from these measures and cut its greenhouse-gas intensity – a measure of emissions against output – by 41 per cent.

As these examples show, harvesting the low-hanging fruit is mostly about changing the way we look at products and processes our companies work with every day. Simple projects, such as replacing bottled water with water filter systems, can bring about significant rewards while getting the company started (just ask Genentech, which saved over $200,000 a year with this action).[358] For many companies we worked with or studied, setting up a small cross-functional team is the best way forward. Regular meetings and off-the-wall brainstorming sessions are a must, so are the actual test projects focusing on finding ways where value for both shareholders and stakeholders can be increased. When pursued, such projects become the important mechanism for training your sustainability muscles, developing new ways of seeing your business, and building credibility for embedded sustainability strategy. Along the way, the harvesting of low-hanging fruit becomes a crucial step for company-wide success: getting the whole organization's buy-in.

Building the buy-in

With the initial experiments to embed sustainability successfully under way, another line of action comes forward as a high priority: the adopted agenda has to become personally relevant to the entire company for true value harvesting to take place. Far too often, visions die prematurely in organizations because of low commitment and the lack of engagement of company employees and key stakeholders. In the case of social and environmental efforts, the potential to encounter skepticism and opposition from employees is even higher, as the issues at large are viewed as marginal or simply about public and government relations, rather than as strategic business opportunities. With many social projects handled by public relations, human resource, or legal departments, line managers in particular have reason to see any socially minded initiative as time-consuming value destruction or an annoying caprice of top management.

The search for a *sustainable value* strategy has to bring specific and clear benefits to the individual minds and hearts in the company – otherwise, there is no reason and incentive for your workforce to engage. Working on pilot projects is one good way to start; here are a few more ideas for building the buy-in.

Walmart found one way to assure such engagement by launching its Personal Sustainability Project (PSP) program –a voluntary initiative designed to help the company's nearly 2 million associates with integrating sustainability principles into their daily lives. Inviting Walmart employees to set up and achieve personal sustainability goals – such as quitting smoking, eating right, and improving family recycling habits – PSPs made a company-wide *sustainable value* effort more understandable, personal, and motivating to employees.

Troika Dialog put its view on the intersection of business and social efforts right into its identity statement:

> We are committed to developing appropriately the infrastructure, mechanics, and rules governing Russia's capital markets. For us at Troika Dialog, Russia is not a hedge or a fly-by-night venture; it is our home, and we are dedicated to building a bright future for it.

The company's identity was then supported by the elaborate *Book of a Thinking Person* – a rule book for all employees that provides guidelines for personal conduct, which has a strong thread of "mutual benefit."

Sodexo, the global food and facilities management company headquartered in France, engaged its employees by creating a community of practices under the title SEED, which stands for Sustainability Education and Expert Development. SEED connects experts from hospitals to museums to corporate offices to share their experience with new technologies and practices and work together on identifying new opportunities.[359]

Bayer, the materials, crops sciences, and health care giant, created a similar program called STEP – Sustainability Thinking and Education Pilot – in its North American subsidiary. The first participants in the STEP program included the CEO and many of his direct reports, before it was rolled out to the rest of the organization.

Trimo, a Slovenia-based global steel building solutions company, created a range of regular sustainability-related events, designed to rally the company's employees and stakeholders and create a universal awareness. The company's traditional Environment & Community Day, for example, serves as an opportunity for rapid company-wide education and engagement while also providing a chance to dialogue with its larger community of stakeholders.[360]

More ideas for effective employee engagement are generated daily. In 2010, for example, the National Environmental Education Foundation put out *The Business Case for Environmental and Sustainability Employee Education* report, filled with clear guidelines and diverse best practices.[361] The jointly produced *Generating Sustainable Value: Moving Beyond Green Teams to Transformation Collaboratives* study is another source of stories and advice on the topic,[362] and so is the GreenBiz.com's *Green Teams* report,[363] both available to the general public.

Across companies and reports, a few best practices appear as crucial for building the buy-in across the entire business system:

- **Creating a community.** Cross-functional and multigenerational interaction is a must, so is a regular meeting schedule. A "green lunch" might just be the way to start

- **Getting your hands dirty.** Starting on real projects proposed and developed by the employees and other members of the team (instead of assigning preplanning projects to the group) is the best way to build excitement and commitment. Visible, tangible, and clear projects with a short timeline are necessary at the early, fragile stages of the change process. A convincing business case is necessary to assure senior management buy-in, so treat sustainability just as you do any other business idea

- **Communicating clearly and consistently.** Studies have long shown that we need to receive information many times, via many channels, and in many forms, to assure lasting comprehension and impact. The task of embedding sustainability is no exception; and many have shown that there is simply no such thing as too much communication – and there is hardly anything more offensive for an employee than to learn about their company's commitment to sustainability via a local newspaper. Newsletters, internal memos, articles, intranet tips of the day, Web 2.0 efforts such as blogs and social media promotions, announcements with rewards and recognition along with cool prizes, video, photo and art competitions, eco-, health- and social causes fairs, guest speakers series, movie and book clubs – the list is endless. What connects these diverse efforts is the commitment to make sustainability the new business-as-usual within and across organizational borders

- **Keeping the attention high.** As the task of embedding sustainability is a long-term commitment, it is important to pace ourselves and find ways to keep the efforts fresh and exciting. Special campaigns and programs are great for this task: with clear tasks and clear deadlines, they bring about a nice punctuation to your social and environmental performances efforts. You can start with simple initiatives such as a fair-trade holiday gifts program, car-pooling days, or e-waste recycling program. With the first programs under way, it is easier to experiment with more complex undertakings, such as a low-carbon diet campaign

- **Engaging customers, suppliers, community activists, and beyond.** Building the buy-in within your organization without achieving commitment beyond its boundaries is a lost war. As most companies quickly discover during the life cycle assessment of their product or service, much of environmental and social impact (and opportunity!) lies outside of company walls, exactly where we all have the least control. With diminished influence, engagement is our best friend. So, make sure to bring in suppliers, customers, and other stakeholders into all the efforts and programs

Building the buy-in is an ongoing process. As the challenge of embedded sustainability demands deeper and deeper integration of social and environmental value into the entire company, value chain, and product line, new levels of commitment are necessary to make sure the transformation stays on track. Functional, geographical, and business unit divisions play a role as well – often, engaging a new subsidiary or a business unit means starting from scratch. Treating the buy-in process as a long-term investment project is the best way to make sure this job does not accidentally fall through the cracks.

Moving from incremental to breakthrough

While the early learnings, baseline assessments, start-up experiments, and commitment building efforts are all crucial elements of embedding sustainability into the core business, the rubber truly hits the road when the company is ready to move from incremental to breakthrough change. This move takes place when the many occasional and scattered sustainable value innovations are extended, elevated, and connected into a comprehensive effort essential for achieving competitive advantage. Essentially, sustainable value creation is about building on your *existing* core competencies and competitive strengths, rather than developing a *new* one. Embedding sustainability into the core of strategy requires finding a clear fit, a sweet spot between business priorities and the new social and environmental efforts.

Finding the fit

For Lafarge, a leading French building materials company present in 76 coun-tries, the analysis of social and environmental risks suggested that local com-munity engagement, better waste management, and investment into green building technologies represent the most important strategic directions for sustainable value creation. Among early successes is the waste management company Eco-processa, created in 2004 as a joint venture between Lafarge and Cimpor in Brazil, set up to supply Lafarge and Cimpor's factories with waste to be used as an alternative fuel. In 2006, the joint venture co-pro-cessed 115,000 tons of waste, and set the target for 2009 at 350,000 tons. In its factories in Cantagalo, Matozinhos, and Arcos, Lafarge has reduced fossil fuel consumption by 25,000 tons and raw material consumption by 10,000 tons thanks to the collection and recycling of waste; similar projects are set up by Lafarge throughout the world.

For Troika Dialog, Russia's largest and oldest private investment bank, poor corporate governance and financial discipline of Russian companies pre-sented a significant social risk. The company turned the risk into an oppor-tunity by introducing a new product as a part of its market research offers. The Corporate Governance Risks Report ranks investment risks associated with corporate governance performance of the nation's largest companies. Since its introduction, the report has grown into one of the most demanded research products, while catalyzing positive changes in governance, trans-parency, and discipline of Russian companies.

For Walmart, cost and supply management stands at the center of its suc-cess and long-term strategy, so the sustainable value efforts introduced by the company in mid-2004 were aligned with its traditional operational strengths and strategic priorities. Redesign of packaging and distribution models allowed for significant reduction of paper, plastic, and fuel expenses – all on top of significant environmental benefits. Walmart took advantage of its scale and deep knowledge of supply chain management to make sure that new eco-smart products are introduced throughout Walmart stores at low prices, helping to attract new customers. Hundreds of similar initiatives have been implemented at Walmart since 2004.

For General Electric, innovation is the core driver for the company's value proposition, and the company's sustainability work is fully aligned with this strategic strength. Connecting its many "green" efforts into one coherent cross-company program, in 2005 GE launched its highly visible "Ecomagi-nation" program, which includes innovations ranging from energy-efficient light bulbs to fuel-efficient and low-polluting locomotives to GE money eco MasterCard which supports greenhouse gas offsetting. In 2007, GE's "green harvest" rose to $14 billion, a revenue level that increased more than 15 per cent from 2006, with revenue of $25 billion projected for 2010. The vision of Jeff Immelt, Chairman and CEO, speaks pointedly about this alignment of corporate strategy, social needs, and company profits: "We are going to solve tough customer and global problems and make money doing it."

For decades, India's Tata Group put the philosophy of "business excellence" at the center of its long-term strategy. It has focused on the area of operations for ongoing quality improvement in ways that benefit Indian society – building hospitals and schools to assure a high-quality workforce long before it was fashionable to do so. So, it makes sense that the recent sustainability efforts of the Group will also lie in the area of operations: more specifically, energy. By 2009, the company's priority targets included energy efficiency improvements, methane recovery to allow for fuel switch in plants, harvesting alternative sources of energy such as solar and wind, steam power generation, and waste heat recovery power generation.

What the experiences of Lafarge, Troika, Walmart, General Electric, Tata, and many others are illustrating is that moving from incremental to breakthrough change requires the discovery of a strong alignment between the sustainability agenda and the business's sources of competitive advantage. If innovative loyal employees are the key source of your competitive advantage, how can sustainability effort contribute to employee effectiveness, creativity, and commitment? If product innovation is something you compete on, in what way can environmental and social performance help you find new and better ways to deliver the desired benefits for your customers? If operational excellence is what distinguishes you among your competitors, how can social and environmental performance help you discover new and more efficient ways to operate? Where is the fit between strategic priorities, existing competitive advantage and the social and environmental opportunities on hand?

All in all, embedding sustainability into the DNA of business for breakthrough transformation offers a number of significant challenges and hurdles. Finding a fit with the existing strategy calls for seeing the business anew. Among the most difficult transitions are:

- **From independence to interdependence.** The three big trends of declining resources, radical transparency, and increasing expectations are redefining the boundaries of a modern company. Now it is not enough to consider the impact and viability of strategic decisions within the borders of the company; to create sustainable value, a company must know and manage social and environmental performance along the entire life cycle value chain, upstream to raw materials and downstream to product end-of-life

- **From marginal PR issue to essential factor of business success.**
  Traditionally, most social and environmental projects have been
  handled by public relations, human resource, or legal departments.
  The vision of embedded sustainability makes a case for social and
  environmental performance as part of everyone's job, particularly
  line managers and business unit heads

- **From maintenance to design.** The rapid change in the competitive environment caused by the massive decline in resources and
  increase in social expectations is creating new business challenges
  the like of which has not been seen before. With no obvious solutions
  and formulas in existence, and little "best practices" accumulated,
  the transition towards a truly sustainable value paradigm requires
  a willingness and appetite for constant innovation, creation, and
  design, rather than maintenance of existing business models and
  approaches

- **From only short-term to balancing short- and long-term.** As
  the opportunities and risks presented by the emerging social and
  environmental terrain change rapidly, it is no longer acceptable to
  operate within the traditional quarterly and yearly focus. Whether
  developing a new product, assessing a new market, or searching for
  a new source of capital, an expanded time horizon is necessary to
  predict and address issues of strategic relevance. Development of a
  new mind-set, supported by new performance measurements systems, is necessary to prevent short-term return maximization at the
  expense of long-term value creation

It is hard to find an approach to change management and strategy development that meets these challenges of sustainable value creation better than
appreciative inquiry (AI) which we touched on in previous chapters. Particularly suited for large-scale organizational change, AI has recently been used
to introduce and enhance sustainability efforts in business.

Changing at the scale of the whole

Built on the conviction that traditional problem solving techniques force
managers to become experts in understanding – and ultimately repeating –
their own mistakes, AI invites companies to apply equally rigorous analysis
to past successes within and beyond company borders. In addition to the
shift in the "what" of strategy analysis and development, appreciative inquiry
also changes the "who" and the "how" of strategic planning, engaging a significant group of company stakeholders – managers, employees, suppliers,

customers, regulatory authorities, and community members – in structured dialogues and action planning aimed at scaling up organizational strengths and engaging the entire system rapidly.

Green Mountain Coffee Roasters, which made it to number one on the list of *Corporate Responsibility Officer Magazine*'s 100 Best Corporate Citizens in 2006 and 2007, has been using AI for its sustainability needs since 2000. Fairmount Minerals ran its first whole-company AI summit in 2005, which allowed for realignment of strategy, and led to new product development, core process improvements, and increased employee engagement. In 2008, Walmart used AI with its sustainability efforts, managing a successful multi-stakeholder process for whole-industry change for Walmart dairy suppliers.

Green Mountain Coffee Roasters, Fairmount Minerals, and the dairy industry all used a well-developed and, perhaps, most tangible methodology within the AI platform, namely the AI Summit. Bernard Mohr and Jim Ludema, seasoned organizational development thinkers, describe the methodology in the following way:

> The Appreciative Inquiry Summit is a method for accelerating change by involving a broad range of internal and external stakeholders in the change process. Typically an event or a series of events of 3–5 days in lengths, a summit brings people together to: (1) discover collective competencies and strengths; (2) envision opportunities for positive change; (3) design the desired changes; and (4) implement and sustain change making it work.

But more than a single event, an AI summit is an extensive process that engages the organization top-down and bottom-up, with the off-site event serving as a high-energy pinnacle of sustainable value creation process. On the opposite page is how the AI summit process looks when utilized for embedded sustainability.

The power of utilizing AI summits for the sustainable value challenge is illustrated in full by the story of Fairmount Minerals, the leading industrial sands manufacturer in the USA based in Chardon, Ohio. On August 29, 2005, over 300 people came together in Eaglewood Resort to take part in the Fairmount Minerals AI Summit, with the imaginative title of "SiO2": the chemical formula for sand silica was chosen to abbreviate the summit theme, "Sustainability in Our Organization." Mixed across functions and stakeholder groups, participants seated at roundtables were quickly led into inquiry, and then on into group dialogue, community votes, rapid prototyping, and post-summit planning. The intense three-day summit was a child of a dedicated summit organization team, which took formal training in sustainability for business advantage and the AI method to launch its summit design and execution work. The particular task of the summit was to ignite change at the scale of

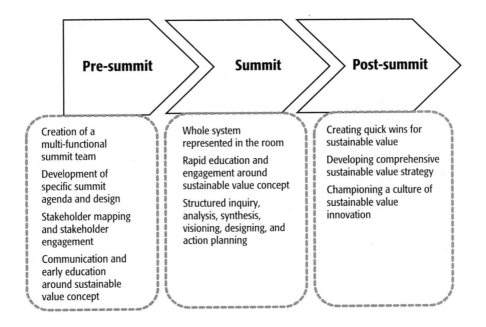

the whole – with the entire system engaged and re-envisioned. It is no surprise, then, that by August 31st the company was buzzing with pilot projects, task groups, and early solutions.

The 2005 summit laid the foundation for a complete overhaul of Fairmount Minerals' strategy and practices. Following the summit, the company has developed new processes, such as the new sand cleaning processes that have significantly reduced the amount of water and energy used; new products, such as a new FDA-approved elastomer used for turf infill, which gives the same shock absorption with minimal environmental and health risk (it is UV-resistant and is 100 per cent recyclable); and new relationships, such as stakeholder dialogues run prior to new mine acquisitions. Moreover, AI allowed the company to go through rapid transformation, elevating diverse and disconnected projects into comprehensive, cohesive business strategy for sustainable value creation.

Collaborative whole-system solutions similar to AI summits tend to leapfrog a company towards an aligned sustainable value strategy, while energizing its employees to follow through on the designed goals and models. At its best, AI answers the call to breakthrough transformation: it expands organizational boundaries to include a wide range of stakeholders in the decision-making process; it fosters cross-functional dialogue that ignites rapid innovation and places sustainability at the core of business; it connects past, present, and future to move beyond the accepted short-term thinking for long-term visioning.

Staying with it

As the train sets in motion, and the dust of the initial excitement settles, it becomes crucial to keep things moving. When it comes to staying with it, the goal of embedding sustainability into the core of business offers particular challenges. Here is how one of our clients puts this challenge into perspective: "It is hard to keep going, as the ultimate goal is to make myself unnecessary. The more successful you are with sustainability, the more invisible it becomes. So, motivation is an issue."

Just as in personal life, having a support infrastructure ready to catch you during small stumbles, big confusions, and overall energy drain is extremely important. Corporate sustainability support groups are popping up across the nation and across the globe. Some of industry's biggest names come together under the umbrella of the Society for Organizational Learning Sustainability Consortium, which allows members like Unilever, Coca-Cola, Seventh Generation, and Schlumberger to exchange ideas, tackle common issues, and join forces around particular solutions.[364] And the power of support groups is not exclusive to large companies. Small and medium enterprises of northeast Ohio get the same benefits through the Sustainability Implementation Group run by Entrepreneurs for Sustainability, also known as E4S, where participating companies co-develop new revenue streams, learn new technologies, and visit each other's facilities to get hands-on experience with sustainable operations. From a tiny group that started in 2000 to an 8,000-member organization in 2010, E4S is a perfect example of how to keep the energy up while making sustainability relevant for a local context.[365]

While the peer learning group is an excellent way to keep your energy and commitment up, metrics and measurements become a critical means to stay with it. As social and environmental performance becomes the new business-as-usual in your company, penetrating products, processes, and business models, it is crucial to take a breather and remind yourself how far you've come.

For Rabobank Group, an international financial services company heavily focused on food and agribusiness, committing to clear key performance indicators (KPIs) and keeping an eye on progress offers a way to keep the energy up around the long-term sustainability goals. The company tracks – and makes publicly available – longitudinal data on such indicators as

"Volume of sustainable and responsible loans and savings products," "Value of sustainable assets under management and held in custody," and "Energy use Rabobank Group by source and activity."[366]

TerraCycle, the "Worm Poop" empire we discussed in Chapter 1, which produces a range of products made out of trash, makes sure that key metrics are front and center on their home page. Live data on the number of people collecting trash (13,773,550 as of January 19, 2011), the units of waste collected (a sizeable 1,862,664,505), the number of products made (209) and the amount of money given to charity ($1,589,276.17) is displayed on the top of the home page.

A number of well-developed guidelines and reports can help you move from baseline assessment to a truly comprehensive – and customized – approach to measurement. There is no question that the Global Reporting Initiative (GRI) offers the most renowned and comprehensive reporting guidelines, alongside valuable resources and events.[367] Big-picture audits such as the one offered by the 2009 MIT Sloan Management Review "The Business of Sustainability" report can provide you with the measurement of progress at the strategic level.[368] Highly customized and technical metrics frameworks are also available: for example, the Sustainable Packaging Coalition offers a highly developed Sustainable Packaging Metrics Framework guiding you through packaging decisions and related measurements.[369]

James Collins and Jerry Porras offer a concept that might come in handy for a company trying to keep the energy up while making real and measurable progress. In their 1996 article entitled "Building Your Company's Vision," Collins and Porras proposed the term Big Hairy Audacious Goal, or BHAG:

> A true BHAG is clear and compelling, serves as unifying focal point of effort, and acts as a clear catalyst for team spirit. It has a clear finish line, so the organization can know when it has achieved the goal; people like to shoot for finish lines.[370]

Setting a BHAG for a specific and manageable period of time gives your company and its value chain a necessary boost of attention, energy, and progress.

In summary

While the above exposition might create an illusion that the movement towards embedded sustainability represents a sequential, linear path, research and practice prove that it is anything but a clear step-by-step process. The task of moving from traditional business strategy towards a truly sustainable value model is a complex and evolving process – so no 'five easy steps' will do.

As the stories of pioneers in the movement from bolt-on to embedded sustainability illustrate, changing the story of the company demands careful management of four interdependent areas of focus. Together, these four areas represent a map of action to guide your own transformation:

Getting the right start	Building the buy-in	Moving from incremental to breakthrough	Staying with it
• Organizational sponsorship • Insight • Baseline • Low-hanging fruit	• Leadership • Organization • Value chain • Key stakeholders	• Vision • Strategy • Co-innovation	• Metrics • Organizational learning • Energy

The four areas interact in an unpredictable and nonlinear way. We might write about low-hanging fruit before we speak about whole-system organizational change, but in reality the two activities are deeply interwoven, interdependent strands of an iterative process.

However, it is useful to separate the conversation about the content of the embedded sustainability strategy from the process of such strategy development and implementation. It is not only about what will be your own strategy – in many cases it is even more important how the strategy was developed and implemented.

But it is now time for us to move from process to content – and consider how it all fits together. In the following chapter, we will get a chance to connect the dots across all the ideas we have covered so far, and come up with one possible way towards developing your own embedded sustainability strategy.

8
Putting it all together

For seven chapters, we traveled through many new concepts, frameworks, and real-life examples. We explored the mega-trends that are reshaping the business landscape and discovered a range of strategic responses available to business leaders. Beyond sustainability as cost, we outlined two strikingly different approaches – *bolt-on* versus *embedded* – that turn sustainability pressures into new opportunities for profit and growth. We advanced *embedded sustainability* as essential to today's core business strategy and delved into the unique competencies required for its execution. But the question remains: how do you design a pathway to integrate sustainability into the business core? How do you strengthen and extend existing strategic choices in support of key business priorities?

While there is no one definitive step-by-step solution – no one-size-fits-all – to meet the needs of every company, there are mileposts to help guide you along the way. These markers offer a chance to rethink, reimagine, and redesign a business strategy that embeds sustainability into the DNA of your organization to create enduring value. Before we map the territory with the suggested markers, consider what we've already encompassed and how it all fits together.

A quick recap: our discoveries so far

To this point we have a covered a lot of ground – a colorful palette of concepts and ideas to paint a new picture of today's business reality:

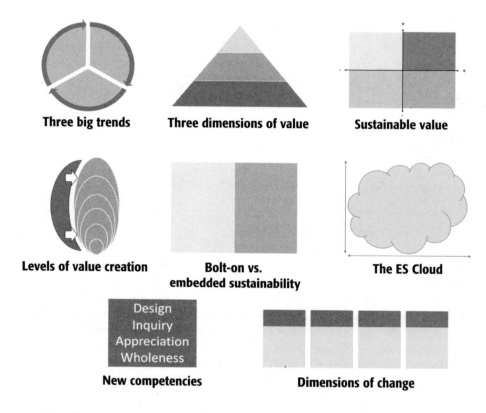

Three big trends   **Three dimensions of value**   **Sustainable value**

Levels of value creation   **Bolt-on vs.
embedded sustainability**   **The ES Cloud**

Design
Inquiry
Appreciation
Wholeness

New competencies   **Dimensions of change**

Now, how do we put them all together in a way that makes practical sense for managers about to embark on their own organizational journey? Let's recap.

In recent years, rising social and environmental pressures created a perfect storm of confusion and frustration for managers around the world. For us, the best way to make sense of these complex, interconnected, and rapidly evolving market forces is to think of them in terms of three interdependent trends: **declining resources, radical transparency**, and **increasing expectations**. Waning natural resources, be it fish stocks, precious metals,

or social equity, threatens the security of our value chains. Consumers and investors (among others) are beginning to demand socially and environmentally savvy products that do not require any compromises in price or quality. Radical transparency, fueled by the growth of the nonprofit sector and supported by evolving social media technologies, makes both declining resources and rising expectations ever more present in the public eye, and therefore ever more a factor of competitive advantage.

Even more central to strategy, the three big trends are reshaping the way business creates value. Long gone are the days when it was possible to focus only on shareholder value – the perverse logic of the "casino economy" – without attention to the product or its end benefits and outcomes.

To compete successfully, companies must now create a **value model** with products and solutions designed to fit consumer and stakeholder needs, producing desired outcomes for business and society without costly externalities. As declining resources, radical transparency, and increasing expectations lie at the core of the new end benefits and outcomes desired by the market, companies have a remarkable challenge to address. They cannot keep pursuing profit at any cost to society. Yet the reverse – a mission of social or environmental activism as the responsible thing to do even if it means sacrificing profit – is also proving undesirable in today's demanding marketplace. Instead of having to choose between profits and social responsibility, **sustainable value** – creating value for shareholders *and* stakeholders – is a third way, a smarter business model in a new competitive environment that demands it. Going well beyond issues of trade-off between social good and business results, sustainable value is a dynamic vision of opportunity, innovation, and synergy.

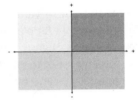

If new social and environmental forces are demanding value for shareholders *and* a wide range of stakeholders without trade-offs, how are we to respond to these pressures?

To answer this question in the most comprehensive and thoughtful way possible, we combed through the strategy discipline, turning to the leading thinkers in the field to help us find the most effective strategic responses.

Two primary ways of approaching sustainability became immediately apparent: sustainability can be treated as a necessary *cost* (and even worse, as an unnecessary distraction), or it can be seen as a business *opportunity*. Yet to our surprise – and in contrast to the "sustainability-as-cost" myths prevailing in so many corporate corridors – when the analytic models and insights of strategy applied to sustainability are assessed, the available data and research conclusions weigh overwhelmingly in favor of business opportunity. More specifically: out of

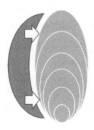

eight possible responses, seven deal with unique and highly attractive ways of creating competitive advantage. These **seven levels of value creation** are: using sustainability as a way to mitigate risks, achieve higher operational efficiency, differentiate your products, enter or create new markets, protect and enhance your brand identity, reshape market rules, and regulatory contexts – all of which have the potential to be amplified by radical innovation. The verdict: there is huge value to be created and captured when sustainability is approached as a business opportunity.

Yet not all opportunity is created equal. Many companies searching for new vistas simply **bolt on** sustainability to their core strategies and operations like a poorly fitted Band-Aid. When bolted on, green initiatives and social responsibility lie at the margins of the business and at best produce symbolic wins that inadvertently highlight the unsustainability of the remaining activities. In contrast,
embedded sustainability calls for an entirely different approach, whereby social and environmental value is integrated into the products and processes across the entire value chain without compromises in price or quality; in other words, with no green or social premium. With sustainability embedded into the DNA of your business, value is created across all seven levels, from risk management to creating new markets, from incremental change to radical innovation, and everything in between. It also became clear that, when embedded, sustainability allows companies to exploit one of two very different pathways. In the first case, companies embed sustainability to strengthen their existing strategic positioning by reinforcing product differentiation or improving cost leadership (the bottom left corner of the *ES Cloud*). In the second case, companies embed sustainability to pursue new and relatively uncontested market space – the blue oceans created by the growing need for business solutions to environmental, health, and social problems (the upper right corner of the *ES Cloud*).

Whether you embed sustainability to strengthen your existing strategy or to develop a new one, a few new competencies are indispensable. While traditional management skills are still necessary – there is no way forward without measurement, solid analysis, and effective project management – a number of new capabilities are needed to bring the embedded sustainability mind-set into reality. While they might come across as an unusual bunch, the experience of early

Design
Inquiry
Appreciation
Wholeness

business pioneers shows that **design**, **inquiry**, **appreciation**, and **wholeness** make a great starter pack for those managers searching to integrate sustainability into the core of their business.

Naturally, such skills and competencies do not emerge in a vacuum or from memos proclaiming the new vision. Practice is the name of the game. And when it comes to the practice of embedded sustainability, it is clear that actions capable of producing quick wins come long before a comprehen-  sive strategy is formulated. While it may sound appealing to start with strategy from the get-go, in reality the change process starts with lots of "playing around" – many experimental projects that help you get the right start, assure early buy-in, and get the company warmed up for bigger strategic conversations. Four different dimensions of change have to be attended to and managed carefully to assure the right transition to embedded sustainability.

Now, with all things explored and considered, what steps should you take in your own company to put these ideas to good use? How do you choose the content and process for beginning a new endeavor?

While examples of companies already successful in embedding sustainability show that no one definitive road map exists for making the right strategic choices, a number of important road signs provide consistent markers of a good strategy. We invite you to treat each of the following steps as exercises aimed at assisting you in your decision making. Together, they offer a guide towards discovering your own embedded sustainability business strategy.

On the road again: discovering your own pathway

It might seem tempting to place strategic discussions of embedded sustainability right at the start of your transformation efforts. Yet in the large majority of companies we worked with or studied, strategic discussions came much later in the game, long after the first wave of experiments and the first low-hanging fruits were harvested. Once those early wins are secured and initial momentum is achieved, the company is ready to shift gears and move to deeper levels of strategy and innovation.

There is no "best way" to organize this shift effectively. Many companies bring together a cross-functional team – with or without external partners – while others assign a coordinating and facilitating role to a single leader. Some choose to hold the bulk of their strategic conversations at one or more multi-day off-site sessions with hundreds of participants at a time, while others split the discussion into sequential meetings of small groups of 8 to 12 individuals. While the format is not what is most important, what is crucial is to allow for the time and resources needed to explore each key business issue in depth – developing a comprehensive, cross-functional, and truly tailored approach to embedding sustainability into your products, processes, business models, and technologies.

Key steps and mileposts for you to conquer are:

1. **Commit.** How do we assure top leadership commitment to move from incremental bolt-on change to breakthrough embedded sustainability in the core business?

2. **Choose where to focus.** Into what core business will we embed sustainability?

3. **Position.** Where on the *ES Cloud* is our business today and where is it going?

4. **Visualize.** What are the life cycle value-added activities from end to end?

5. **Listen.** Who are the key stakeholders of the business and what are their issues and wants?

6. **Anticipate.** How are their expectations changing? What will they be in five to ten years?

7. **Assess value**. How does the sustainability footprint of your business convert into business risks and opportunities? In what ways will the opportunities create business value?

8. **Set goals.** What are the sustainable value objectives for your business?

9. **Take action.** What actions will we take? With whom and with what resources?

10. **Measure.** What is the financial return on investment of each proposed action?

11. **Prioritize.** What are the quick wins, incremental changes, and disruptive innovations and in what order will we undertake them?

In the following pages, we invite you to take a look at each step and discover the questions, tools, and approaches that might come in handy along the way. We hope that, when completed, these conversations will leave you with a set of clear cohesive strategic options. Along the way, we thank the countless companies that helped us develop and polish these steps in recent years.

Commit

How do we assure top leadership commitment to move from incremental bolt-on change to breakthrough embedded sustainability in the core business? is a crucial inquiry for setting the right foundation for your embedded sustainability strategy. To make sure executive commitment is secured, it is important to understand what is happening in the company already, and how social and environmental issues can be framed as a source of business opportunity.

To start, it is useful to meet with sustainability advocates inside the company to understand what has been accomplished to date, how sustainability is defined (or not) within the organization, and how environmental and sustainability issues have been integrated into business decision making. Using this data, engage, educate, and enroll a broad leadership group on sustainability as a source of innovation and business advantage. Often, the quick wins already achieved within the company are not widely known, and the diverse sustainability-related activities in different parts of organization are not connected under one potent strategic umbrella. Presenting and discussing the accomplishments of today and strategic directions for tomorrow is one way to acquire and build the support of top leadership.

Choose

Once the initial leadership commitment is assured, the first big decision to make is: *Into what core business will we embed sustainability?* The more specific the selection, the better – often it is a single brand, product line, and geographic market. Two criteria are paramount in the choice.

First, what are the products, processes, business models, and technologies that are central to our ability to compete today and tomorrow? What activities are at the core of our strategy? What represents the essence of the current value capture model? For example, for an electric utility, the type of fuel (coal, geothermal, nuclear . . .) used in power generation is central to the business; office recycling and the choice of cars for the corporate fleet are not.

Second, what are the significant sustainability pressures on the business today? Where do we feel some pressure already? What areas of the business offer some promise to do something different?

Often, companies brainstorm a long list of potential products and processes – as well as business models and technologies – to focus on, and then narrow it down to a shorter list to be explored in parallel. It can be helpful to allow small teams to choose their own focus, and support them as they explore the following steps.

Position

Where on the ES Cloud *is our business today?* is the next big conversation to hold. As the Cloud serves as a sort of map to make sense of your personal sustainability terrain, it is helpful to have in-depth, cross-function conversations about your current position as the starting point of your transformation.

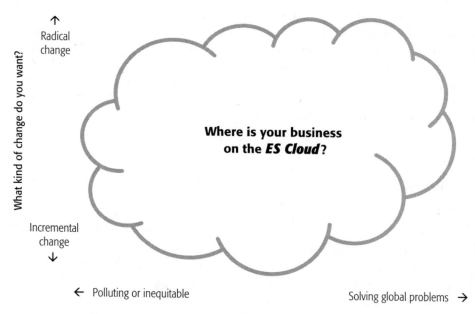

As you hold these discussions, you might notice that representatives of different departments, functions, and geographical locations have dramatically different assessments of the business's current position. Discussions with external stakeholders can bring in even more disparity. However, putting all of the perceptions and visions on the table early is the best way to have a productive and realistic conversation necessary for designing a successful pathway to sustainable value.

Visualize

What are the life cycle value-added activities from end to end? is another key conversation to have early across the company. To answer this question, managers find it helpful to develop a simplified life cycle drawing of the business they are targeting. Begin with your organization's own activities (such as manufacturing or distributing) and add upstream activities of your suppliers all the way to raw material extraction or resource planning activities, as well as downstream activities to product end-of-life. Here are some of the key activities you might consider:

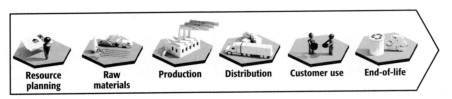

Your drawing should be specific to your industry and is likely to look quite different from the generic life cycle value chain above. For example, in the pharmaceutical industry the life cycle starts with the discovery of new molecules (R&D, validation, screening, optimization). The next activity stage is clinical trials and submission for approval to regulatory bodies. Only then are raw materials procured for the sourcing of active pharmaceutical ingredients (APIs) and excipients that go into the manufacturing, marketing, and sales of drugs. The final activity of interest is the disposal of pharma products, both unused and unmetabolized, which are thrown away or excreted into waste water systems.

Listen

With the value chain in front of you, the next question is: *Who are your business's key stakeholders and what are their issues and wants?* It is helpful to consider the full range of stakeholders along each activity step in the value chain – and you might find yourself surprised to discover groups and individuals who have a stake in your business way outside of the usual set of suppliers and customers.

As you are making your analysis of stakeholder issues and wants along the life cycle value chain, a simple tool such as the table below might come in handy. As you are working with the table, the key question is: for your business the way it currently stands – with its existing strategy and activities – what are the key stakeholder perspectives on the economic, environmental, and social value *created* or *destroyed* by your business?

Stakeholder group	What are the key issues and existing frustrations?	What are the main interests and wants?
Communities		
NGOs		
Governments		
Customers		
Employees		

For the left-hand column, we have chosen five generic stakeholders as a mere illustration. We invite you to choose those stakeholders that are essential to your organization's success – and you might find it helpful to list specific organizations or groups as well.

Now, to the search for answers. In addition to dialogue with stakeholders to get their perspective on the environmental, social, and economic impacts of your business, you can draw on existing management systems and external data to determine a baseline sustainability footprint.

The process so far should result in a map of all the stakeholder impacts that your business has – whether they are under your organization's control or not. For example, if you sell cotton T-shirts, you must include the health and environmental harm of growing conventional cotton with pesticide-intensive farming and mono-irrigation techniques (and not only the ginning, sewing, and distribution of the T-shirts). Once the stakeholder needs and issues are identified, the life cycle sustainability footprint is mapped in your own customized visual similar to this:

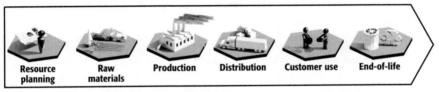

Resource planning	Raw materials	Production	Distribution	Customer use	End-of-life

- Energy-in-extraction
- Sustainable sourcing
- Waste, toxics
- Human rights
- Fair wages
- Community outreach
- Regional development

- CO_2 emissions
- Use of fossil fuels
- Water use
- Worker health & safety
- Social equity
- Community integration
- Growth, jobs, tax base

- Energy efficiency
- Product disposal
- Biodiversity impacts
- Consumer health & safety
- Well-being
- Transparency
- Meeting unmet needs

If we have not made it clear yet, here is the key point to emphasize: when it comes to understanding your stakeholders, *listening is the best strategy.* Stakeholder perceptions and emotions – which cannot easily be discovered with many of our traditional hard data-driven approaches – are essential to the footprinting exercise. Engaging stakeholders in dialogue about environmental, health, and social impacts helps to build relationships and also shapes their perceptions and emotions. Collecting and analyzing impacts data are foundational but complementary activities.

However, let us say a few words on hard data collection. In data-intensive approaches, managers have the option of conducting a simplified life cycle review focused on key "hot spots" or they can conduct a more sophisticated data-intensive life cycle assessment (LCA) with primary data collection for carbon, water, waste, and other stakeholder impacts. The choice of data-driven approach depends on what you are trying to accomplish at this stage. To communicate externally with a high level of sophistication or to position itself as a sustainability leader in the industry, a business may wish to conduct a full LCA. Alternatively, if it is looking to optimize client satisfaction and business value from sustainability performance, a simplified approach will be more cost-effective.

Anticipate

Now that you know where your stakeholders stand on the issues today, it is time to ask: *How are stakeholder expectations changing? What will they be in five to ten years?* Take the baseline of impacts along the life cycle value chain and ask, "What if?" Develop scenarios of stakeholder expectations to help ready your organization for change. As described in an earlier book, *Large Scale Organizational Change*:[371]

> What-if scenarios are not undertaken as an exercise in prediction; they are part of creating a mind-set that is open to radical change. If you are asking yourself what your company would do in case its future proves radically different from the past, it is probably already too late. Companies must integrate into their strategies a number of scenarios for radically alternative futures. Such envisioning of the future can remain fact based and issue driven, even if it represents a discontinuity with the past and present . . . The syndrome of compiling quarterly reports and annual budgets can be extremely limiting to a company's ability to adapt to fundamental change. Although these short-term exercises are efficient and necessary for a host of reasons, they must not allow senior management to privilege the short term at the cost of sustainability by optimizing existing structures and processes in a world in which these structures and processes are becoming irrelevant.

What if the price of oil goes to $200 per barrel or even $500 per barrel? What if total water usage in every business becomes routinely reported on product labels? What if your supply chains are disrupted because key raw materials become difficult or costly to obtain?

Managers need to consider high-probability, long-term trends in expectations (such as reducing dependence on coal and oil) as well as short-term events.

A simple visual exercise is to review the completed stakeholder table developed earlier and to identify the top three to five issues, frustrations, needs, and wants. Conducting stakeholder dialogues and outreach on these expectations, complemented by hard data, provides the foundation for the next set of tools.

Assess value

By now, you have selected a specific line of business to focus on; visualized its value-added activities and impacts; explored stakeholder frustrations and needs; and have a list of social and environmental risks for today and tomorrow. Now, the question becomes: *How does the environmental and social footprint of your business translate into* business *risks and opportunities? In what ways can altering the footprint create new business value?*

Very often, environmental managers and CSR heads stop at the previous stage of quantifying environmental and social impacts, with a glossy report that presents the (positively spun) sustainability impacts of the business. In contrast, we have to go further and convert sustainability impacts into core business risks and opportunities.

Begin by making a list of the business risks of continuing with the negative stakeholder impacts already identified. Consider the rising expectations of customers, employees, governments, NGOs, and other stakeholders. What will happen if you continue for the next five to ten years with your current business strategy? Example risks might include customer deselection, loss of market share to greener or more socially responsible competitors, preemptive government regulation, loss of reputation, and fines and penalties.

Now, imagine that the existing social and environmental damages are minimized or eliminated, and that the associated business risks are mitigated. Then make a mirror image list of business opportunities that come from minimizing harm and from providing environmental, health, and social *benefits* to stakeholders along the life cycle value chain. Competitive opportunity might include gaining market share, enhancing brand image, become supplier-of-choice, motivating employees, and discovering new markets based on solving customer sustainability problems through Blue Ocean Strategies.

You can organize your sustainability-related business risks and opportunities using the seven levels of value creation:

7 sources of business value

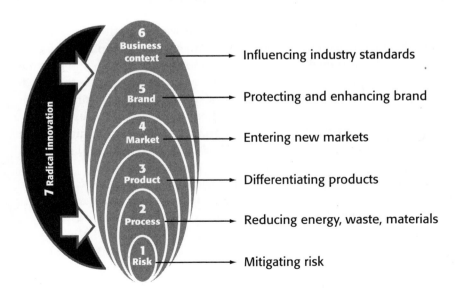

From *The Sustainable Company* (Figure 11-8), by Chris Laszlo. Copyright © 2003 Chris Laszlo. Reproduced by permission of Island Press, Washington, D.C.

For every opportunity to reduce negative impacts on stakeholders or to provide ecological and social benefits to them, consider how business value is created along the seven levels. What can begin as a "low-level" opportunity to conserve energy or reduce waste can extend beyond cost savings to product and brand benefits as well as opportunities to enter new markets driven by the need for sustainability solutions.

Set goals

Now that the general scope of value creation opportunities is understood, the question becomes: *What are the sustainable value objectives for your business?*

Your choice depends on where you are today and whether you are pursuing incremental or disruptive change to your business strategy. In essence, there are two types of option available to your business:

- Improving your strategic positioning in an *existing* market, or

- Pursuing a Blue Ocean Strategy of creating *new* uncontested market space

Within these two categories, your goals can include incremental or disruptive innovation.

To help you with the goals, the *ES Cloud* provides a useful visual tool. By now, after much deliberation within the company and beyond its walls, you have already positioned yourself on the Cloud. Now the question becomes what ultimate position you will pursue and what are the possible intermediary stops along the way. Based on the sustainability-driven business opportunities and value creation levels identified in the previous step, establish your objectives in a five- to seven-year horizon. Embedding sustainability for better positioning or embedding sustainability for creation of uncontested market space are both valid and potent options (see opposite).

Here any of your favorite existing strategic planning methods can be used. Once the strategic direction is set, make sure to use your "habitual" strategic thinking to develop the strategy in depth.

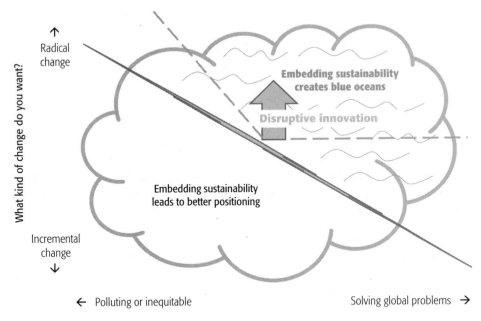

↑
Radical
change

What kind of change do you want?

**Embedding sustainability
creates blue oceans**

Disruptive innovation

Embedding sustainability
leads to better positioning

Incremental
change
↓

← Polluting or inequitable   Solving global problems →

How green and socially attuned is your business? (now and in the future)

Take action

With the general strategic direction and pathway outlined, it is time to turn to concrete steps and actions. With the product, process, business model, or technology in focus, and the end-state envisioned: *What actions will you take? With whom and with what resources?*

It is time to turn opportunities and goals for embedding sustainability into one or more specific projects. Begin by describing each project in general terms. What is it intended to accomplish? Over what time period? What resources will it need? What are you asking your company to say "yes" to? Describe the main components of the project you are proposing to undertake.

Here stakeholder collaboration plays a critical role in embedding sustainability for business advantage. Developing your projects via ongoing partnerships with government bodies, NGOs, outside experts, local communities, and others, you will have access to specialized knowledge about environmental and social performance that is simply unavailable internally. Virtual social networking collaboration tools offer new platforms for stakeholder engagement in day-to-day actions to improve buy-in and market acceptability for business activities and products or services.

Measure

As the projects begin to take shape, numbers matter. *What is the financial return on investment (ROI) of each proposed initiative?* Using the seven levels of value creation explored earlier, you can begin to make a quantified business case for the proposed actions. The spreadsheet below offers one possible template for quantifying the expected financial value of any given project:

	Year 1	Year 2	Year 3	
Investment:				
Project-related revenues: • New sales from "green" products" • New sales from improved reputation/brand image • New customers or markets accessed • Other project revenues (+/−)				
Project-related costs: • Energy conservation/waste reduction, raw materials savings • Avoided fines and penalties (pollution/carbon emissions, . . .) • Increased employee productivity, lower employee turnover • Other project costs (+/−)				
Nonfinancial value (balanced scorecard): • Improved community relations, number of sustainability awards • Diversity of workforce, number of volunteer hours • Other nonfinancial (+/−)				

Based on the streams of value generated relative to the initial investment, you can also calculate a return on investment including the projected payback period.

However, not all value created can be easily quantified financially. Market confidence from investors who perceive embedded sustainability as an indicator of management quality is one such example. Customer preferred purchasing status can be difficult to translate into immediate sales numbers. Organizational alignment and learning from a shared vision of sustainable value are also difficult to measure. A useful reference for best practices in measuring and managing sustainability-driven business projects is Marc Epstein's *Making Sustainability Work.*[372]

Prioritize

With the key projects identified and explored, it becomes prime time to prioritize. *What are the quick wins, incremental changes, and disruptive innovations and in what order will you undertake them?* The process of embedding sustainability can result in a portfolio of projects aimed at strengthening an existing business strategy or aimed at migrating the business to a new strategy. Because many of the skills and capabilities that we discussed throughout the book will be new to the organization, it is important to learn-by-doing and to build momentum and credibility for embedding sustainability by starting with quick wins that demonstrate tangible business results.

Once you have a new set of sustainability-driven goals and a prioritized pathway for achieving them, it is helpful to go back and ask: how does embedded sustainability fit into the overall strategy of the company? What makes it credible and compelling? You started this process by selecting one or more products, processes, business models, or technologies into which sustainability is embedded. Now, after much analysis, deliberation, and imagination, does your original choice hold? Does it support your existing business priorities? Does it make your business stronger?

In summary

Embedding sustainability into the core of your business strategy is a deliberate, nonlinear, and iterative process. In most cases, conversations about strategy become relevant only once the company has already harvested some low-hanging fruit, engaged its employees in practical day-to-day action, and created the foundation for transitioning from incremental to deeper change.

But once the foundations are built, finding the right fit in the core business becomes paramount. To work, sustainability must be embedded into existing business priorities, making your company stronger, rather than creating a new side project for the already busy – and frequently overwhelmed – managers.

With this chapter, we conclude the practice-oriented conversation around the vision of embedded sustainability. We hope that it will offer you an effective starter kit for finding your own way towards creating sustainable value. It was our deliberate choice to provide a set of steps capable of meeting companies wherever they are in the sustainability journey, and to focus on a business point of view on social and environmental pressures. Yet there is no question that the issues raised go well beyond competitive advantage and that the realities of creating a sustainable world are complex and equivocal.

In the last part of the book, we turn to the bigger picture and leap into deeper conversations about business, society, and the future of the world at large. To get us started, in the next chapter we invite you take a trip with us to the year 2041. As we travel through time, we hope you will experience in a very real way the possibility and challenges of creating a world that works for all and over time. And in the concluding chapter, we bring those challenges to the surface, exploring the big-picture questions surrounding embedded sustainability.

Welcome to the future.

Part IV
LEAPING INTO THE FUTURE

Fruits of the future
Introduction to Part IV

So far, we have relied heavily on proven facts and rigorous analysis to make our arguments. We attempted to demonstrate the conceptual and practical foundations of embedding sustainability for competitive advantage using the data-driven, quantitative, reductionist methods of social science. Because our subject matter is inherently about whole systems – business-in-society and society-in-nature – such methods have their limitations. Just as we cannot explain the functioning of the human body by analysis of the individual organs, muscles, and bones, so we cannot capture embedded sustainability by its individual elements of strategy and organizational change. What we need is some way to get at the creative design implicit in embedded sustainability or, to paraphrase architect William McDonough, the *signals of human intent* that lie at its core.

Chapter 9 is an attempt to take such a whole-brain approach that engages our emotions as well as our logic. It is a fictional account of a young man in the year 2041 in which many of the ideas and leading practices of this book are brought to life. In the story, after major wars and economic collapse, there is a "reset" period in which business takes a strong leadership role in profitably solving many of the world's toughest social and environmental problems. It does so not only out of moral reawakening but because the economic, social, ecological, cultural, technological, and mind-set factors of that future era align to make it a matter of self-interest. It tries to make clear the role of mind-set and to suggest the main features of a mind-set that will make possible a positive role for business.[373]

Chapter 10 addresses the limits of business and markets as mechanisms for solving the world's problems. It explores the risks of expecting too much of business and the corollary responsibility of government regulation and public activism. The debate about the impossibility of continued economic growth on a small planet is touched on. Additional questions reflect those that managers most often ask in our seminars on embedded sustainability.

One feature of the story is the complete absence of the word "sustainability." There are no sustainability strategies (at least not in the social and ecological sense) and no sustainability managers in a future in which it is fully embedded. Sustainability is invisible and yet permeates every aspect of business.

The decision to use storytelling is motivated by the desire to provide yet another learning style. As we have tried throughout the book, our goal is to make the book engaging and generative. It draws on the creative and empathetic "whole brain" that lies at the heart of the new competencies needed to embed sustainability (see Chapter 6). Best-selling author Daniel Pink, in *A Whole New Mind: Why Right-brainers will Rule the Future*, says,[374]

> When our lives are brimming with information and data, it's not enough to marshal an effective argument. Someone somewhere will inevitably track down a counterpoint to rebut your point. The essence of persuasion, communication, and self-understanding has become the ability also to fashion a compelling narrative.[375]

Based on the feedback received from readers of *Sustainable Value* (2008), the inclusion of a compelling narrative makes a sustainable business book more accessible – it is an easy read – and perhaps even better, it becomes more memorable. Such stories are "sticky'" with readers.

The products and business models imagined in the following chapter are thoroughly researched and science-based. They represent potential innovations and technological breakthroughs based on cutting-edge developments in areas such as biomimetics, genomics, and photochemistry. For example, scientists are already able to build artificial molecules that convert sunlight to usable energy at high efficiency rates, although on a very small scale and only under controlled lab conditions.[376] We draw on the futuristic thinking of experts in fields such as urban planning, agronomy, transportation, and waste management. Readers should note that we have taken the liberty of imagining certain specific developments. These cases are obviously not based in facts; the companies, brands, and products mentioned do not reflect actual entities or events.

Jake's story is intended to be fictional but not fictitious. While predicting the future may not be possible, an informed outline of a promising scenario can be a grounded exercise in strategy. As Professor David Cooperrider has pointed out, positive images of the future can lead to positive actions.[377] We hope that readers who have been convinced by our research and analysis will also be inspired by our dreams.

9
The world in 2041
A job interview

> The future is already here – it's just unevenly distributed
> **William Gibson**

Jake Marstreng pulled into the swap station in a hurry. His final job interview – this one with Ellen Chen, the new CEO of Septad Corp – was less than an hour away. As he pulled into a swap-lock, he could hear the robotic arm under his old jalopy. For the hundredth time he wished he could afford one of the fast-charge ultracapacitors instead of lithium-air for his aging electric roadster. Fast-charging in 90 seconds instead of the usual ten minutes would mean he could skip battery swap stations altogether and be good for nearly 500 miles.

A dreamy look came into Jake's eyes. He would turn 30 in June. He was facing the biggest career opportunity of his life, and he intended to seize the moment. *Carpe diem.* He lit a tobacco-free e-cig and felt the nicotine unwind him, slowly letting a long stream of smoke find its way out the window, barely cracked against the summer heat. With this job, in five years he would be in line to be general manager of a business unit, perhaps even officer of the parent company. Prestige, money, the good life . . . He could almost taste it.

The year 2041 was promising to be a good one. Taking another pull, Jake reflected on how much better things had gotten. In his early teens, the future had seemed grim, not because he wasn't excelling, but because the Water Wars and heavy government regulation had combined to bring the world economy to a near standstill. The prospect of almost any job had briefly disappeared and general morale – particularly in the business world – had hit an all-time low. His mother, Deena, had fought hard to keep her own company from going under. The strain at home had been palpable.

Now, a decade and a half later, opportunities were everywhere. Economic growth was high and with little end in sight; companies were fighting for talent and fortunes were being made. A sense of optimism – even for the long term – infused his generation. It was true that the best opportunities and highest standards of living were now in Eurasia and Brazil, but the North American Zone (NAZ) was roaring back. Even China was gradually recovering. In fact, for the first time in history, most of the world's 9 billion inhabitants were flourishing.

Recently the private sector had made major breakthroughs that restored Jake's faith in business and reminded him why he had pursued his MBA in the first place. Jake wasn't an Earth-Firster and he didn't particularly care for their causes or tactics. He wasn't willing to give up his car and air travel, both now carbon-free but still taxed and disparaged. But he could see that all the big innovations – the ones that made a lot of money – dealt with solutions to the world's toughest environmental and social problems.

Hearing the battery slide into place, he thought again about Septad, as he gunned it back into traffic. One couldn't really think in terms of the private sector anymore; the biggest corporations all had webs of partnerships with universities, government, and nonprofits. Joining one of the big market leaders had become the single most desired career path of his generation, whether it was to make a lot of money or the world a better place. Business was now part of the solution; a handful of top companies were helping to restore climate stability and food security – and closing the rich–poor gap by meeting the needs of the world's poor – among other challenges that had eluded governments and nonprofits for decades. Imperceptibly, business had become cool.

One of the biggest and most profitable breakthroughs had come five years earlier, when BioSOL – a Septad competitor and Jake's former employer – had commercialized photo-receptor cells that grew in ambient conditions and converted sunlight to usable energy with 95 per cent efficiency. Engineered molecules had finally been assembled into artificial cells capable of membrane potential – essentially molecular batteries – that were easy to grow and maintain for energy generation into electric grids and for powering homes around the world.

Decoding chloroplasts – the cell-like organelles of leaves that photosynthesize – had produced *two dozen* Nobel Prizes and revolutionized the world economy. Researchers had found a way to build inexpensive solar cells capable of turning light into electricity and storable fuels. From Jake's bioengineering classes at Stanford, he remembered the seeming impossibility of duplicating what weeds, pine needles, and some bacteria could do: capture the sun's energy with chlorophyll pigments, funnel it into a molecular reaction center where electrons were activated to split water, free oxygen, and turn carbon dioxide into sugar. The breakthrough had come when research- ers first commercialized artificial molecules capable of mimicking photosyn- thesis at nature's background efficiency rate. It was an innovation that led to the founding of BioSOL. The company's first product was a can of rooftop paint containing billions of these molecules that harvested the sun's energy in summer or winter. It was self-sustaining and maintenance-free. The com- pany's second product was a road surface sealant that turned a country's highways into electricity generators.

Decoding photosynthesis led to a lot of other things besides clean energy. Artificial cells were used to do chemistry with sunlight and water at room tem- perature. Photozymes searched out and destroyed polychlorinated biphe- nyls (PCBs) – the widespread carcinogen that had sent up mortality rates and health care costs in the early part of the century. These photozymes acted like micro-reactors, using energy from sunlight to scavenge for PCBs, even in remote Arctic waters, breaking their chlorine bonds and turning the toxins into harmless, nonchlorinated, biodegradables. Since their widespread use, the world had become a little healthier.

Jake was not a microbiologist and even less a photochemist, but like many business leaders after the year 2030, he had acquired an interdisciplinary familiarity with these sciences. He was going to have to draw on all of it if he had any chance of getting the job.

Pulling into a free plug port, he quickly put in his Virtual Retinal Display contact lenses. If anything unfamiliar came up, he could always do an eye- motion controlled web search.

The borg in the lobby scanned him in before taking him to the executive suite's private elevator.

The interview begins

After a nail-biting 20 minutes outside Chen's office, during which time he could hear the pitched conversation of a high-end 3-D virtual conference, the door opened wide. Out stepped Septad's CEO, smiling warmly, ushering him in to a well-worn leather seat. Jake was shocked at how youthful she was – he had calculated her age at 55 but would easily have guessed half that. Her large brown eyes sparkled with energy.

Gesturing to the wall panels, Chen spoke animatedly. "That was our high- performance materials team in Uruguay. They are getting ready to launch our next-generation whisper-thin coatings and surface proteins business

– essentially intelligent skin for portable devices. These skins not only use sunlight to power the devices, they also scrub CO_2 from the air, for which we get tax credits. And in our newer version, they self-repair until deactivated by the user. That's because our protein scientists finally developed templates that allow self-assembly without having to use living cells. We can now synthesize DNA segments directly into designer crystals to produce the polymers we want."

She added, "Our skins are not only abrasion- and corrosion-resistant, they're going to have the best compressive and torsional strengths on the market."

Jake jumped in. "My team at BioSOL had a similar project. We were working on inserting the DNA segments into bacteria and using them to manufacture the target proteins – essentially a farming operation. Our hope was that we could harvest these materials in water solutions, at room temperature and without a toxic draw across the Periodic Table." With Chen nodding encouragingly, he continued. "It worked well in the lab but not on a commercial scale. When it does, whichever company gets there first will have a way to produce cement-like polymers – even glass and ceramic – that can be used in everything from beam bridges to nano-optical devices."

"What do you think is the key to making it work on a large scale?" asked Chen.

"It's the amino acid sequencing," replied Jake. "Getting it right will help fiber designers link the structure of proteins and their function; that's going to be key to assembling polymers with precision on a large scale."

"Without high temperatures or harsh chemicals," he added, "or any manufacturing waste."

Chen, trying not to look impressed, scanned his resume on the desk in front of her. "I see your MBA concentration was in business innovation," she said with a smile. "What do you think our business model should be for new coatings and surface proteins? How do we roll them out to our customers to create a return on our investment?"

"I would look across market segments, not just portable devices but also medical, furniture, transportation, and even housing applications. And I would start with low-income consumer segments."

The CEO looked intrigued. "Why low-income consumers? Are you suggesting some sort of social justice strategy to increase market acceptance? How are we going to make a profit with such low margins?"

"Well, first of all, none of Septad's competitors is in these markets. It's a wide blue ocean. If you can force enough efficiency in the supply chain to profitably price for low-income groups, then selling in higher-income markets will be easy. I would look at new distribution channels where you can cut intermediaries and build loyalty directly with end-users, based not only on technical but also social and environmental benefits. Move manufacturing to these markets and position the skins as a social innovation to get brand backing from nonprofits and financial support from governments."

He got up and walked over to the panoramic window. "With enough product volume, the CO_2 reductions and new jobs for low-income groups will make a real difference. That'll further boost Septad's reputation as a true global leader. Everyone will want to work for you."

Jake could see that had got her full attention. She stared at him a moment longer before reaching to make a call. "One second," she motioned. "I'm checking to see if Mack Davies is in." After a brief conversation, she turned to Jake. "Mr. Davies is a member of our Managing Board. I'd like him to meet you."

Two minutes later, a gentleman in his sixties, with a shock of white hair and deep black eyes that matched the color of his skin, warmly extended his hand. "Mack, I thought the two of you should meet. You have Jake's CV along with the notes from our earlier interviews of him. I have to run to a Capex meeting . . . should be back in 20 minutes." And, with that, she was gone.

The board member

Davies sat quietly in the high-back leather chair, leafing through the papers Chen had given him, a kindly expression on his face. Then without preamble, he began in a firm, gentle voice.

"I'd like to know a little more about you," he asked. "Tell me about yourself – what things would you say helped define who you are today?"

Jake settled into his chair and knocked back half his coffee. He could have used something stronger.

"I grew up in Chicago," he said somberly. "I saw the world of my parents fall apart in the 2020s, when the Water Wars triggered global conflict and food simply stopped being available. Our middle-class neighborhood suddenly went hungry. I still remember the day the price of oil hit $400 and you couldn't buy imported food. That was the same year Manhattan and Florida went under water, the same year we had those Category 5 storms hit inland all the way up to Atlanta and even Montreal in the north. The wave of migrants from the east coast nearly overwhelmed us, until the city finally barricaded itself in. Of course, that was nothing compared to what was going on in Bangladesh and China – or even Italy and Spain."

For a brief moment Davies, listening intently as he stared out the window, no longer seemed a senior member of the board; he looked vulnerable, remembering his own years during the terrible decade.

"Yes, and we all saw what government did at that point," Davies grumbled, "or rather failed to do. The military was supposed to save the day, closing borders and targeting extremists. Governments clamped down on business around the world, turning a bad situation into a much worse one. Political alliances fell apart; it became each country and each region – every city – for itself."

Davies added, "What was frightening was being able to see how quickly things spiraled downwards. At the time I was traveling regularly to Asia and South America. Everywhere it was the same – air quality and access to water in the big cities, where everyone lived, had dropped below safety thresholds. Public health fell apart. The poorer sections of cities – with illnesses going through the roof, no jobs, and only junk food to feed them – began raiding the richer neighborhoods."

"I suppose," acknowledged Jake," that bad as we had it, Chicago hardly saw the worst of those years. I heard about the uprisings in Hong Kong–Guangzhou–Shenzhen. Rio–SãoPaulo, what people called the endless city, became a haven for narco-traffickers, arms dealers, and terrorism. Disease and famine in the Mumbai–Delhi corridor and the Nigeria–Ghana 400-mile stretch of urbanization spawned wars and social conflict that spilled across continents."

"But we were talking about what shaped your life." Davies's focus came back to Jake. "How did you deal with the Dark Years? It's hard to imagine a young person finding positive influences back then."

"My friends and I were still in our teens," he replied, "but we could see and feel what we called 'the Abyss.' We knew without being told that the entire global system had come to a screeching halt at the edge of a cliff. It became obvious that we had hit a point of no return: it was either rebuild or close shop."

Suddenly Jake's mood shifted. His face relaxed and a bit of lightness came into his words. "But you know what else was extraordinary about that time? As people everywhere saw and experienced the Abyss, there was a collective shift. People's core values were transformed, not because of politicians, moral visionaries, or Earth First activists – although we had heard them preach for decades about the need for change – but out of self-interest."

"What do you think drove the change?" Davies prodded.

"Well, at one level we went from just trying to hold on and survive, to a deep desire to build a better future. We went from patching up problems to wanting to find real solutions that would lead us away from the Abyss and toward a healthy world."

"It all sounds very idealistic," was the curt observation.

"Not really," replied Jake. "What is idealistic is telling people they *should* change their behavior. Or that they *should* be more morally responsible. This was a collective self-organizing movement of billions of people who experienced the failure of what had led up to the Abyss and who became inspired by images of a better future. It became crystal clear that Band-Aid fixes were not going to work. At the same time, we had leading examples of fundamental solutions and alternatives to the old system. It amounted to an unspoken cultural rebirth – an awakening of people's minds and hearts. Reflexive behavior shifted from doing less harm to regenerating our social and natural capital. People wanted to invest themselves in a positive future. They wanted to be a part of restoring a sense of well-being."

"But what do you think led people to behave differently?" Davies pressed.

"Well, instead of reacting to events like we had for decades, in the 2020s the patterns of destructive behavior suddenly became clear. People were forced to see the underlying forces that were leading to disaster. They saw the consequences of destructive practices in energy, food, water, waste. They saw what happens when the middle class earns $130 per day while the masses of poor earn $4 per day with no safety net. The results couldn't be ignored any longer. There was no way to push the consequences into the future. It was change now or die."

"That still sounds a bit conceptual," Davies said with a twinkle in his eyes.

"But it involved very practical and immediate problems. Take agriculture. In the fields outside Chicago, I remember seeing tractors so large the driver sat two stories high, checking his six television monitors to see what was going on the ground, as he sprayed chemicals to control weeds, fertilizers to promote growth, herbicides, defoliants, growth regulators . . . In retrospect it seems crazy. By 2020, pesticide use had risen thousands of per cent while crop loss to pests actually got worse. With a single-minded focus on cash crops, these farmers stripped their fields to the point of least diversity. Topsoil disappeared, washed and blown away, desiccated and used up from mono-irrigation and chemical blends. Suddenly our ability to produce enough food was at risk – with no quick fix in sight."

"By comparison," nodded Davies, "the focus of agriculture today is on healing the soil while growing food. It really is a completely different approach."

"And at an even deeper level," Jake forged ahead, vaguely thinking: is this helping or hurting my chances of getting hired? "The Abyss forced a shift in our mental models – the thinking that led to the patterns of destructive behaviors."

This *was* getting deep, thought Davies. But why not let Jake go on? It would tell him who he was and how he thinks; after all, they were thinking of hiring this young man – less than half his own age – for a relatively senior position.

"You mean that business people began seeing the larger systems of which they were a part and they worked more collaboratively to offer solutions to the global problems?" Davies made the question into a statement.

"Exactly," said Jake as he stood and walked over to one of the large touch screens. "There was a change in our collective consciousness without any one person or institution setting direction."

"Here is how I would describe the shift in thinking that took place." He picked up the digital pen and began to write a list. "After people experienced the slide toward the Abyss's edge, new core beliefs emerged. Some of the most important ones are these."

We are a global family, not isolated nations and tribes

We are a part of Nature, not separate from it

Cooperation rewards individual competitors

"You almost sound like an Earth First-er," Davies said skeptically.

"Not at all," Jake replied, trying not to appear defensive. "My friends and I had ambitions to go into business. In fact, we were pro-business and pro-growth. We wanted the good life. It's just that all the new beliefs simply made sense given what we wanted. The world had changed and so had our ways of thinking about it."

"I'm actually trying to be really practical here," he continued, wishing he could light his e-cig. "At BioSOL, being able to see the larger system – not only complex supply chains and cross-industry clusters but the interests of society and nature – allowed us to find new business opportunities that we would never have otherwise. Being able to collaborate with lots of different groups – including those with very different perspectives – made it possible to develop customer solutions that BioSOL couldn't have otherwise."

"I would say that also defines our culture," said Davies. "Each of our lines of business pursues its profits in ways that promote the health of the company, the industry, society, and nature. But in a marketplace where the demand driver is rebuilding a better world, that's just smart business. I like to think of it as resembling a set of 19th-century Russian dolls. Each business sits inside the company, the company inside the industry, and so on all the way up to the global system. I suppose you are right to give so much weight to core beliefs. It explains a lot how we came to do business today."

After a brief pause, Davies continued. "When I began my career in 2002, it was almost the opposite. The investment bank I worked for was only inter-ested in its own bottom line, which frequently came at the expense of the banking industry and the public. We all saw where that led us in the financial meltdown of 2007–2009. Economic value was too often at the expense of society. Even within the financial services industry, what one bank did to maximize its cut of profits was frequently at the expense of the others. Short-term profits were inconsistent with long-term value creation."

Jake became animated. "Exactly! And there were lots of other business benefits to changing our core beliefs. Compared to the old way of working, seeing things in terms of larger systems – reflexively stepping back to ask what our decisions mean for society and nature – engaged, motivated, and inspired employees like nothing else. As soon as it became obvious that "doing good" could be a way to *do even better* for customers and investors, people everywhere wanted to work for companies that were seen as contributing to rebuilding and restoring a better world."

"Before the Abyss," concluded Jake, "the energy in business came from reacting to crises. Afterward, there was a frenzy of creativity that seemed to draw its energy from the hopes and dreams people had of a better future. Inspiration turned out to be a much better motivator for change than fear."

An urgent call was flashing on Chen's desk. At that very moment, Chen herself walked in. As Davies and Jake stood, she stepped over to take the call, speaking a few rapid words in Mandarin, before joining them around the mahogany table.

Davies thanked Jake warmly for the interview. With a few words to Chen to say that he was expected in another meeting, he excused himself and left.

The Chen interview continues

"So what motivated you to pursue a career in business?" she asked as they resumed the conversation. "I see you started at the Sloan School in 2032, when the economy was still shaky to say the least."

"My biggest influences – and strongest role models – were Wes, Raj, and Emma, three Chicago entrepreneurs who started a food business downtown in the Loop near Millennium Park. This was in 2027 or 2028. That year they financed the conversion of an abandoned 50-floor skyscraper into a vertical farm that made them rich and literally helped save the city. Their success turned them into local stars – a few years later they were given the keys to the city."

Chen smiled wryly. "I remember a lot of vertical farms springing up in inner cities back then. Basically these were urban high-rises turned into large-scale greenhouses using hydroponics and crop stackers to produce fruits, vegetables, and grains year round. What made this one so successful?"

"Most vertical farms were clever adaptations of skyscrapers and food-growing techniques. But they still needed city water and power. With lighting, heating, and cooling for crops split across 30 floors, electricity consumption was huge. Also, each building only fed 20,000 people a year at most.

"Wes was a self-taught agronomist, Raj was a bio-engineer and Emma was an architect. Between the three of them, they rethought vertical farming literally from the ground up. They asked heretical questions: could a vertical farm be totally independent of outside sources for water, energy, and nutrients? Could one building feed 200,000 people a year instead of 20,000?"

Chen looked amused. "I bet there were a lot of disbelievers."

Jake laughed. "They had no choice. In the late 2020s Chicago had regular brown-outs and lasting electricity outages. Everyone had severe restrictions on water use. It would have killed crop yields. But they wanted to go further than just resource independence: they asked whether their farm could be a net generator of power, whether it could be a source of potable water. And could it create jobs for the unemployed?"

"Even considering such a project must have been heresy," she reflected.

"Creativity and incredible ambition under pressure. That's essentially what it boiled down to. They used existing techniques like evapotranspiration recovery to collect plant water vapors floor by floor and microbial treatments to turn city sewage into gray water for irrigation. But they also came up with entirely new solutions: ventilated double-sided glass panels with solar sprays that prevented rain from beading and cleaned pollutants on the way to collection troughs. They came up with crop cultivation techniques like reflectometers to test for ripeness and bio-photoperiod manipulation, which led to 16 times more plant production than traditional greenhouses. They also added farm-bred tilapia, chicken, and pigs."

Then he added, "The waste product alone from all the plants and animals was enough to meet the farm's energy needs."

This startled her. "You mean they used methane digestion to power the entire operation?"

"Yes," replied Jake. "Anaerobically rather than by composting. Along with solar, wind, and kinetic energy collectors, that gave them enough extra to put 20 million kWh back into the grid."

Chen whistled softly. Far from being a net importer of electricity, this farm was a mini-generator. And by substituting for farmland in rural areas, it was allowing reforestation to reduce CO_2 emissions.

Jake continued. "They also hired the unemployed and previously unemployable. In a move worthy of Henry Ford, the farm paid everyone twice minimum wage – drawing huge crowds, reducing turnover to almost zero, and putting money into a community that could once again afford to buy fresh produce."

"By 2030, the three entrepreneurs had added 15 more farm towers, a cluster that fed 85 per cent of the city's nearly 4 million residents. It also made the trio fabulously wealthy. That's what I remember most about them: they revitalized the city and made a fortune in the process."

Chen looked at him appraisingly. "So did you go to business school to make a lot of money or to have a social impact?"

"Both," he replied. "I can't understand why people didn't see more such opportunities earlier. The world needed solutions to food, climate, energy, water, fair wages, social inclusion . . . . and what better institution than business to innovate on a dime?"

It was time for a short break. Two hours into the interview, Jake was feeling exhilarated but relaxed, his jodhpuri jacket thrown over one of the chairs. The richly grained mahogany table had been cleared so that he could use it for the occasional holographic display. Chen got up to make a few calls and then announced that another Septad senior manager would be joining them. "Lora Estefan is in our offices today – she's based in Munich and head of our Advanced Vehicles division. It'll be good for her to meet you. She should be here in about ten minutes."

The General Manager of Advanced Vehicles

While they were waiting for Estefan to arrive, Chen asked, "What other disruptive innovations impress you as smart business decisions? How many of them are like the vertical farm – profitable solutions to seemingly intractable social and environmental problems? As you know, Septad has divisions not only in advanced vehicles but also in building materials, energy, and emerging markets."

Jake thought about her question. Economic growth had been strong for almost a decade but most economists considered the nature of international business to be fundamentally different from what had existed pre-2020. Instead of focusing on doing less harm and pushing consumerism for its own sake (as long as it could be considered green and socially responsible), business had taken a leading role in something more profound. Recently, the two co-presidents of Eurasia had described it as "knitting together the very fabric of civilization." The growth in market demand reflected a collective craving for integrated solutions, not quick fixes. Whether business clients or end consumers, the demand was for products and services that embedded personal health, social well-being, and caring for the natural world. Business leaders had seemingly undergone a transformation in their pursuit of profits – yet it was driven not only by moral reawakening but by the realization that doing good would allow them to do even better.

He cleared his throat. "Well, there are almost too many deep business innovations to know where to start." After a brief pause he added, "But a few do stand out in my mind. They are as big as mass production and information technology were in the last century."

"As a young kid I remember transportation being a real mess. Car accidents, long commutes, city smog, air travel disruption, an aging rail infrastructure. At the time, the sector depended on oil imports and accounted for almost a third of all CO_2 emissions. Then, in the space of only a few years, I saw massive change. Almost overnight it became a more efficient, more connected, cleaner, and safer system. And it made traveling a lot more fun too."

Calling up a real-time holographic map of the United States, he said, "This is what I see today. It's not perfect, but it's as different from what existed pre-2020 as cars were from horse-drawn carriages. Now we have whisper-quiet rail with full office, club or home VR options while you travel. High-efficiency planes have become quiet and almost zero-emission. Flying drones deliver everything from packages to pizza and groceries." Zooming in on Chicago, he pointed to a dozen arteries filled with two-wheelers heading to and from the city center. "I know you know this already, since Septad was involved in its construction, but it amazed me to see the network of e-cycle superhighways for commuters who prefer that way to get to work."

Just then Lora Estefan walked in, her sharp cream-colored business suit offset by a brilliant silk scarf and black hair pulled neatly back. "Perfect timing!" said Chen. "We were just talking about disruptive innovations in transportation." After Estefan and Jake shook hands and exchanged a few pleasantries, he knew the conversation would now turn to cars.

"I would very much like to learn about Septad's Advanced Vehicles division and its projects," he began politely. But Estefan demurred, asked him instead what he thought about recent innovations in the industry.

Secretly Jake was delighted to be asked: he loved sports cars and followed developments with more than impartial interest. "When the Chinese and Indians formed their partnership that led to the development of the zero-impact intellicar, the newly created joint venture became the biggest and most profitable car manufacturer in the world. It happened almost overnight. Here was a car that weighed 400 lbs instead of ten times that, built entirely with reusable or biodegradable materials. With fewer materials and pieces, the company could sell it at half the average price of a family sedan and still make a profit.

"One of the changes that made the biggest impression on me was fully automated navigation – an expensive option but fortunately subsidized by tax breaks and insurance companies. Suddenly, drivers could just say where they want to go and the car takes them there. My grandparents, both in their nineties, use it all the time. It gives them a freedom that a lot of elderly people never had before. It means always finding the least traffic route and avoiding accidents while being able to safely give their attention to friends and family along the way.

"But the most disruptive innovation by far," he continued, "was the shift from cars that were less harmful to the environment to a new generation of zero-emission vehicles that cleaned the air while driving. As you know, these cars now make money for their owners by serving as a distributed source of peak power to the grid. Transmission operators pay them to connect their vehicles during peak demand."

Estefan nodded. "Cars along with everything else in the economy were going from less harmful to delivering positive benefits like restoring clean air and topping up power to the grid."

Jake assented, happy to let her go on.

"Behind these new functionalities, our division has been hard at work on every aspect of the vehicle, from solar photovoltaic (PV) thermoelectric generator (TEG) hybrid systems to flexible seating designs using our "total safety" technology. We were the first to commercialize variable polarity surfaces to shed weight and increase aerodynamic flow. We build all the parts that go into clean propulsion systems. But the most interesting innovations came from our partnerships to redesign the actual transportation networks. We've been working with competitors, outside experts, and IT companies to connect the trillions of RFID tags, tracking instruments, and IP flows, allowing our cars and systems to speak to each other so that travel is adjusted automatically in real time. No matter what the traffic and weather conditions. These partnerships are embedding interconnectivity, system knowingness, and security by design."

"Incredible," said Jake, his eyes wide. "And what's amazing to me is that during this transformation, all the major automotive players became so hugely profitable."

"And why do you think current efforts succeeded where so many previous attempts had failed?" Chen asked.

Jake was starting to feel a little out of his depth but chose to hazard a guess. "Well, besides good science and technology management, the cross-industry collaboration and partnerships with government and nonprofits brought outside perspectives that led to much richer ideas for product and process redesigns. That plus the ability to leverage distributed virtual collaboration platforms. Your partnerships were able to build on system strengths using an open-source approach, yet still capture a portion of the value chain profits for the company."

Chen and Estefan exchanged glances. He felt he was at least on the right track and decided to pause while he was still ahead. Before leaving, Estefan asked him how he felt the interviewing process was going and encouragingly told him she looked forward to seeing him again. A few moments later, when Chen's V3D assistant materialized to whisper a question, she too stepped out of her office. Alone for a moment, Jake reflected that it was turning into a much longer afternoon than he could ever have imagined.

The interview concludes

"So, what's next?" Chen asked when she returned after a few minutes. "How about recent innovations in another one of our markets: building materials and building designs?"

Jake couldn't believe there was still more to the interview, but he had to admit it was a fascinating question. "This may be nothing new to you, but I remember being shocked in high school to learn that residential and commercial buildings guzzled 70 per cent of all electricity in the U.S., half of which was wasted. Inefficient lights left on in empty rooms, air conditioners cooling empty offices at night, every appliance on standby. Back then, heating came mostly from oil and gas, which explains in part why buildings emitted 40 per cent of all CO_2 emissions. You also had billions of tons of nonrenewable raw materials that went into construction, never to be reused or recycled. I once read that commercial buildings used to lose as much as 50 per cent of the water that flowed into them. It's crazy when you think about it.

"Today with Septad's leadership we have hyper-efficient buildings that cost a lot less to build and maintain than they did 30 years ago. With more daylight, better air circulation and less toxic chemicals in the materials used, they are a lot more livable. Waste and water is now completely reclaimed. I'm sure it took a lot of cross-industry partnerships for Septad to find solutions that worked for everyone. Architects, building materials manufacturers, urban planners, energy providers, and the builders themselves had to come up with innovations that fit together to produce an entirely different type of building."

"What do you think is the biggest change in design approaches to buildings and building materials?" asked Chen.

"By far I would say it's the shift from trying to be less wasteful and harmful to 'designing in' health benefits – to making buildings curative in their social and natural environments. Like cars, buildings went from reducing negative impacts to having zero impacts – the ZEBs [zero-energy buildings] of the 2010s – to then being net energy producers with on-site renewables. They also became net freshwater suppliers with rain catchment systems and hydro botanic water treatment. Buildings became essentially living systems integrated into local communities and ecologies."

Chen readily assented, adding that she too would have chosen that as one of the most significant aspects of doing business in the 2040s. With a smile that gave nothing away, she thanked him and asked if he would mind waiting outside her office.

It was starting to get dark outside. Jake installed himself in one of the oversized sofas, wondering what the next step would be. It had already been an incredible afternoon when he saw Mack Davies and Lora Estefan enter Chen's office. Ten minutes later, Chen herself stuck her head out and asked Jake to come in. All three stood by her desk. Jake looked at each face in turn, trying to gauge his chances and wondering what would be next.

10
Sustaining inquiry

As you make your way back from 2041, the journey may well leave you with more questions than answers. Indeed, the entire vision of embedded sustainability introduces big-picture uncertainties, naturally leading many of us to reflect on the essential nature of business and its future role.

Exactly how much *can* we expect from companies as agents of world benefit? What is the role of government and of the nonprofit sector? Some of the questions concern the context required to realize the benefits of embedded sustainability. For example, the kind of spiritual transformation and collective consciousness needed to support a wholesale shift in business. Must we move away from consumerism and the pursuit of unlimited individual wealth? And just how much cultural transformation can we expect from inspiration and creativity compared to desperation and the fear of impending disaster?

Viewed from the prevailing *cost* or *bolt-on* approaches to sustainability, many of these questions take the form of contradictions. They appear to be *either–or* choices. A question about growth becomes one of *choosing between* economic prosperity and environmental protection. Sustainability is portrayed *either* as a moral obligation to be socially responsible *or* as a business opportunity to profitably solve global problems. We are left wondering whether the agenda is really about ethical values or marketplace value. In such a perspective, trade-offs and contradictions are much more frequent because actors pursue their interests without regard to the interests of the whole of society and nature.

But what happens if we attempt to find another way to look at these questions? Using a whole-systems perspective, many of the apparent contradictions resolve into healthy tensions:[378] business profits and ethical behavior become entangled; incremental change is compatible with long-term transformation; and economic, ecological, and social benefits become mutually reinforcing. Whole-systems thinking drives better decision making in every business unit.

In practice, this means that companies pursue profits in ways that promote the health of their industries and the larger world in which they operate. Like Russian dolls – what Arthur Koestler first termed nested holons[379] – the various levels interlock: the business unit within the company, the company within the industry, and so on up through the global system.

In the following pages, you will find a series of inquiries designed to address the big picture issues raised by the previous chapters. Each question is accompanied by background information and supporting data to help you explore, question, and draw your own conclusions.

By no means will you find the following list exhaustive. Rather, it is a short springboard to an inquiry that we hope will be continued far beyond the pages of this book.

Our starter-kit of Big Picture questions:

1. Growth or no growth?

2. What is the role of government and of the nonprofit sector?

3. Stopping the bad or creating the good?

4. *Having* or *being*?

5. Evolution or revolution?

6. Restoring or transforming nature?

7. Fear or enlightened self-interest?

Now we dive into a diversity of perspectives and inquire beyond simple "right" and "wrong." Exploring, questioning, and redesigning our own assumptions is the name of the game.

1. Growth or no growth?

Is growth itself sustainable? Within the sustainability debate, it is hard to find a question that appears more black-and-white or that has more strongly defended arguments on both sides.

NO is the first simple answer. "To truly stop ruining the planet," says environmental activist Bill McKibben, "society must break its most debilitating habit: growth."[380] He argues that growing ourselves out of problems is "not going to happen fast enough to ward off enough change to preserve the planet we used to live on." McKibben is one of a long line of environmentalists and philosophers who advocate the need for economic restraint and voluntary simplicity. Notes one observer: "Environmentalists define their interest as limiting human intrusions upon nature . . . They have tended to view economic growth as the *cause* but not the *solution* to ecological crises."[381]

YES is the equally compelling opposite response. Pro-growth advocates point out that the naysayers fail to distinguish between intensive and extensive growth, a distinction of neo-classical economics now extended from labor and capital – and wealth creation – to include natural resources. Extensive growth, in which twice the economic output requires a doubling of land, energy, and raw materials, has a very different environmental impact than intensive growth, in which twice the economic output leads to *less* space, materials, and carbon intensity – think of the vertical farm example from the previous chapter.

Related to the concept of intensive growth are growth-qualified definitions of sustainable development, such as Goodland and Daly's "development without growth in throughput of matter and energy beyond regenerative or absorptive capacities."[382] Author Ervin Laszlo suggests that intensive growth can be grasped through the three "C's" of *connection, communication,* and *consciousness.*[383] Connecting people to each other and to nature, and facilitating their communication and the continued evolution of our consciousness, meets a growing market demand with a potential to reduce negative social and environmental impacts.

Maslow's pyramid of needs suggests that poor people are necessarily more concerned with satisfying physical and material needs – often without regard to ecological consequences – whereas better-off populations pay attention to post-material needs such as quality of life and environmental preservation. Observers note that ". . . around the world there is a very strong association between prosperity and environmental values."[384]

So . . . will growth in China and India necessarily increase the environmental burden on the planet, or is it possible that such growth could actually reduce the burden? To answer this question, one interesting avenue of inquiry comes from the so-called I.P.A.T. equation developed by Barry Commoner, Paul Ehrlich and John Holdren in the 1970s to describe the impact of human activity on the environment.[385] In the original formulation, a multiplicative effect of population, affluence, and technology determine the impact, where I = impact, P = population, A = affluence (a measure of income per person), and T = technology (the processes used to obtain resources and transform them into goods and services):

$$I = P \times A \times T$$

The assumption here is that increases in technology necessarily lead to increases in environmental impact – a relationship that seems to have held for much of the 20th century. But what if 21st-century technology is focused on reducing negative impacts and increasing positive impacts? In effect the variable T becomes a denominator in the equation[386]

$$I = \frac{P \times A}{T}$$

In this latter scenario, technologically driven growth can lead to reduced harm and increased social and environmental benefits in products, processes, and business models. With the world's population set to peak at 9 to 10 billion by mid-century, the revised I.P.A.T. equation – in which technological innovation offsets the rise in people and incomes – suggests a vision of a global economy capable of sustainably meeting the needs of everyone.

An example of a pro-growth vision is provided by reformed environmentalists Nordhaus and Shellenberger. In their 2007 book, *Breakthrough: From the Death of Environmentalism to the Politics of Possibility*, they argue for "an explicitly pro-growth agenda that defines the kind of prosperity we believe is necessary to improve the quality of human life and to overcome ecological crises."[387] For them, it is only through prosperity and strength that humans become compassionate, generous, and responsible to each other and for the larger world they inhabit.

2. What is the role of government and of the nonprofit sector?

In *Deceit and Denial*, historians Gerald Markowitz and David Rosner recount how the chemical industry was dragged kicking and screaming toward regulatory standards that safeguarded human health and the environment, often lying and making exaggerated claims that their products and industrial processes were safe when they were not. The eventual regulation of vinyl chloride monomer – used in the manufacture of PVCs – is particularly illuminating on the role of government and its often conflictual relationship with business.

In 1954, exposure to vinyl chloride monomer above 500 ppm (parts per million) became the threshold limit value (TLV) for workers in polyvinyl chloride factories. But already in the late 1950s, managers at Dow Chemical suspected that this threshold value was insufficient and could lead to "appreciable injury" to full-time workers exposed to it. In 1961, Dow recommended a lower TLV but the American Conference of Governmental Industrial

Hygienists failed to change it. "Often the industry saw itself at war with regulatory agencies or environmental and labor groups and established a pattern of hiding information about vinyl chloride's dangers."[388]

By the mid-1960s it became apparent that workers who entered the polymerizer vats, where PVC was synthesized from vinyl chloride monomer, suffered from acroosteolysis, a previously undefined condition involving "skin lesions, absorption of bone of the terminal joints of the hands, and circulatory changes."[389] A 1969 University of Michigan study presented to the Manufacturing Chemists Association (MCA) Medical Advisory Committee suggested that "sufficient ventilation should be provided to reduce the vinyl chloride concentration [to] below 50 ppm."[390] The validity of the report was roundly rejected by PVC producers but their reactions to the link between vinyl chloride and acroosteolysis was nothing compared to their reaction to the news of a link to cancer – including kidney, liver, and lung tumors. "When cancer became an issue, the industry took more extreme and potentially explosive actions to cover up the danger. The industry moved from denial and obfuscation to outright deception."[391]

In spite of evidence from Italian laboratories that proved the carcinogenicity of vinyl monomer even at low dosages, the industry decided not to revise the Material Chemical Safety Data Sheet (MCSDS). By now, PVC had become central to the viability of many American and European chemical companies. Between 1966 and 1971, PVC production in the U.S. alone had doubled. Internal memos from the major industrial players speak of being "honor-bound" to maintain secrecy regarding potential health risks. Then in January 1974, the American public learned that vinyl chloride monomer had been implicated in the deaths of four workers at a B.F. Goodrich plant in Louisville, Kentucky. A *Rolling Stone* article described the PVC plant as a "Plastic Coffin."[392]

Crisis followed, with the industry arguing that any dramatic reductions in the TLV would be impossible to meet and could lead to total industry collapse. Yet despite these protestations, on April 4, 1974, OSHA issued an emergency temporary standard setting a permissible exposure limit of 50 ppm.[393]

A short time later, an independent lab conducting animal tests phoned the MCA with the news that mice exposed to 50 ppm of the monomer were developing angiosarcomas. Worse still, there was a creeping view of the evidence that suggested there was *no known safe level* of exposure, no matter how low. In mid-May OSHA published in the *Federal Register* its long-awaited proposal including a "no detectable level" of 1 ppm permissible exposure limit.[394] The plastics industry continued to do battle, arguing that the epidemiological evidence was ambiguous and that a standard of 1 ppm would "be so economically unfeasible that it could wreak havoc with the national economy."[395] Despite industry's petition to the U.S. Supreme Court, a stay was denied and on April 1, 1975 the 1 ppm standard went into effect.

What was the result? Despite all their objections, the plastics manufacturers quickly and efficiently adapted to the new standard. The *New York Times* wrote, "One year later not one of the doomsday predictions has proven accurate." Prices had not increased, supplies of the vinyl monomer were plentiful, and the industry was actually expanding, not contracting.[396]

In this and many other cases, government regulations designed to limit harm became a powerful stimulus to innovation. If necessity is the mother of invention, then new tougher environmental laws and regulations can be a boon to next-generation products, processes, business models, and technologies. Of course radical transparency makes it impossible for business today to engage in the kind of "deceit and denial" portrayed in the vinyl monomer case. But still today, left to its own devices, industry tends to justify why sustainability-driven change is impossible. Through means ranging from criminal enforcement to financial subsidies and voluntary programs, governments can powerfully shape sustainable business practices.

Now consider the role of diverse stakeholder groups from NGOs and bloggers to academia, unions, and local communities. The nonprofit sector – increasingly managed to the same efficient results-driven standards as the private sector – has moved from merely condemning business (the old Greenpeace model) to partnering with industry leaders to shape sustainable market outcomes. Today a constellation of individuals and nonprofit organizations is helping to raise public awareness of global challenges, inexorably raising the aspirations of consumers and investors by promoting environmental and social values in the marketplace.

3. Stopping the bad or creating the good?

The sustainability camp is increasingly divided into market optimists, who believe that business innovation will solve all our problems, and radicalized market pessimists, who argue for regulatory controls and government protection. The former advocate "creating the good" while the latter focus on "stopping the bad." Which faction is right? Or are they both right and mutually dependent for desired outcomes?

Business is facing a growing schism among environmentalists with important implications for its ability to effect change fast enough to satisfy rising expectations. In 2003 author Alex Steffen first applied the term "bright greens" to those who believe that innovation and entrepreneurialism within the market system will solve our environmental and social problems. He contrasted these with "dark greens" who tend to view the market system as the problem rather than the solution. That same year, environmentalists Ted Nordhaus and Michael Shellenberger decided to break away from the "regulate-and-protect" framework they had being using, to propose a new Apollo project for clean energy jobs, R&D, infrastructure, and transit for a more prosperous America.[397] In their 2007 book, they argue that

> Today we have new choices to make. We must choose between a politics of limits and a politics of possibility; a focus on investment and assets and a focus on regulation and deficits . . . And, most of all, we must choose between a resentful narrative of tragedy and a grateful narrative of overcoming.[398]

But do we have to choose? Are managers stuck between regulation and innovation, between focusing on "stopping the bad" and "creating the good?" Or are both needed?

Here is what Professor Andrew Hoffman says on the topic, originally as part of his longer Foreword to our book.[399] Given its insightful analysis of this question, we've included the entire passage.

> The reality is that both sides are mutually dependent. Scholars who have studied the civil rights movement and other periods of change argue that more extreme groups within a movement actually help the moderate, consensus-building groups with a kind of "radical flank effect." When radicals pull the tail of the political spectrum further in one direction, they shift the center of the debate and create a category of moderates. Think of Martin Luther King. He was seen as a moderate because Malcolm X pulled the political flank so far to the left that mainstream America found King's message palatable. Russell Train, second administrator of the EPA, once echoed a similar sentiment when he said, "Thank God for the David Browers of the world. They make the rest of us seem reasonable."
>
> Together, the two seemingly different branches really form a broad spectrum. Sometimes this has been described as a tension between purity and pragmatism, or between confrontation and consensus – and the movement needs both. Where the bright greens put environmental issues into a language and frame that is palatable and easily digestible by the broader public and, importantly, business, dark greens warn us about the dangers of compromise and push the frontier of environmental issues.
>
> But I want to end . . . with a warning that the dark greens are losing their power and voice. They're becoming marginalized, either by their own activities or the way they're often cast in extreme relief against the more moderate bright greens. In my own research, I have found a strong positive correlation between the number of

corporate ties an NGO has and the size of its budget. The implication is obvious: the bright greens actively engage with corporations, they have more money and therefore they have more influence than the dark greens. This is both unfortunate for dark green groups and bad for the environmental movement as a whole.

While the bright greens can help to bring about change, the dark green message is needed now more than ever. Dark greens need to remind us that, regardless of how mainstream green becomes, the concept as it is presently envisaged does not go far enough. For many within the corporate sector, it is nothing but a label for actions or strategies that are actually driven by the standard social, economic, and institutional mechanisms. Thus while there are many good ideas for reform driven by the bright greens – such as for increased transparency and increased accountability in markets and in environmental policy; for greater use of intelligent subsidies and market-based approaches to change; for elimination of perverse incentives; and for technologies that facilitate better relations with the environment – such remedies are necessarily limited in scope and impact. In short, these are attempts to use the flawed tools of a flawed system to fix it. Blind adherence to metrics such as internal rate of return and net present value is a large part of what got us into the environmental mess we're now in. Rather than harmonizing economic and environmental considerations into a synergistic whole, the prevailing institutions within which bright greens engage remain that of making trade-offs while holding to economic growth as the paramount objective.

Where dark greens tend to be "doomers" as Steffen puts it, their message rests on the point that we need to reassess and restructure the fundamentals of our existing social, political, and economic systems if we are going to really address the environmental problems we face. We must augment economic reasoning with a shift in values. Without an examination of our values – moral, spiritual, ethical, and otherwise – we will never go far enough in our solutions. Sustainability challenges widely held assumptions, including: the necessity of increasing economic growth; the perception of nature as a limitless source for materials and sink for wastes; the superiority of technological development for controlling natural systems; the social and physical autonomy of the firm; and the profit motive as a singular objective of the firm. In addition, sustainability challenges the moral precepts underlying debate about economic development. The Stern Report questions whether discounting the future is inherently immoral. George Soros questions whether the mobility of capital flows has an inherently moral component to it. Recent squabbles over patent rights to AIDS drugs in Africa question the pre-eminence of profit streams over human needs. And a growing list of companies are finding themselves the target of well-orchestrated campaigns to call attention to grievances produced through standard modes of business. Examples include: Royal Dutch Shell for dealings with a repressive regime and egregious environmental abuses in Nigeria; Coca-Cola for environmental issues in India and labor issues in Colombia; and Exxon-Mobil for its resistance to action on climate change.

Before all, sustainability challenges the idea that the market as presently defined can and will provide for a secure environment and that corporations can and will provide for security and prosperity. Can a sustainable world be guaranteed by the market's "invisible hand" which joins self-seeking buyers with profit-seeking suppliers? No doubt the invisible hand is invaluable, but is it enough? What else is there to the story? Citizens are more than consumers and care for more than selfish satisfactions. And business entrepreneurs are more than opportunists moved by avarice or cupidity. New questions need to be raised that challenge the fundamentals of standard business practices. Within the halls of academe, questions are today being raised about the adequacy of economic theory in explaining business behavior. Does it suffice to treat human relationships as transactions, human aspirations as market opportunities, human motivations as only pecuniary, and corporate social responsibility as limited to shareholders? Such logic dismisses calls for greater attention to environmental (and social) issues within market environments and in so doing disdains calls for sensitive attention to core values and beliefs, aside from a pure market logic. Where this logic imagines the economic system of market capitalism to be socially and morally inert, the problem of sustainability today suggests otherwise. As Robert Heilbroner explains, "a general subordination of action to market forces demotes progress itself from a consciously intended social aim to an unintended consequence of action, thereby robbing it of moral content."

So, while the bright greens continue to work for change within the existing systems, dark greens call our attention to the fact that these systems are inherently flawed and changes in them will not yield the ultimate outcomes we seek unless we examine the core values and beliefs that underlie them. As John Ehrenfeld points out, being less unsustainable is not the same as being more sustainable. And right now, the efforts of the bright greens are largely helping us to become less unsustainable. While important in the immediate term, in the long term appeals to economic and political solutions will get us only part of the way.

The ultimate goals of sustainability involve aspirations of a better life, equal opportunity, justice, security, community, responsibility and full realization of human experience and potential. For Ehrenfeld, sustainability is about flourishing, and "flourishing means not only survival, but also the realization of whatever we humans declare makes life meaningful – individual satisfaction, dignity, freedom, justice." But as long as solutions for sustainability draw on the same logic and beliefs that created the problem in the first place, these ultimate goals of sustainability cannot be fully realized. Bright greens can help us to attain successes in the short term. But dark greens must keep us alert to the long-term actualities of the ultimate goals of environmental sustainability.

We might sound like a broken record, but it is hard to overemphasize the importance of the *both–and* perspective of whole systems. Viewed from the larger global perspective, the pro-growth innovation agenda of the bright greens is consistent with the regulate-and-stop agenda of the dark greens.

As a business manager, next time you hear a "dark green" preach about carbon cycles and the need to respect the Laws of Nature, remember that declining resources, radical transparency, and rising expectations are forcing markets to respond to and integrate such on-the-surface extreme points of view. Dark greens are helping to raise awareness among consumers, investors, and employees; they are catalyzing a transformation in the values of business leaders; they are engaging individuals and stakeholders in dialogue about what constitutes a meaningful society. In short, dark greens are helping to raise individual and collective consciousness and promoting ethical behavior in mainstream markets.

4. Having or being?

Is a collective spiritual transformation, such as a greater emphasis on *being* rather than *having* and on living in harmony with nature, a prerequisite for embedded sustainability? Can such a transformation be mandated, catalyzed . . . or will it emerge on its own?

In responding to this question, we reiterate the John Ehrenfeld assertion, quoted by Andrew Hoffman, above: "flourishing means not only survival, but also the realization of whatever we humans declare makes life meaningful – individual satisfaction, dignity, freedom, justice." Ehrenfeld goes on to say that "flourishing is not something to *do* or to *have*. One can flourish only by *Being*. This story is very different from one about ecoefficiency, solving technological problems, or getting the price right."[400]

Many executives and line managers are left scratching their heads at such metaphysical mumbo jumbo. What exactly does Ehrenfeld mean when he says that we must "shift back to the flourishing fullness of 'Being' from its impoverished modern form of 'having' " – and do we really need to understand old-world philosophers like Erich Fromm and Martin Heidegger to embed sustainability in everything we do?

Well, yes, says Ehrenfeld, a respected doyen of sustainable business who taught at MIT for many years. How we act and interact with the world depends on our view of reality: for example, that we are separate from each other and from nature rather than part of an interconnected whole. "Our everyday objective way of holding reality is one of our root causes of unsustainability," he says.

> This belief leads to the potential of domination at all levels of social interaction, from family to workplaces to whole societies . . . the idea of the separation of the mind from the world supports the idea of human mastery over nature, as we see ourselves as outside rather than as a part of the natural world.[401]

This idea is echoed by fellow MIT systems guru Peter Senge, who stresses the importance of our "mental models" – the internal images of the world we all carry. "How the system works," says Senge, "arises from how we work; how people think and act shapes how the system as a whole operates."[402]

In *Worldshift 2012*, Ervin Laszlo imagines a sustainable future in which

> being rich is defined not by *having*, but by *being*. Possessing material goods beyond what's needed to ensure a decent quality of life is not an achievement; on the contrary, it's an indication of backward thinking. Real wealth lies not in the possession of money, but in living a fulfilling life, with loving families, healthy and happy children, a caring community, and a healthy environment. Living well means living wisely, comfortably, even luxuriously, yet comfort and luxury are not measured by the quantity of the goods we own and control, but by the quality of our life and lived experience.[403]

These views beg several questions. Who defines the world-view we ought to hold? If sustainability is a question of living the right values (rather than creating sustainable value), who determines which ones? Clearly many businesspeople are rubbed the wrong way by exhortations to live a greener lifestyle or to shun materialism – "don't buy that gas guzzling car or that big house because it's not sustainable!"

And yet a collective spiritual transformation that de-emphasizes material acquisition and domination over nature (and each other) may best be seen *not* as driven by political or ideological considerations in the sense of attempting to impose the beliefs of one group on another group, but simply as dictated by the stark realities of 7 (soon 9) billion people living on a small planet. As author Ross Gelbspan put it so well, "Throughout history it has been philosophers, religious leaders, and revolutionaries who have asked us to reexamine our values, our relationships, our purposes, and the way we live. Now we are being asked by the oceans."[404] Bill McKibben sums it up this way: "We're moving quickly from a world where we push nature around to a world where nature pushes back – and with far more power. But we've still got to live on that world, so we better start figuring out how."[405]

Is a collective moral awakening a necessary part of embedding sustainability in business? We invite you to reflect on this question, not in opposition to sustainable value creation but as integral to meeting new market expectations in a world of declining resources and radical transparency. As Senge notes, "At a certain point, expanding boundaries and facing deeper problems opens people's eyes to totally new opportunities."[406]

There is little doubt that, to avoid disaster, we will need collectively to move toward lower carbon- and material-intensity in our consumption habits; pay more attention to the accessibility for all people to shared goods such as clean air, water, and land; build sustainable habitats; increase fair-trade products and services; reduce toxic releases into the environment; and meet the unmet needs of the world's poorest. Such transformations cannot easily be mandated at a global scale. The political institutions simply do not exist to decree solutions to global problems. But the world can self-organize to bring about a new collective mind-set and a new set of shared values as businesses, governments, nonprofits, and the average person realize that it is in their self-interest to do so.

5. Evolution or revolution?

Is it realistic to expect a global breakdown and rebuild to occur within a few decades? Or is the long arc of history more gradual and smooth?

In Jake's story painted in Chapter 9, the global system reaches a point of total collapse – the Abyss – sometime in the 2020s; it is followed by rapid and total rebuild over the course of about a decade. By the year 2041, business regains a role of leadership in a world that is by no means perfect – environmental damages still occur and social injustices continue to reflect human proclivities – but in the Brundtland spirit of living in a way that doesn't compromise the ability of future generations to meet their needs, it is once again sustainable.

The issue here is not whether we can predict the future but whether it is possible to have insight into the nature of coming economic, social, and environmental change. Businesspeople often act as if sustainability trends such as soil erosion or water scarcity are incremental and linear; for evidence of this behavior, consider the number of companies that are setting 2020 targets such as "10 per cent less XYZ than 2010 levels," where XYZ is CO_2 emissions, energy consumption, waste, packaging, or water usage. Such target setting assumes that doing a little less bad is sufficient.

The 16th-century naturalist Francis Bacon famously said, "Natura non facit saltum" ("Nature does not proceed by leaps"), which 19th-century thinkers interpreted to mean that evolution is slow and piecemeal. But 20th-century Harvard evolutionary biologist Jay Gould and Nobel Prize-winning physicist Ilya Prigogine argued that complex systems – of which the global economy and the Earth itself are prime examples – undergo disruptive bifurcations and evolutionary leaps over very short periods of time. The Earth's climate is a good example of a complex system that can reach a critical threshold in just one or two degrees, with so-called positive feedback processes such as melting tundra which releases additional CO_2 and methane, in turn further speeding up climate change. Hitting sensitive thermal milestones can lead to the routine failure of nonirrigated crops, new disease vectors such West Nile virus in areas previously untouched by the disease, and coral deaths linked to very slight ocean acidification.

In other words, our collective experience of breakdown is unlikely to be gradual or predictable. We will not see additional gigatonnes of CO_2 emissions lead always to the same degree of change in hurricane activity or crop failure. Instead, we are likely to see sudden changes tending toward uncertain outcomes. The move from 450 to 500 ppm of CO_2 in the atmosphere will not have the same speed, magnitude, or extent of species extinction as the move from 500 to 550 ppm. Just exactly how much faster and how many more species will die out are not known; nor is the differential impact of biodiversity loss on our ability to produce medicines.

But there is also good news in the nonlinear dynamics of complex systems.[407] With the vision and will imagined in Jake's story to rebuild a world on the brink of catastrophe, businesses can rapidly innovate solutions to global problems. Companies in every sector working in tandem with government and nonprofits can come up with new products and services that not only do less harm but also offer curative and restorative benefits. Communities with infrastructure such as buildings that clean the air, generate clean energy, filter gray water, and grow food sustainably are not the airy dreams of misguided optimists; they are a technological reality today.

The insights from complex adaptive systems tell us that we are likely to experience increasingly eventful years ahead. The high degree of instability in our financial, economic, energy, food, and other interrelated global systems promise great risk but also major opportunities. Those who seize the opportunities – and innovate business solutions that embed sustainability – will create profits and growth while contributing to a better world.

What is your vision of change in the environmental and social parameters key to your business? And are you pursuing only incremental change or are you also asking heretical questions and pursuing potentially game-changing innovation?

6. Restoring or transforming nature?

Should an outcome of sustainable business be to preserve and restore nature, or to transform it into new and improved forms for human benefit? Where do powerful new technologies such as genetic modification and nanotechnology fit into a sustainable future?

John Muir (1838–1914), the American naturalist, was among the earliest to advocate the preservation of nature in its untouched state. At a time when the Earth and its abundant resources were seen as almost limitless, he advanced the view that it needed protecting, in the form of national parks and preserves, for future generations.[408] It was then – over a century ago – that a controversy erupted between Muir and fellow environmental pioneer Gifford Pinchot (1865–1946), whose progressive views called for extracting from nature "whatever it can yield for the service of man." Although both men opposed the reckless exploitation of natural resources, Muir advocated preserving nature for its own sake while Pinchot took a utilitarian view of managing nature for commercial use.

Muir's preservationist philosophy stemmed from an early systems view – the recognition of the deep interconnectedness of the global ecosystem. He famously said, "When we tug at a single thing in nature, we find it attached to the rest of the world." Today's opposition to tinkering with nature – such as genetic engineering – is similarly based on fears of the potential unintended consequences at a global level. As geneticist Barry Commoner wrote in *Harper's Magazine*,

> there is persistent public concern not only with the safety of genetically engineered foods but also with the inherent dangers in arbitrarily overriding patterns of inheritance that are embedded in the natural world through long evolutionary experience . . . What the public fears is not the experimental science but the fundamentally irrational decision to let it out of the laboratory into the real world before we truly understand it.[409]

Modern advocates of Pinchot's utilitarian views argue that trying to preserve or restore nature to what it once was is not only infeasible but undesirable. "We must abandon the environmentalism that thinks of itself as representing and defending . . . nature," argue 21st-century environmentalists Ted Nordhaus and Michael Shellenberger:

> Overcoming the ecological crises and realizing humankind's potential will require abandoning efforts to return to some Edenic past . . . As the earth warms, forests disappear, and the Arctic melts into the oceans, new natures will emerge all over; it will become increasingly untenable for anyone to claim to represent some essential nature or environment.[410]

Will genetically modified organisms (GMOs) help feed the world or are they the stuff of nightmares, a Pandora's Box of Frankenfoods that once opened can never again be closed? On the one hand, we have global famine and climate change with the prospect of increased droughts and extreme weather pushing subsistence farming to ever more precarious (and damaging) states. On the other hand, environmentalists such as Stewart Brand argue that "open source biology" in which genetic pools are manipulated everywhere is already a reality, whether we like it or not. Farmers cross-breed and hybridize crops, agriculture companies radiate seeds to produce new variants, research institutions such as the Philippines International Rice Institute pursue a range of biotechnology programs.[411] Plants grown under heat or drought stress, or plants modified by electroporation, agrobacterium genetic transfer, and marker-assisted breeding make it difficult to draw the dividing line between GMOs and organisms with more "natural" genetic mutations.

Pro-GMO advocates argue that genetic accidents happen in nature all the time, and that superweeds such as Palmer amaranth (pigweed) are unavoidable, but that genetic engineering is an opportunity to be purposeful and deliberate in how we increase food yields, reduce pests, and even tackle human disease. Anti-GMO activists worry that GMOs introduced into the wild could affect the fitness of whole species and delicate ecologies, with risks of serious damage or even extinction, and that transgenic foods will cause human health problems such as cancer. They compare the potential for disaster to thalidomide-related birth defects, asbestosis, and Creutzfeldt-Jakob disease (mad cow disease) – past proofs that human interventions can cause unthinkable catastrophe.

New technologies that re-engineer the natural world will be pervasive in the years ahead. For example, companies in a wide range of sectors are already using nanotechnology – cosmetic companies for titanium dioxide nanoparticles to block UV rays, food companies to enhance flavors and colors, and pharma companies to deliver drugs to diseased cells. Banks will have to decide whether to finance such R&D and related ventures, and insurance companies whether to cover their associated risks.

Yet the choice between preserving and transforming is still to be made – by all of us. Should corporations push into biotechnology and other manipulations of nature? Is fundamentally altering molecular structures, genetic pools, or ecosystems a necessary and desirable part of embedding sustainability in business? Or do we need to go back to our roots – and find ways to restore the environment to its most pristine of ways?

7. Fear or enlightened self-interest?

What is the main motivator for change? Is it fear of disaster or positive images of the future? The issue is what enables a collective shift – for example, is it more driven by problem analysis or by imagining desirable solutions? Can connecting strength to strength and creating generative spaces for everyone speed the transformation to a more sustainable world?

Throughout human history, we have seen powerful movements created for different reasons. Fear and hate have been behind some of the most important developments of the 20th century. Yet fear does not explain planetary victories such as the eradication of smallpox or the remarkable, rapid, but completely decentralized spread of Internet-based global connectivity. Martin Luther King Jr.'s *I Have a Dream* speech is famous because, as one observer put it, "it put forward an inspiring, positive vision that carried a critique of the current moment within it. Imagine how history would have turned out had King given an *I Have a Nightmare* speech instead."[412] Yet, the media on every continent and on every network continues to convince us that it is negative images that turn us on[413] – and your own evening news is, perhaps, the most direct proof of this motivation theory.

What role you attribute to business is influenced by your underlying view of human nature, which in turn influences your view of what motivates change. What do you think is the basis for getting your company moving? Is it Lester Brown's *Plan B 4.0: Mobilizing to Save Civilization*?[414] Or is it James Howard Kunstler's *The Long Emergency: Surviving the Converging Catastrophes of the 21st Century*?[415]

Some of the best and brightest scholars of change have put forward their theories of what motivates and creates change. John Kotter, perhaps the most celebrated writer on the subject, makes a strong case for crisis and urgency as the first foundational step in his eight-step approach to leading change.[416] For Kotter, crisis is so necessary that it can even be artificially engineered:

... in the more successful cases I have witnessed, an individual or a group always facilitates a frank discussion of potentially unpleasant facts: about new competition, shrinking margins, decreasing market share, flat earnings, a lack of revenue growth, or other relevant indices of a declining competitive position ... In a few of the most successful cases, a group has manufactured a crisis. One CEO deliberately engineered the largest accounting loss in the company's history, creating huge pressures from Wall Street in the process. One division president commissioned first-ever customer-satisfaction surveys, knowing full well that the results would be terrible. He then made these findings public. On the surface, such moves can look unduly risky. But there is also risk in playing it too safe: when the urgency rate is not pumped up enough, the transformation process cannot succeed and the long-term future of the organization is put in jeopardy.[417]

Sounds convincing, doesn't it? Indeed, scientific discourse aside, we all see – and live through – countless examples of fear, pain, or discomfort serving as key motivators for change. Working on this very text, we asked some of you on Facebook to think with us on what moves humanity towards change. Dan Croitoru's honest and powerful answer goes to the core of the question: "I believe that we move when we don't have other choices. It seems that somehow we human beings are not able to sacrifice immediate profit, our well-being for that distant benefit that would work for all . . ."

Yet, before you rush back to your company or community to stage a crisis, let's question the axioms of deficit- and fear-based change, and turn briefly to the growing movement of strength-based change and positive organizational scholarship. Unlike their deficit-based counterparts, proponents of strength-based change invite us to use positive emotions and desirable visions of the future as the main motivator for change. Here is how David Cooperrider and Leslie Sekerka speak about the forces behind this approach:

Prior research links positive affect with broader thinking and associates positive emotions with improved psychological health. For instance, coping strategies related to the occurrence and maintenance of positive emotions . . . serve to help buffer against stress. These types of strategies help individuals handle crises with effective coping, sustain closer relationships, and hold a richer appreciation for life – all of which predict increased psychological well-being. Given these findings, inquiry into the appreciable world is a vehicle for creating and developing positive change, not just within the present moment but also over time.[418]

Maybe it is time for us to draft our own *I Have a Dream* speech?

Conclusion

We hope that the big-picture inquiry offers you an opportunity to think more deeply about contextual issues: the assumptions and beliefs that lie behind embedded sustainability as an essential driver of business strategy and change management. Our intention is practical rather than philosophical. It's simply another layer in the exploration of "what will it take for companies to succeed in the years ahead?" Becoming aware of the hidden assumptions and beliefs that surround the challenge of embedding sustainability can give all of us a newfound ability to act on it.

When sustained, such an inquiry offers us a solid foundation for taking action. Embedded sustainability is proving to be a smarter business model for companies of every stripe. Mainstream managers who may or may not believe in environmental and social causes are discovering that customers and investors expect sustainability in their core business. Every day it's becoming more apparent that embedding sustainability is first and foremost about responding to a new market reality, rather than only a moral injunction (important as that is).

As managers, we now have a fiduciary responsibility to shareholders to listen to a broad set of stakeholders – such as local communities and NGOs – because doing so is a source of business value at the heart of competitive strategy. Paying attention to vanishing natural resources is no different than competing for scarce talent; supply chains and operations are at risk when these are neglected. Radical transparency is not a choice; it is a fact of corporate life whether managers want it or not. Sustainability-related skills and competencies increasingly separate winners and losers.

This book's frameworks, tools, and competencies provide a new competitive arsenal for managers who recognize the changed market reality. Inexorably, business is being led to care for human health, social well-being, and ecological integrity because – very simply – that is what successful businesses do in today's marketplace. The question is no longer *why* managers need to embed sustainability in their core business; it is about *how* to do it. We hope this volume of work provides a useful platform for practitioners searching for a more profitable way forward.

Afterword
Sustainability for strategy
(not strategy for sustainability)

David Cooperrider[419]

After the euphoria of the Internet bubble, the hard work of good management took over.

The Internet, everyone soon realized, would not be a replacement for bricks and mortar. Well-managed just-in-time manufacturing would not give way to virtual "not-at-all manufacturing." And the wisdom of crowds would not supersede the need for outstanding senior leadership. Indeed, once the bubble popped there were many companies, often in confused overreaction, who wanted to ignore the Internet altogether. But in reality the Internet had already changed the game.

Meanwhile it was through the tools of good business analysis that the Web was leveraged, transformed, and customized into an indispensable source of integrated value creation not just for an organization as a whole but for every level and function imaginable. Every company in the world, of course, needed to engage the Internet at least at a minimal level – just to stay in the game, to compete and keep up. But a few stepped up to leadership: Walmart with its industry-leading, web-based logistics and efficiencies; Apple with its dazzling new product lines made possible through iTunes; and Google with its disruption of whole industries. What each had in common was a focused and disciplined business question: under what conditions does the Internet create wealth, and how can we play to our strengths to make its long-term payoff strategically significant?

It's also important to underscore that it was not a simplistic black and white debate: "will the Internet be good for our business and customers or not?" Instead, it was a relentless, penetrating question of *how*: "How will we harness the new discontinuities in information technologies to create value across the stakeholder spectrum, from customers and communities to suppliers and shareholders?"

Today, sustainability is at the same stage; there are billion-dollar opportunities in this discontinuity. So now is the exact time, propose the authors of this book, to turn from the hype of the sustainability revolution (who isn't going green?) to the bricks and mortar of disciplined management. Like the Internet that certainly had its share of early-stage mismanagement, the euphoria of the sustainability scene is leaving many people confused and far too many companies remain only superficially committed. Some, perhaps with a sense of betrayal after "green to gold" failed to materialize, want to ignore the sustainability wave altogether, as if it hasn't happened. But this is a huge business mistake. The trends are not invisible.

Remember when Toyota began investing in the "long shot" of the Prius? For Toyota executives the hybrid synergy series was positioned as a huge business opportunity. And what was GM doing at the same time? Of course we all know about their investment in the Hummer. But the issue is deeper than that. One company looked at the sustainability landscape as a kind of "social responsibility" sideline to the real business. The other said that the lens of sustainability must be approached through serious market economics and business strategy. Market shifts, they pragmatically reasoned, create disruptive opportunities. Agility is required. Risk is ever-present. But more than anything else it requires a shift in the fundamental question. The old and tired question – does social responsibility pay or is it even required? – is more than irrelevant. It is bad business. Today's strategy question is a managerial one. It's about how. How will we turn the lens of sustainable value into wealth-creating, world-benefiting opportunity – for risk mitigation, radical resource and energy productivity, for opening unexpected doorways to new markets, for strengthening and protecting brands, strategically altering industry standards, and catalyzing radical win–win–win innovation?

Toward this end, there is not a better book in the entire strategy literature than the one you hold in your hands if your goal is to harness the power of sustainability to create long-term competitiveness, new wealth, and shareholder value. This book is not about strategy for sustainability. This book is about sustainability for strategy – what it does for strategy, how it transforms the work of strategy, and ultimately, how it enriches it.

While many companies entertain the call for sustainability as a moral imperative, there is an odd and puzzling paradox to be reckoned with: when companies embrace sustainability as a strategic lens for creating shareholder value, they invariably do more and better for the world than those approaching this work as a social responsibility sideline. When sustainability is competently and systematically managed to create newly minted sources of value, it automatically creates a more effective platform for corporate responsibility. The reverse is rarely true. Yet this is not in any way meant to say that moral intention is not good. It's just not good enough. To bring sustainability to scale in business, it needs to be good for business, the total business.

Just last week I met with the senior team of a Fortune 500 corporation. Initially they had an approach to sustainability that was, to use Laszlo and Zhexembayeva's graphic term, "bolted on." The simple story was that they succeeded with a remarkable new product that helped their manufacturing customers dramatically reduce product waste, energy costs, and environmental footprint. That single product's unexpected success in the marketplace caused the CEO to extrapolate to the future and reconceptualize the company's long-standing mission statement. His reboot was bold. It was inspiring. This multinational would be reconceived as company providing solutions to ten of humankind's most significant global problems. Without exception, across the executive team, there was a collective gasp when the CEO read the new mission as it was written on a napkin. The implications would be enormous.

So I asked each senior leader – the chief financial officer, the head of operations, legal counsel, the executive vice president of human resources, and others – to consider how the focus on sustainability might become not just an incremental but an unprecedented innovation engine for each of their domains. To the HR executive I asked, "Can you imagine it, that sustainability might well be the biggest HR opportunity of the 21st century – a pathway to take employee engagement and talent management to a whole new octave? How will you communicate this to your global HR group, and what, exactly, will they be asked to do?" I framed similar questions for the chief financial officer, and others. Then I asked the CEO, "Are you ready, with this new positioning of the business, to declare your intention to Wall Street and describe the objectives not just for a single sustainable value-creating product line, but your transformation plan for an embedded culture of sustainability that calls upon your entire workforce, makes customers your inspired partners, and creates the kind of business growth that is only possible through new sources of innovation?" Everyone wondered if Wall Street would buy it, the reality of it, and if stakeholders would believe it.

Drawing on experiences we've had with Walmart, Fairmount Minerals, and Green Mountain Coffee Roasters – companies with business results all described in the book – I suggested the clearest, simplest, and most powerful three first steps I could think of for moving forward.

The three steps are easy. The steps work. And they can your help your system move fast because they reach beyond silos, generate leadership deep in the organization, and make stakeholder strengths more productive than ever.

1. Prepare the senior team at the highest level with the strategy tools outlined in this book

This is what Walmart did as an early step, for example. Using an early version of the sustainable value framework in this volume, the CEO asked each of his senior team members to envision two strategies: one called a "compete strategy," meaning a strategy designed to simply keep up with where the marketplace might likely be heading, and a second to create a "strategy to lead," that is, something that demonstrated ways to thoughtfully position the company for the future – to discover blue ocean opportunities never yet discussed or rarely considered. From the greening of markets for organic cotton, healthy foods, and sustainable fisheries, to the opportunities to be discovered in sustainable electronics and solar facilities, every part of the business would be scanned through careful stakeholder analysis, seeking both the tiniest and boldest signals of opportunity.

This kind of results-focused "homework" – reading the book in relation to real-time strategy considerations – can serve as a basis for setting in motion a shared view of the business importance of sustainable value. Nothing fancy yet. If you undertake this exercise, just treat it as a solid step for becoming familiar with the language and tools of stakeholder analysis and the 6 + 1 sources of value model. Reading a book is one thing. But working with it is a hundred times better. The only ground rule: each strategy proposition must be able to demonstrate how it could generate sustainable value to stakeholders and new value to shareholders. That's all. Each senior executive is, therefore, invited to bring forward their best strategy to compete, and one strategy to lead. And each should articulate the value-capture pathway. This is the simple assignment.

Using the management tools in this book, you will be amazed at the outpouring of opportunities. There will be quick wins. There will be provocative insights. There will also emerge, almost instantly, a collaborative exchange with a collective passion and executive team focus too rarely experienced. Likewise – and this is predictable – there will be an automatic desire to take immediate action, to put shape to a plan. But don't. Remember that your aim is to create a corporation that embeds sustainability. That won't happen through traditional planning methods. This time sustainability won't be bolted on.

2. Take advantage of state-of-the-art large-group planning: it is easy, fast, and productive

It's odd that after all these years we do not have a good term for the opposite of micro-management. While we will leave it to historians to trace the shift from micro-managing practice to macro-management – what Peter Drucker described as "bringing in the meaningful outside" – it is clear that sustainability, with its search for new and unexpected sources of stakeholder value, is leading the way with its large-group planning methodologies.

As Laszlo and Zhexembayeva demonstrate, a tool like the appreciative inquiry (AI) summit – used for strategy work at the U.S. Navy, Walmart, HP, Interface Carpets, the BBC, and hundreds more – is revolutionizing the way we do strategy work. As the authors sum up, "AI summits tend to leapfrog a company towards an aligned sustainable value strategy."

Let me give a testimonial on this. I was there at one of the summits that Laszlo and Zhexembayeva helped lead. The company was Fairmount Minerals, one of the largest sand mining and manufacturing organizations in the United States. The company decided to embed sustainability into the heart of the enterprise, and use it to reshape the company mission, strategy, and vision. On June 24, 2005 they launched their first sustainability strategy summit. The large-group "whole system in the room approach" proved successful beyond aspirations. Between 2005 and 2007 revenues almost doubled, while earnings took a gigantic leap of more than 40 per cent per year. The company's engagement scorecard also soared as it documented a workforce on fire. Likewise, plans from the strategy work were implemented with passion, focus, and unusual speed. In addition, Fairmount soon received the nation's "top corporate citizen" award from the United States Chamber of Commerce. This, combined with the company's unprecedented move in their marketplace leadership, is the kind of performance one might expect from a fast-moving design firm such as IDEO. Not an old industrial sand company based near Cleveland, Ohio.

To get a feel for it, I want you to imagine that you are a concerned citizen and environmentalist. You know Fairmount Minerals. And you have real questions about the next mine they might want to open. Then you receive an invitation letter from the CEO. You are invited not to be an observer, but to engage as full collaborator in Fairmount's strategic planning meeting. So imagine the start of the three-day summit:

> You enter a Grand Ballroom. It is teeming with 350 people from the sand company. There is no central podium or microphone. As many as 50 round tables fill the room – each has a microphone, a flip chart, and packets of materials including the summit's purpose, three-day agenda, and a pre-summit strategy analysis and

fact base. As an external stakeholder of the company you've been invited to roll up your sleeves and participate in a real-time strategy session devoted to the future.

You sit down at your assigned round table and you are struck by the complex configuration of individuals: the CFO of the company; a sand loader operator; a marketing specialist; a potential solar energy supplier (external); a product designer; a corporate lawyer; an IT professional; and a middle manager from operations. Soon the "whole-system-in-the-room" summit begins.

The CEO of the company stands up from one of the 50 tables and speaks to the "state of the business" and the task of this strategic session. He speaks about the difference between being a sustainability leader versus a sustainability laggard – and vows that this company will not be caught flat-footed by the future. An external moderator then calls attention to the key questions for the summit, each one designed to elicit discovery into strategic strengths, hidden opportunities, aspirations, and valued future scenarios – all with a focus on future results and game-changing industry possibilities. People are instructed to use the questions in the form of an interview with the person or key stakeholder sitting next to them. Within 30 minutes of the CEO's welcome people are into deep exploration, sharing, and listening, The Grand Ballroom is buzzing.

The moderator, after almost an hour, calls people to reconvene and describes the 4-D cycle of Discovery; Dream; Design; and Deployment that will unfold over the three days. "The key point" states the moderator "is that we are creating the innovation and change agenda together – this meeting is not about speeches or pre-negotiated plans, nor is it simply about dialogue – this meeting is a co-design and collaborative creation of the future of the company . . . we need your best thinking."

An appreciative inquiry summit is a large-group planning, designing, or implementation meeting that brings a whole system of internal and external stakeholders together in a concentrated way to work on a task of strategic, and especially creative, value. Moreover, it is a meeting where everyone is engaged as designers, across all relevant and resource-rich boundaries, to share leadership and take ownership for making the future of some big-league opportunity successful. The meeting appears bold at first, but is based on a simple notion: when it comes to embedding sustainability, there is nothing that brings out the best in human systems – faster, more consistently, and more effectively – than the power of "the whole." Flowing from a larger tradition called "strengths-based management," the AI summit says that, in a multistakeholder world, it is not about (isolated) strengths per se, but about configurations, combinations, and interfaces. It's all about the chemistry of relationships – about the concentration effect of strengths – and it's surprisingly easy.

While at first it seems incomprehensible that large groups of hundreds of people in the room can be effective in unleashing system-wide strategies, making organizational decisions, and designing rapid prototypes, this is exactly what is happening in organizations around the world. Fairmount's experience was not an isolated or atypical triumph. For you – an earlier critic of the company – the experience was eye-opening. First, you saw the integrity and sincerity of the company. Then you saw one new business idea after another being discovered. One that amazed you most was the new multi-million-dollar business that was designed to take old, spent sand – the stuff that is discarded after its use in factories – and turn it into clean biofuel for powering the company's heavy trucks. How could this be? Well a chemist in your group shared how spent sand, when placed on farmland, has been shown to help grow higher yields of biomass. Another person observes that the company's sand mining facilities are located in rural locations near many farms. Between the two observations a light bulb went on. How might we create a new business for spent sand? And why not create a new partnership with farmers – a partnership where sand-assisted biomass growth becomes the basis for lower-cost, green biofuels to power the heavy truck fleet.

This single innovation, coupled with a dozen other win–win–win sustainability breakthroughs, soon doubled Fairmount's already superior double-digit growth rates, and set it on a pathway of differentiation unheard of in an industry that's just the opposite of Silicon Valley. Headlines in a Wisconsin business paper told the story well in an article: "The Tale of Two Sand Companies."

There is a formula emerging among industry leading stars that says Sustainability = Innovation. But the real question is how? If there is one part of this book that I urge you to reread – this time for the details on how – it's Chapter 7's section on "getting the right start." Embedding sustainability may be just this simple. Do you want to embed? Then engage. And watch how sustainability and strategy together become a powerful tandem force for overcoming silos, making customers part of your team, speeding up the arithmetic of innovation, pushing the envelope on speed, and generating more leadership deep in the organization.

3. Start with your strengths

I have discovered through my own career in the field of change management that it simply does not work to introduce sustainability through the fear-based approach of "burning platforms" or diagnostic focus on "where are our biggest weaknesses." Instead it is becoming clear that all the most success-ful, innovative, and long-lasting deep work happens through the assumption that organizations, even industries, grow most effectively and fastest in their areas of strength and business competence. It is no accident, for example, that the most efficient organization in the world is now fast becoming the most eco-efficient organization in its industry. Walmart could have spent millions diagnosing its value-destroying footprint – and then used this as a way "to inspire" its managers to adopt a sustainability mind-set. But did it need to do this? Didn't Walmart – and the world – already know its ecological footprint, the negative one, was huge? If so, then why not direct those same resources into surfacing business competencies – signature capabilities – and imagine new ways those capabilities could be magnified into sustainable value opportunities?

I'll never forget when I first heard that Walmart wanted to offer the high-est-quality organic food in their stores. The amounts they were talking about would create a new demand that would transform agriculture. There were analysts who objected to the idea – for everyone knows that organic foods are not low-cost. But Walmart leaders saw the world through the prism of strengths. They said they could harness and leverage their logistic manage-ment skills to help lower the costs of organics, and in so doing could make organic foods not a luxury of the rich and famous, but a staple for working families at every level and class. The upward spiral here is important: more investment in strengths leads to confident, even game-changing innovation, and confident innovation in the sustainable value realm generates value for the world and the company. To be sure, areas of weakness need to be man-aged and mitigated, but non-incremental breakthrough happens where there is a concentration effect of strengths.

One of my favorite conversations of my entire career was with Peter Drucker, when he was 93 years old. I asked Peter about leadership. I asked: "Can you put it in a nutshell, what's the essence?" Drucker said, "That's easy." He paused and continued: "The task of leadership is to create an alignment of strengths in ways that make the system's weaknesses irrelevant." I wrote that down.

And that to me is the underlying message in this great book. Tie the strat-egy lens of sustainable value to your **strengths**. Leverage the strategy lens to surface **opportunities**. Create multistakeholder design events that lead to the discovery of common-ground **aspiration**. And keep the business eye on real **results**. Then, if you spell out the acronym taken from the first letter in each of these words, you have spelled "soar."[420]

That's what happens when you do these three simple steps: prepare the senior team at the highest level with the strategy tools outlined in this important book; take advantage of state-of-the-art large-group planning – it is easy, fast, and productive; and start with your strengths.

David Cooperrider
Fairmount Minerals Professor of Social Entrepreneurship
Case Western Reserve University, Weatherhead School of Management,
Cleveland, Ohio, U.S.A.

Endnotes

Foreword: Greg Babe

1 Greg Babe is the President and Chief Executive Officer of Bayer Corporation and Bayer MaterialScience LLC.
2 G. Pinchot, *The Fight for Conservation* (New York: Doubleday, 1910): 50.
3 Pinchot 1910: 45.

Foreword: Andrew J. Hoffman

4 Andrew J. Hoffman is the Holcim (U.S.) Professor of Sustainable Enterprise at the University of Michigan, a position that holds joint appointments at the Ross School of Business and the School of Natural Resources & Environment. He is also Associate Director of the Erb Institute for Global Sustainable Enterprise.

The wasp and the frog: an introduction

5 "Notes On The Way," in *George Orwell: The Collected Essays, Journalism and Letters. Volume 2: My Country Right or Left, 1940–43* (ed. S. Orwell and E. Angus; Harcourt Brace Jovanovich, 1968).

Chapter 1: Business reality reshaped

6   M.E. Porter and M.R. Kramer, "Business & Society: The Link between Competitive Advantage and Corporate Social Responsibility," *Harvard Business Review* 84.12 (2006): 78-92.

7   C.K. Prahalad, *The Fortune at the Bottom of the Pyramid: Eradicating Poverty through Profit* (Upper Saddle River, NJ: Wharton School Publishing, 2004).

8   V. Sole-Smith, "70 New Reasons to Live Green," March 6, 2009; us.glamour. com/magazine/2009/03/70-new-reasons-to-live-green, accessed July 27, 2009.

9   Think MTV, "About"; think.mtv.com/Info/About.aspx, accessed March 8, 2010.

10 "Green is Good," *Fortune* 155.6 (2007): 42-74.

11 M. Berns, A. Townend, Z. Khayat, B. Balagopal, M. Reeves, M. Hopkins, and N. Kruschwitz, "The Business of Sustainability," *MIT Sloan Management Review* Special Report (2009); www.mitsmr-ezine.com/busofsustainability/2009, accessed January 10, 2010.

12 Habitat Media, "Longlining, Overfishing & Atlantic Bluefin Tuna"; www.pbs. org/emptyoceans/eoen/tuna/viewpoints.html, accessed March 9, 2010.

13 N. Gronewold, "Is the Bluefin Tuna an Endangered Species?" *Scientific American*, October 14, 2009; www.scientificamerican.com/article.cfm?id=bluefin-tuna-stocks-threatened-cites-japan-monaco&page=2, accessed May 10, 2010.

14 "Fish Story: Big Tuna Sells for Record $396,000," *MSNBC News*, January 5, 2011.

15 D. Biello, "Overfishing Could Take Seafood off the Menu by 2048," *Scientific American*, November 2, 2006; www.scientificamerican.com/article. cfm?id=overfishing-could-take-se, accessed April 24, 2010.

16 The Natural Step, "The Funnel"; www.naturalstep.org/en/the-funnel, accessed July 27, 2009.

17 J.A. Krautkraemer, "Economics of Natural Resource Scarcity: The State of the Debate" (Resources for the Future, Discussion Paper 05–14, April 2005); www.rff.org/Documents/RFF-DP-05-14.pdf, accessed November 17, 2009.

18 B. Jowett, *The Dialogues of Plato* (translated into English with Analyses and Introductions by B. Jowett; 5 vols.; Oxford, UK: Oxford University Press, 3rd edn, 1892): Book V.

19 T.R. Malthus, "An Essay on the Principle of Population" (1798); www.econlib. org/library/Malthus/malPop.html, accessed November 17, 2009.

20 H. Barnett and C. Morse, *Scarcity and Growth: The Economics of Natural Resources Availability* (Baltimore, MD: Johns Hopkins University Press, 1963): 163-217.

21 D.H. Meadows, D.L. Meadows, J. Randers, and W.W. Behrens, *The Limits to Growth* (New York: Universe Books, 1972).

22 Julian Simon claimed in 1994, "We now have in our hands – in our libraries really – the technology to feed, clothe, and supply energy to an ever-growing

population for the next 7 billion years"; N. Myers and J. Simon, *Scarcity or Abundance: A Debate on the Environment* (New York: WW Norton, 1994): 65.

23 WWF, "Living Planet Report 2008"; assets.panda.org/downloads/living_ planet_report_2008.pdf, accessed November 17, 2009.

24 "Oil Reserves"; en.wikipedia.org/wiki/Oil_reserves, accessed November 17, 2009.

25 "Living on a New Earth", *Scientific American*, Special Report on Sustainability, April 2010; and J. Foley *et al.*, "Boundaries for a Healthy Planet," *Scientific American*, April 2010.

26 With 15,000 liters of water required to produce one kilogram of grain-fed beef, and beef production increasing dramatically over the past years, the growth in meat production alone can account for a significant strain on the world's water resources.

27 Goldman Sachs 2007.

28 World Water Council, "Water Supply and Sanitation"; worldwatercouncil. org/index.php?id=23, accessed April 30, 2010.

29 The FAO food price index of internationally traded basic food commodities reached a historic high in 2008 and, despite a global recession, by May 2009 it still stood at 152 relative to the 2002–2004 baseline, and nearly 70 per cent higher than in 2000. See the following note for source.

30 Food and Agriculture Organization of the United Nations, "The State of Food and Agriculture 2009"; www.fao.org/docrep/012/i0680e/i0680e.pdf, accessed March 10, 2010.

31 D.R. Davis, M.D. Epp, and H.D. Riordan, "Changes in USDA Food Composition Data for 43 Garden Crops, 1950 to 1999," *Journal of the American College of Nutrition* 23.6 (2004): 669-82.

32 Goldman Sachs Global Investment Research, *GS SUSTAIN* (New York: The Goldman Sachs Group, Inc., 2007).

33 International Energy Agency, "World Energy Outlook 2009 Fact Sheet"; www.worldenergyoutlook.org/docs/weo2009/fact_sheets_WEO_2009.pdf, accessed March 11, 2010.

34 The Millennium Ecosystem Assessment assessed the consequences of ecosystem change for human well-being. From 2001 to 2005, the MA involved the work of more than 1,360 experts worldwide. See www.maweb.org/en/index.aspx accessed February 16, 2011.

35 Millennium Ecosystem Assessment, "Living Beyond Our Means: Natural Assets and Human Well-Being" (2005); www.maweb.org/documents/document.429.aspx.pdf, accessed February 16, 2011.

36 P. Hawken, *Blessed Unrest: How the Largest Movement in the World Came Into Being, and Why No One Saw it Coming* (New York: Viking Press, 2007).

37 Ibid.

38 www.gapminder.org

39 Dru Oja Jay, "Greenpeace's Corporate Overreach: Controversial Hire is an Opportunity to Start Building a Democratic Environmental Movement,"

Pacific Free Press, March 11, 2010; www.pacificfreepress.com/news/1/5798-greenpeaces-corporate-overreach.html, accessed January 10, 2011.

40 www.edf.org/article.cfm?contentID=5634, accessed May 10, 2010.

41 H. Rheingold, *Smart Mobs: The Next Social Revolution* (Cambridge, MA: Perseus Publishing, 2002).

Chapter 2: To the desert and back

42 C. Meyer, and J. Kirby, "Leadership in the Age of Transparency," *Harvard Business Review*, April 2010.

43 You will find more information on PeaceWorks on their site, peaceworks.com (accessed January 10, 2011).

44 World Economic Forum, "Redesigning Business Value: A Roadmap for Sustainable Consumption" (Deloitte Touche Tohmatsu and the World Economic Forum, January 2010); www.weforum.org/pdf/sustainableconsumption/DrivingSustainableConsumptionreport.pdf, accessed May 20, 2010.

45 GMA and Deloitte, "Finding the Green in Today's Shoppers: Sustainability Trends and New Shopper Insights" (2009); www.deloitte.com/assets/Dcom-Shared%20Assets/Documents/US_CP_GMADeloitteGreenShopperStudy_2009.pdf, accessed February 16, 2011.

46 See *2009 BBMG Conscious Consumer Report: Redefining Value in a New Economy* by the branding and marketing agency BBMG.

47 Consumer unwillingness to pay more is reaffirmed by MIT's 2009 "The Business of Sustainability" report, which finds that, currently, "insufficient customer demand or needs" is ranked as the most significant roadblock to addressing sustainability concerns (with 26 per cent of managers ranking it as number one).

48 J. Dublin, "Will the Mainstream Buy Green to Save the Earth?" Sustainable Life Media, 2010; www.sustainablelifemedia.com/content/column/brands/will_mainstream_buy_green_to_save_earth, accessed May 20, 2010.

49 CEA, "Consumer Desire for 'Green' Electronics on the Rise, says CEA" (press release, December 10, 2008); www.ce.org/Press/CurrentNews/press_release_detail.asp?id=11649, accessed May 20, 2010.

50 Walmart, "Walmart Stores, Inc., Offering Environmentally Friendly Textile Options to Customers" (factsheet, May 2008); walmartstores.com/download/2310.pdf, accessed May 21, 2010.

51 Thomas Miner, "P&G Launches Supplier Scorecard," Sustainable Life Media, May 11, 2010; www.sustainablelifemedia.com/content/story/design/p_g_launchces_supply_chain_scorecard, accessed January 10, 2011.

52 Environmental Leader, "Businesses Fail to Engage Consumers on Environmental Issues," May 20, 2010; www.environmentalleader.com/2010/05/20/americans-want-to-share-environmental-responsibility-with-businesses, accessed May 21, 2010.

53 Trendwatching.com, "10 Crucial Consumer Trends for 2010"; trendwatching. com/trends/10trends2010, accessed May 21, 2010.

54 C. Fishman, "Hire This Guy," *Fast Company*, November 1, 2007; www. fastcompany.com/magazine/120/hire-this-guy.html?page=0%2C1, accessed May 11, 2010.

55 E.G. Chambers, M. Foulton, H. Handfield-Jones, S.M. Hankin, and E.G. Michaels III, "The War for Talent," *The McKinsey Quarterly* 3 (1998): 44-57.

56 R. Knight, "Business Students Portrayed as Ethically Minded in Study," *Financial Times*, October 25, 2006; www.ft.com/cms/s/ee45a804-63c5-11-db-bc82-0000779e2340.html, accessed May 21, 2010.

57 D.A. Ready, L.A. Hill, and J.A. Conger, "Winning the Race for Talent in Emerging Markets," *Harvard Business Review* 86.11 (November 2008): 62-70.

58 See, for example, D.B. Turban and D.W. Greening, "Corporate Social Performance and Organizational Attractiveness to Prospective Employees," *Academy of Management Journal* 40 (1997): 658-72, or World Business Council for Sustainable Development, "Driving Success: Human Resources and Sustainable Development" (2005); www.wbcsd.org/web/publications/hr.pdf, accessed July 10, 2007.

59 "Employee Engagement"; en.wikipedia.org/wiki/Employee_engagement, accessed May 21, 2010.

60 A.M. Saks, "Antecedents and Consequences of Employee Engagement," *Journal of Managerial Psychology* 21.7 (2006): 600-19.

61 F. Luthans and S.J. Peterson, "Employee Engagement and Manager Self-efficacy: Implications for Managerial Effectiveness and Development," *Journal of Management Development* 21 (2001): 376-87.

62 M. Buckingham and C. Coffman, *First, Break All the Rules: What the World's Greatest Managers Do Differently* (New York: Simon & Schuster, 1999).

63 J.K. Harter and F.L. Schmidt, *Employee Engagement, Satisfaction, and Business Unit-Level Outcomes: Meta-analysis* (Washington, DC: Gallup Technical Report, 2002).

64 See, for example, A. Glavas and S.K. Piderit, "How Does Doing Good Matter? Effects of Corporate Citizenship on Employees," *Journal of Corporate Citizenship* 36 (December 2009); www.greenleaf-publishing.com/productdetail. kmod?productid=3124, accessed May 21, 2010.

65 Business as an Agent of World Benefit, "Green Mountain Coffee Goes to Source," January 17, 2005; worldbenefit.case.edu/innovation/bankInnovationView.cfm?idArchive=195, accessed July 10, 2007.

66 Website accessed January 14, 2011.

67 Junior Achievement, "The Benefits of Employee Volunteer Programs: A 2009 Summary Report"; www.ja.org/files/BenefitsofEmployeeVolunteerPrograms. pdf, accessed February 16, 2011.

68 L. Story, "Can Burt's Bees turn Clorox Green?" *New York Times*, January 6, 2008; www.nytimes.com/2008/01/06/business/06bees.html?pagewanted=all, accessed May 30, 2010.

69 Cause Capitalism, " 'What's the Social Compensation Package?' 5 Ways to Attract Talent without the Checkbook," August 28, 2009; causecapitalism. com/social-compensation, accessed May 30, 2010.

70 Gap Inc., "Gap Inc. Employees Honored with Global Founders' Award for Dedication to Giving Back to their Community" (press release, August 25, 2009); www.csrwire.com/press/press_release/27522-Gap-Inc-Employees-Honored-With-Global-Founders-Award-for-Dedication-to-Giving-Back-to-Their-Community, accessed May 30, 2010.

71 See full details of the Pepsi Refresh Project at www.refresheverything.com, accessed January 10, 2011.

72 See Social Investment Forum's 2007 Report on "Socially Responsible Investing Trends in the United States," available at www.socialinvest.org/resources/pubs, accessed February 16, 2011.

73 Social Investment Forum, "Socially Responsible Investing Basics for Individuals"; www.socialinvest.org/resources/sriguide, accessed May 23, 2010.

74 Investor Network on Climate Risk, "Investors File a Record 95 Climate Change-Related Resolutions: A 40% Increase Over 2009 Proxy Season," March 4, 2010; www.incr.com/Page.aspx?pid=1222, accessed May 23, 2010.

75 Carbon Disclosure Project, "Carbon Disclosure Project 2009: Global 500 Report"; https://www.cdproject.net/CDPResults/CDP_2009_Global_500_Report_with_Industry_Snapshots.pdf, accessed January 10, 2011.

76 London Climate Change Partnership: Finance Sub-Group, "Adapting to Climate Change: Business as Usual?" (November 2006); www.london.gov.uk/lccp/publications/docs/business-as-usual.pdf, accessed May 23, 2010.

77 D.J. Lynch, "Corporate America Warms to Fight against Global Warming," USA Today, May 31, 2006; www.usatoday.com/weather/climate/2006-05-31-business-globalwarming_x.htm, accessed May 23, 2010.

78 The Equator Principles, "About the Equator Principles"; www.equator-principles.com/documents/AbouttheEquatorPrinciples.pdf, accessed May 23, 2010.

79 G. Shipeng and E. Graham-Harrison, "China Launches Surprise Crackdown on Plastic Bags," Reuters, January 8, 2008; www.reuters.com/article/idUSPEK25589820080108, accessed May 30, 2010.

80 C. Goodyear, "S.F. First City to Ban Plastic Shopping Bags," SFGate, March 28, 2007; articles.sfgate.com/2007-03-28/news/17235798_1_compostable-bags-plastic-bags-california-grocers-association, accessed May 30, 2010.

81 CBC News, "Calgary Moves against Trans Fats," December 29, 2007; www.cbc.ca/canada/story/2007/12/29/calgary-fats.html, accessed May 30, 2010.

82 Follow the updates on electronics waste management at the Sustainable Electronics Initiative page on International Legislation and Policy at www.sustainelectronics.illinois.edu/policy/international.cfm, accessed February 8, 2011.

83 Ceres, "Regulators Require Insurers to Disclose Climate Change Risks and Strategies" (2009); www.ceres.org/Page.aspx?pid=1062, accessed May 23, 2010.

84 Carbon Trust, "Carbon Reduction Commitment"; www.carbontrust.co.uk/policy-legislation/business-public-sector/pages/carbon-reduction-commitment.aspx, accessed May 30, 2010.

85 Polity.org.za, "Warburton Attorneys Monthly Sustainability Legislation, Regulation and Parliamentary Update," March 2010; www.polity.org.za/article/monthly-sustainability-legislation-regulation-and-parliamentary-update-march-2010-2010-04-09, accessed May 30, 2010.

86 Whirlpool, "Cash for Appliances: Every Kind of Green"; www.whirlpool.com/content.jsp?sectionId=1338&dcsref=http://www.whirlpool.com/assets/images/home/wp_homepage_031609.swf, accessed May 23, 2010.

87 Apollo Alliance, "Whirlpool Website Helps Consumers Access Energy-Efficient Appliance Rebates," January 27, 2010; apolloalliance.org/blog/whirlpool-website-helps-consumers-access-energy-efficient-appliance-rebates, accessed May 23, 2010.

88 A Piece of Cleveland, "Why APOC?"; www.apieceofcleveland.com/history_mission.asp, accessed May 23, 2010.

89 IBM, "Smarter Water Management"; www.ibm.com/smarterplanet/us/en/water_management/ideas/?&re=sph, accessed May 23, 2010.

90 Hydrolosophy, "Vision"; www.hydrolosophy.com/Vision.html, accessed May 23, 2010.

91 www.sourcemap.org, accessed January 14, 2011.

92 Answers.com, "Charles Revson"; www.answers.com/topic/charles-revson, accessed June 14, 2010.

93 F. Braudel, *The Wheels of Commerce: Civilization & Capitalism 15th–18th Century* (New York: Harper & Row, 1979).

94 Braudel 1979: 23.

95 H. Bourgin, *L'Industrie et le Marché* (1924), quoted in Braudel 1979: 31.

96 The characteristic feature of concentrated manufacture was the "bringing together under one roof, usually in a large building, of the labor force; this made possible supervision of the work, an advanced division of labor – in short increased productivity and an improvement in the quality of the products" (Braudel 1979: 300).

97 Braudel 1979: 304.

98 Braudel illustrates this prevalence of community over shareholder value in this portrait of an early capitalist: "Our capitalist, we should not forget, stood at a certain level in social life and usually had before him the decisions, advice and wisdom of his peers. He judged things through this screen. His effectiveness depended not only on his innate qualities but also on the position in which he found himself . . . Nor should we believe that the profit maximization so frequently denounced entirely explains the behavior of capitalist merchants" (Braudel 1979: 402).

99 M.S. Albion, *Making a Life, Making a Living: Reclaiming your Purpose and Passion in Business and in Life* (New York: Warner Books, 2000).

100 Gramota.ru, "Delo"; www.gramota.ru/slovari, accessed August 3, 2007 (Russian language only).

101 "Business"; dictionary.reference.com/browse/business, accessed August 2, 2007.

102 Ibid.

103 Braudel 1979: 455.

104 Braudel 1979: 343.

105 J. Diamond, *Collapse: How Societies Choose to Fail or Succeed* (New York: Penguin Books, 2005).

106 U.S. Census Bureau, "Historical Estimates of World Population"; www.census.gov/ipc/www/worldhis.html, accessed January 10, 2011.

107 The IPAT equation was developed by Barry Commoner, Paul Ehrlich, and John Holdren in the 1970s to explain the impact of human activity on the environment.

108 Meyer and Kirby 2010: 38-46.

109 Braudel 1979: 178.

110 J. Bendell, *Barricades and Boardrooms: A Contemporary History of the Corporate Accountability Movement* (Technology, Business and Society Programme Paper Number 13; Geneva: UNRISD, 2004).

111 D. Korten, *When Corporations Rule the World* (London: Kumarian, 1995): 59.

112 A. Bierce, *The Devil's Dictionary* (first published in book form by Doubleday, Page, and Company, 1911; New York: Neale).

113 M. Friedman, "The Social Responsibility of Business is to Increase its Profits," *New York Times*, 13 September 1970.

114 A. Rappaport, *Creating Shareholder Value: The New Standard for Business Performance* (New York: Free Press, 1986).

115 J. Howe, "No Suit Required," *Wired* 14.09 (September 2006); www.wired.com/wired/archive/14.09/nettwerk_pr.html, accessed June 14, 2010.

116 R.E. Freeman and D.L. Reed, "Stockholders and Stakeholders: A New Perspective on Corporate Governance," *California Management Review* 25.3 (1983): 88-106.

117 B. De Wit and R. Meyer, *Strategy: Process, Content, Context* (London: Cengage Learning EMEA, 2004): 604.

118 World Commission on Environment and Development, *Our Common Future* (Report of the Brundtland Commission; Oxford, UK: Oxford University Press, 1987).

119 P.F. Drucker, "The New Meaning of Corporate Social Responsibility," *California Management Review* 26.2 (Winter 1984): 53-63.

120 T. Cannon, *Corporate Responsibility* (London: Pitman, 1992).

121 A. Demb and F.F. Neubauer, *The Corporate Board: Confronting the Paradoxes* (Oxford, UK: Oxford University Press, 1992).

122 M. Yoshimori, "Whose Company Is It? The Concept of the Corporation in Japan and the West," *Long Range Planning* 28 (1995): 33-45.

123 S.L. Hart, "Beyond Greening: Strategies for a Sustainable World," *Harvard Business Review*, January–February 2007.

124 Bendell 2004.

125 The Global Compact, "Who Cares Wins: Connecting Financial Markets to a Changing World"; www.unglobalcompact.org/docs/issues_doc/Financial_markets/who_cares_who_wins.pdf, accessed February 16, 2011.

126 SustainAbility, *Buried Treasure* (SustainAbility, February 6, 2001); www.sustainability.com/library/buried-treasure, accessed January 10, 2011.

127 SustainAbility, International Finance Corporation & Ethos Institute, "Developing Value: The Business Case for Sustainability in Emergent Markets" (SustainAbility, July 17, 2002); www.sustainability.com/library/developing-value, accessed January 10, 2011.

128 This particular take on the concept of sustainable value is explored in depth in C. Laszlo, *The Sustainable Company: How to Create Lasting Value through Social and Environmental Performance* (Washington, DC: Island Press, 2003, 2005) and C. Laszlo, *Sustainable Value: How the World's Leading Companies Are Doing Well by Doing Good* (Sheffield, UK: Greenleaf Publishing/Stanford, CA: Stanford University Press, 2008).

129 November 6, 2008 remarks of Jeffrey Immelt at the BSR Conference, "Sustainability: Leadership Required," New York.

130 Ibid.

131 In 2009 Mike Duke asked his employees, "Sustainability is even more critical now, isn't it?" and went on to say that "we want to accelerate our efforts in sustainability" – not the language of a company that wants to slow down its greening efforts because of a recession.

132 See the Bloomberg news report, January 6, 2010, at www.bloomberg.com/apps/news?pid=20601109&sid=aJEVrzt2t.8o&pos=10, accessed January 8, 2010.

133 Laszlo 2005, 2008.

134 Environmental Leader, "IKEA Eliminates Incandescent Bulbs," June 16, 2010; www.environmentalleader.com/2010/06/16/ikea-eliminates-incandescent-bulbs, accessed January 10, 2011.

135 Retail electricity prices actually fell steadily from 1985 to 2005 (in real terms), and by 2008 were still well below historic levels (see "Figure 8.10: Average Retail Prices of Electricity" in U.S. Energy Information Administration/Annual Energy Review 2009; www.eia.doe.gov/emeu/aer/pdf/pages/sec8_38.pdf, accessed January 10, 2011).

136 "SUVs: The High Costs of Lax Fuel Economy Standards for American Families," Public Citizen, June 2003; www.citizen.org/documents/costs_of_suvs.pdf, accessed January 10, 2011.

137 M. Porter and M.R. Kramer, "The Competitive Advantage of Corporate Philanthropy", *Harvard Business Review*, December 2002.

138 P.J. Cescau, "Foreword," in C. Laszlo, *Sustainable Value: How the World's Leading Companies are Doing Well by Doing Good* (Sheffield, UK: Greenleaf Publishing/Stanford, CA: Stanford University Press, 2008): 12.

139 A. Rappaport, "Shareholder Value and Corporate Purpose", adapted from *Creating Shareholder Value: The New Standard for Business Performance* (New York: The Free Press, 1986).

140 Ibid.

141 De Wit and Meyer 2004: 602.

142 The authors are indebted to Gilbert Lenssen of the Academy of Business in Society for drawing our attention to the ICI example.

143 John Kay, speaking at the 2004 EABIS colloquium, "The Challenge of Sustainable Growth: Integrating Societal Expectations in Business," hosted by Vlerick Leuven Gent Management School in Belgium on September 27–28, 2004.

144 *Financial Times*, March 13 and 16, 2009. Quoted in V. Sathe, "Strategy for What Purpose?" in *The Drucker Difference* (New York: McGraw-Hill, 2010).

145 *The Economist*, May 8, 2004: 64. Quoted in Sathe 2010.

146 R.E. Freeman, *Strategic Management: A Stakeholder Approach* (Boston, MA: Pitman, 1984).

147 Cited in R.E. Freeman and D.L. Reed, "Stockholders and Stakeholders: A New Perspective on Corporate Governance," *California Management Review* 25.3 (1983): 88-106.

148 Berle and Means 1932 and Chester Barnard 1939, cited in De Wit and Meyer 2004: 616.

149 H.I. Ansoff, *Corporate Strategy* (New York: McGraw-Hill, 1965).

150 De Wit and Meyer 2004: 616.

151 De Wit and Meyer 2004: 604.

152 Clarkson 1995 and Alkhafaji 1989, cited in De Wit and Meyer 2004: 604.

153 J. Wallace, "Value(s)-Based Management: Corporate Social Responsibility Meets Value-Based management", in *The Drucker Difference* (New York: McGraw-Hill, 2010).

154 R.E. Freeman and D.L. Reed, "Stockholders and Stakeholders: A New Perspective on Corporate Governance," *California Management Review* 25.3 (1983): 88-106.

155 Freeman and Reed 1983: 88-106, cited in De Wit and Meyer 2004: 619.

156 Yet Freeman foresaw the need to collapse the separate treatments of different stakeholder groups and shareholders into a single strategic management approach. "Issues which involve both economic and political stakes and powerbases must be addressed in an integrated fashion. No longer can public affairs, public relations, and corporate philanthropy serve as adequate management tools" (De Wit and Meyer 2004: 621).

157 Cited in J. Wallace, "Value(s)-Based Management: Corporate Social Responsibility Meets Value-Based Management," in *The Drucker Difference* (New York: McGraw-Hill, 2010).

The tree of profit: introduction to Part II

158 "SEC Charges Goldman Sachs with Fraud in Structuring and Marketing of CDO Tied to Subprime Mortgages" (SEC press release, April 16, 2010); www.sec.gov/news/press/2010/2010-59.htm, accessed May 15, 2010.

Chapter 3: What would a strategist do?

159 A. Chandler, *Strategy and Structure: Chapters in the History of the Industrial Enterprise* (Cambridge, MA: MIT Press, 1962). Reprinted in *The Essential Alfred Chandler* (Cambridge, MA: Harvard Business Press, 1988): 174.

160 Ansoff 1965.

161 E.P. Learned, C.R. Christensen, K.R. Andrews, and W.D. Guth, *Business Policy: Text and Cases* (Homewood, IL: Irwin, 1965).

162 D.C. Hambrick and J.W. Frederickson, "Are you sure you have a strategy?" *Academy of Management Executive* 15.4 (November 2001): 48-59.

163 M. Porter, *Competitive Strategy: Techniques for Analyzing Industries and Competitors* (New York: The Free Press, 1998).

164 Chandler 1962: 174.

165 M.E. Porter, *Competitive Strategy* (New York: Free Press, 1980). See also his *Competitive Advantage* (New York: The Free Press, 1985).

166 R.D. Buzzell and B.T. Gale, *The PIMS Principles: Linking Strategy to Performance* (New York: Free Press/London: Collier Macmillan, 1987).

167 M. Treacy and F. Wiersema, *The Discipline of Market Leaders* (New York: Basic Books, 1995, expanded edition January 10, 1997).

168 R. D'Aveni, *Hypercompetition: Managing the Dynamics of Strategic Maneuvering* (New York: The Free Press, 1994).

169 S.L. Brown and K.M. Eisenhardt, *Competing on the Edge: Strategy as Structured Chaos* (Boston, MA: Harvard Business School Press, 1998).

170 H. Mintzberg and J.B. Quinn, *The Strategy Process: Concepts, Context, Cases* (Englewood Cliffs, NJ: Prentice Hall, 3rd edn, 1996).

171 Brown and Eisenhardt 1998.

172 C.M. Christensen and M. Overdorf, "Meeting the Challenge of Disruptive Change," *Harvard Business Review*, March–April 2000. See also C.M. Christensen and M.E. Raynor, *The Innovator's Solution* (Boston, MA: Harvard Business School Press, 2003).

173 Christensen and Overdorf 2000.

174 H. Mintzberg, B. Ahlstrand, and J. Lampel, *Strategy Safari: A Guided Tour through the Wilds of Strategic Management* (New York: The Free Press, 1998).

175 Ibid.

176 H. Mintzberg and J. Lampel, "Reflecting on the Strategy Process," *Sloan Management Review*, Spring 1999: 21-30.

177 This suggestion comes from a personal conversation between Henry Mintzberg and Nadya Zhexembayeva on June 29, 2010.

178 Responses one through six and the "nested holons" visual are drawn from an earlier book by Chris Laszlo, *Sustainable Value: How the World's Leading Companies Are Doing Well by Doing Good* (Greenleaf Publishing and Stanford University Press, 2008). In this chapter, each of the responses is researched and documented to a much greater extent than was the case previously.

179 K. Palmer, W. Oates, and P. Portney, "Tightening Environmental Standards: The Benefit-Cost or the No-Cost Paradigm?" *Journal of Economic Perspectives* 4 (1995): 121.

180 F. Reinhardt, *Down to Earth: Applying Business Principles to Environmental Management* (Boston, MA: Harvard Business School Press, 2000): 5.

181 S. Sharma and J. Alberto Aragon-Correa, "Corporate Environmental Strategy and Competitive Advantage: A Review from the Past to the Future," in S. Sharma and J. Alberto Aragon-Correa (eds.), *Corporate Environmental Strategy and Competitive Advantage* (Cheltenham, UK: Edward Elgar Publishing, 2005): 1.

182 N. Walley and B. Whitehead, "It's Not Easy Being Green," *Harvard Business Review*, May–June 1994: 46-51.

183 A. Hoffman, *Competitive Environmental Strategy* (Washington, DC: Island Press, 2000): 134.

184 M. Epstein, *Making Sustainability Work: Best Practices in Managing and Measuring Corporate Social, Environmental and Economic Impact* (Sheffield, UK: Greenleaf Publishing/San Francisco: Berrett-Koehler, 2008): 113.

185 The resource-based view of competitive advantage is described in the context of sustainability in A. Marcus, "Research in Strategic Environmental Management," in S. Sharma and J. Alberto Aragon-Correa (eds.), *Corporate Environmental Strategy and Competitive Advantage* (Cheltenham, UK: Edward Elgar Publishing, 2005): ch. 2.

186 M. Porter and C. van der Linde, "Green and Competitive: Ending the Stalemate," *Harvard Business Review*, September–October 1995: 125.

187 Reinhardt 2000: 79 and Laszlo 2008: ch. 5.

188 De Wit and Meyer 2004: 238.

189 Reinhardt 2000: 18.

190 Reinhardt 2000: 17.

191 Freedonia, "Air Pollution Control in China to 2010" (a report of the Freedonia group, April 2007); www.freedoniagroup.com/Air-Pollution-Control-In-China.html, accessed January 11, 2011.

192 C. Tait, "Clean Water: Most Precious Resource," *Vancouver Sun*, May 16, 2010; www.vancouversun.com/business/Clean+water+Most+precious+resource/2963500/story.html, accessed July 21, 2010.

193 Prahalad 2005.

194 World Resources Institute, *The Next 4 Billion: Market Size and Business Strategy at the Base of the Pyramid* (Washington, DC: WRI/IFC, 2007).

195 See the Case Western University case study, "Shakti: Growing the Market While Changing Lives in Rural India," August 22, 2005; worldinquiry.case.edu/bankInnovationView.cfm?idArchive=362, accessed January 11, 2011.

196 Competitive Advantage, "Project Shakti: A Win Win Situation," June 4, 2010; competitiveadvantage.thecompanymarketing.com/comparative-advantage/project-shakti-a-win-win-situation, accessed July 21, 2010.

197 Laszlo 2008: ch. 10.

198 Laszlo 2008: 161.

199 J. Hand and B. Lev (eds.), *Intangible Assets: Values, Measures and Risks* (Oxford, UK: Oxford University Press, 2003).

200 D. Fortson, "BP Offers Barack Obama Clean-up Billions," *The Sunday Times*, June 13, 2010; business.timesonline.co.uk/tol/business/industry_sectors/natural_resources/article7148985.ece, accessed January 11, 2011.

201 MSNBC News, "As spill costs mount, BP shares tumble anew"; www.msnbc.msn.com/id/37602159/ns/business-world_business, accessed June 10, 2010.

202 www.environmentalleader.com/?s=Advertising+Standards+Authority. For example, on May 6, 2010 an article appeared titled, "Renault Ad Banned Over Misleading Green Claims." See www.environmentalleader.com/2010/05/06/renault-ad-banned-over-misleading-co2-claims, accessed January 11, 2011.

203 C. Nehrt, "Maintainability of First Mover Advantages when Environmental Regulations Differ between Countries," *Academy of Management Review* 23 (1998): 77-97 showed that organizations that outstrip their competitors in advanced environmental practices and investments in technologies may obtain benefits if environmental legislation affecting the firm and the competitive scenario met certain conditions.

204 The U.S. Climate Action Partnership was founded in January 2007 (www.us-cap.org, accessed January 11, 2011).

205 For DuPont's leadership in low carbon technologies, see Laszlo 2008: ch. 5.

206 Reinhardt 2000: 56.

207 Chamber of Mines of South Africa, "Position Statement: The Potential Impact of REACH Authorisation Requirements on Mining in Developing Countries"; www.bullion.org.za/Departments/SafetySusDevl/Downloads/REACHinfo/REACH%20position%20statement.pdf, accessed January 11, 2011.

208 Reinhardt 2000: 106.

209 Traditional cement makers are one of the largest carbon-emitting industries, contributing about 5 per cent of global emissions.

210 The visual draws on Figure 10.4, "The Six Levels of Strategic Focus," published in Laszlo 2008: 155.

211 The resource-based view of competitive advantage is described in the context of sustainability in A. Marcus, "Research in Strategic Environmental Management," in S. Sharma and J. Alberto Aragon-Correa (eds.), *Corporate Environmental Strategy and Competitive Advantage* (Cheltenham, UK: Edward Elgar Publishing, 2005): ch. 2.

212 S. Sharma and J. Alberto Aragon-Correa, "Corporate Environmental Strategy and Competitive Advantage: A Review from the Past to the Future," in Sharma and Aragon-Correa 2005: ch. 1.

213 Ibid.

214 Ibid.

215 M. Porter, "America's Green Strategy," *Scientific American*, April 1991: 168.

216 A. Marcus, "Research in Strategic Environmental Management," in Sharma and Aragon-Correa 2005: ch. 2.

217 Sharma and Vredenburg, cited in Sharma and Aragon-Correa 2005: ch. 1.

218 Sharma and Aragon-Correa 2005: ch. 1.

219 Summarized in Sharma and Vredenburg, cited in Sharma and Aragon-Correa 2005: ch. 1.

220 C.K. Prahalad and G. Hamel, "The Core Competence of the Corporation," *Harvard Business Review*, May–June 1990: 79-91.

221 Prahalad and Hamel 1990: 84.

222 A. Winston, *Green Recovery: Get Lean, Get Smart, and Emerge from the Downturn on Top* (Boston, MA: Harvard Business School Press, 2009).

223 Marcus 2005.

224 "The LifeStraw® Concept"; www.vestergaard-frandsen.com/lifestraw, accessed June 5, 2010.

225 Laszlo 2005: 58.

226 MotorTrend reported in 2004 that "the two-seat Insight was first to market in late 1999, and the Prius sedan arrived soon after. Each accelerated like an economy car from a decade earlier. They both rode on rock-hard, high-efficiency tires that offered minimal grip and followed pavement grooves and ruts with a fundamentalist's zeal. Both cars often accelerated and braked in a jerky and nonlinear fashion as the electric motor's assistance phased in and out." Frank Markus, "Road Test: 2004 Honda Civic Hybrid, 2004 Toyota Prius, 2004 Honda Insight, 2003 Toyota Prius," *Motor Trend*, May 2004; www.motortrend.com/roadtests/alternative/112_0405_hybrid_car_comparison/index.html, accessed March 8, 2010.

227 Reinhardt 2000: 38.

228 Sustainability-led innovation leads to new product processes and designs, business models, and technologies that incorporate environmental and social benefits, such as low carbon intensity, without adding cost or lowering performance.

229 Reinhardt 2000: 17.

230 B. Piasecki and P. Asmus, *In Search of Environmental Excellence: Moving Beyond Blame* (New York: Simon & Schuster, 1990).

231 The 1995 Brent Spar incident between Greenpeace and Shell is a well-known example of this antagonistic relationship between environmentalists and big business. It contrasts with the constructive partnerships that now exist between major corporations such as Walmart and NGOs such as WWF or Environmental Defense.

232 Reinhardt 2000: 80.

Chapter 4: Cool strategies for a heated world

233 De Wit and Meyer 2004: 250.

234 De Wit and Meyer 2004: 252.

235 H. Mintzberg, "Five Ps for Strategy," in H. Mintzberg and J.B. Quinn (eds.), *The Strategy Process* (Englewood Cliffs, NJ: Prentice-Hall International Editions, 1992): 12-19.

236 Porter 1980.

237 C. Baden-Fuller and J. Stopford, *Rejuvenating the Mature Business* (London: Routledge, 1992); and C. Kim and R. Mauborgne, *Blue Ocean Strategy* (Boston, MA: Harvard Business Press, 1999) argue in different ways that the generic strategies are limiting because they do not consider middle grounds between the three generic strategies.

238 M.C. Porter, "What Is Strategy?" *Harvard Business Review*, November–December 1996: 64.

239 Ibid.

240 S. Chatterjee, "Core Objectives: Clarity in Designing Strategy," *California Management Review* 47.2 (Winter 2005): 33-49.

241 Laszlo 2008: ch. 6.

242 "Lexus Hybrid Interactive Guide: LS 600 h L"; www.lexus.com/hybridbrochure/ls_600h_l.html, accessed July 27, 2010.

243 J. Ewing, "BMW Inaugurates a Factory for Electric Cars," *The New York Times*, November 5, 2010.

244 Cited in a blog, "BMW To Make Electric Cars Pure Luxury," by Alice Winchester; www.tinygreenbubble.com/eco/environmental/item/1039-bmw-to-make-electric-cars-pure-luxury, accessed November 8, 2010.

245 M.E. Porter 1985, cited in De Wit and Meyer 2004: 264.

246 E. Iwata, "Small businesses take big steps into green practices," *USA Today*, December 7, 2007; www.usatoday.com/money/smallbusiness/2007-12-02-greenbiz_N.htm, accessed January 11, 2011.

247 A sector of the market defined by the Roper ASW Green Gauge Report as the most interested in "green" or environmental issues. In 2007, these customers jumped dramatically from only 9 per cent to 30 per cent of the total American consumer population and they tend to be educated, have higher incomes, and influence other consumers.

248 Lifestyles of Health and Sustainability; www.lohas.com, accessed January 16, 2011.

249 www.culturalcreatives.org, accessed January 11, 2011.

250 C. Kim and R. Mauborgne, "Blue Ocean Strategy," *Harvard Business Review*, October 2004: 2.

251 Kim and Mauborgne 2004: 3.

252 C. Kim and R. Mauborgne, *Blue Ocean Strategy: How to Create Uncontested Market Space and Make the Competition Irrelevant* (Boston, MA: Harvard Business School Publishing, 2005): 12.

253 Kim and Mauborgne 2005: 13.

254 D. Biello, "Pulling CO_2 from the Air: Promising Idea, Big Price Tag," *Environment 360*, October 8, 2009; e360.yale.edu/content/feature.msp?id=2197, accessed January 11, 2011.

255 Comment communicated in an email from Professor Vijay Sathe, The Drucker School, in July 2010.

256 Kim and Mauborgne 2005: 17.

257 Kim and Mauborgne 2005: 7-8.

258 Yellow tail is a brand of the Australian winery, Casella Wines.

259 Kim and Mauborgne 2005: 49.

260 For a University of Michigan case study on Cemex's Patrimonio Hoy program, see www.bus.umich.edu/BottomOfThePyramid/CEMEX.pdf, accessed January 11, 2011.

261 Kim and Mauborgne 2005: 73.

262 Kim and Mauborgne 2005: 124.

263 Conversation between Renée Mauborgne and Chris Laszlo on the INSEAD campus in December 2005.

264 Christensen and Overdorf 2000: 7.

265 See the IPCC *Fourth Assessment Report*, issued in 2007, available at www.ipcc.ch.

266 C. Christensen, *The Innovator's Dilemma* (New York: Collins Business Essentials, 1997): 7.

267 C. Morrison, "30 Electric Cars Companies Ready to Take Over the Road," *GreenBeat*, January 10, 2008; green.venturebeat.com/2008/01/10/27-electric-cars-companies-ready-to-take-over-the-road, accessed March 24, 2010.

268 Christensen 1997: 235.

269 Dealer prices as of March 28, 2010. Manufacturer websites.

270 Christensen 1997: 36.

271 A. Hoffman, *Competitive Environmental Strategy* (Washington, DC: Island Press, 2000): 163.

Chapter 5: Embedded sustainability

272 D.L. Cooperrider, D. Whitney, and J.M. Stavros, *Appreciative Inquiry Handbook* (San Francisco: Berrett-Koehler, 2008): 172.

273 Please see up-to-date information on Erste Group Bank at www.erstegroup.com.

274 good.bee, "Our Team"; www.goodbee.com/feed-back-contact/our-team/#section1, accessed August 14, 2010.

275 "The Richline Group"; www.richlinegroup.com/responsible.html, accessed January 11, 2011.

276 www.greenworkscleaners.com, accessed January 11, 2011.

277 Quoted in Winston 2009: 68.

278 For more information on the 2010 U.S. Presidential Green Chemistry Award, please see www.epa.gov/gcc/pubs/pgcc/past.html.

279 Dr. Charles P. Gerba, Bulk Soap Contamination, unpublished studies, University of Arizona 2006, 2007.

280 GOJO Industries, Inc. The authors would like to thank Argerie Vasilakes, Nicole Koharik, and David Searle for providing information on the company.

281 M. Katakis, "Chevy Cruze Engines to Get Easy Change, Environmentally Friendly Oil Filter," *GM Authority*, May 26, 2010; gmauthority.com/blog/2010/05/chevy-cruze-engines-to-get-easy-change-environmentally-friendly-oil-filter, accessed January 11, 2011.

282 See, for example, "Rising to the Sustainability Challenge: Remarks by Sherri K. Stuewer, Vice President of Environmental Policy and Planning, Exxon Mobil Corporation, Business and Sustainability Conference, Washington, D.C., June 17, 2009"; www.exxonmobil.com/corporate/news_speeches_20090617_sks.aspx, accessed July 11, 2010, in which sustainability is referred to as a balancing act.

283 For details on Exxon-Mobil Corporate Citizenship efforts, see www.exxonmobil.com/Corporate/community.aspx.

284 EMF stands for electromagnetic field, also the abbreviation for electromagnetic frequency.

285 D. Abell, "What Makes a Good Case?" *ECCHO: The Newsletter of European Case Clearing House* 17 (1997): 4-7.

286 C. Christensen, *The Innovator's Dilemma* (New York: Collins Business Essentials, 1997).

287 C.K. Prahalad and R.A. Mashelkar, "Innovation's Holy Grail," *Harvard Business Review*, July–August 2010: 132-41.

288 We owe this example to Stuart Hart, *Capitalism at the Crossroads: Next Generation Business Strategies for a Post-crisis World* (Upper Saddle River, NJ: Wharton School Publishing, 3rd edn, 2010): 118-20.

289 Hart 2010: 120.

290 The company's website is www.burco.com, accessed January 11, 2011.

291 Hart 2010: 40.

292 QuickMBA (www.quickmba.com/strategy/competitive-advantage, accessed March 5, 2010) provides a succinct definition: "When a firm sustains profits that exceed the average for its industry, the firm is said to possess a competitive advantage over its rivals."

293 De Wit and Meyer 2004: 231.

294 De Wit and Meyer 2004: ch. 5.

295 D. Meadows, D.L. Meadows, J. Randers, and W.W. Behrens III, *Limits to Growth* (New York: New American Library, 1972).

296 H. Kohler, *Intermediate Economics: Theory and Applications* (Glenview, IL: Scott, Foresman & Company, 1982): 526.

297 A.C. Pigou, *The Economics of Welfare* (London: Macmillan, 4th edn, 1946).

298 A.T. Kearney and WRI, "Rattling Supply Chains: The Effect of Environmental Trends on Input Costs for the Fast-Moving Consumer Goods Industry"

(November 2008); pdf.wri.org/rattling_supply_chains.pdf, accessed May 28, 2010.

Chapter 6: Hot competencies for a cool world

299 See, for example, an excellent and hands-on book on the power of left- and right-brain capabilities in business: D.H. Pink, *A Whole New Mind: Why Right-brainers will Rule the Future* (New York: Riverhead Books, 2005).

300 The fascinating world of Cultural Creatives is explored in P.H. Ray and S.R. Anderson, *The Cultural Creatives: How 50 Million People are Changing the World* (New York: Harmony Books, 2000).

301 We ran an advanced Google search for "management decision making" on July 25, 2010, and in a matter of 0.07 seconds received about 360,000 results.

302 "Decision making"; en.wikipedia.org/wiki/Decision_making, accessed July 16, 2010.

303 R.J. Boland and F. Collopy, *Managing as Designing* (Stanford, CA: Stanford University Press, 2004).

304 Ibid.

305 E.L. Plambeck and L. Denend, "The Greening of Walmart," *Stanford Social Innovation Review*, Spring 2008: 53-57.

306 L. Scott, "Twenty First Century Leadership," Wal-Mart, October 24, 2005; walmartstores.com/sites/sustainabilityreport/2007/documents/21stCenturyLeadership.pdf, accessed July 16, 2010.

307 Plambeck and Denend 2008.

308 Boland and Collopy 2004.

309 T. Brown, *Change by Design* (New York: HarperCollins, 2009): 3.

310 Ibid.

311 William McDonough + Partners, "Design is the First Signal of Human Intention"; www.mcdonoughpartners.com/design_approach/philosophy, accessed July 16, 2010.

312 Pink 2005: 70.

313 Brown 2009: 18.

314 TED, "William McDonough on Cradle to Cradle Design," February 2005; www.ted.com/talks/lang/eng/william_mcdonough_on_cradle_to_cradle_design.html, accessed July 16, 2010.

315 Media.Ford.Com, "Ford installs world's largest living roof on new truck plant," (press release, June 3, 2003); media.ford.com/article_display.cfm?article_id=15555, accessed July 16, 2010.

316 TED, "William McDonough on Cradle to Cradle Design."

317 "Nestlé Boycott"; en.wikipedia.org/wiki/Nestlé_boycott, accessed January 11, 2011.

318 Nestlé S.A., Public Affairs, "The Nestlé Creating Shared Value Report" (March 2008); www2.nestle.com/Common/NestleDocuments/Documents/Reports/CSV reports/Global report 2007/Global_report_2007_English.pdf, accessed July 16, 2010.

319 S.J. Fulton, *Thoughtless Acts? Observations on Intuitive Design* (Watertown, MA: Chronicle Books, 2005).

320 T. Brown, "Strategy by Design," *Fast Company*, June 1, 2005; www.fastcompany. com/magazine/95/design-strategy.html?page=0%2C1, accessed July 16, 2010.

321 GE Reports, "On the hunt for sunken treasure at GE"; www.gereports.com/on-the-hunt-for-sunken-treasure-at-ge, accessed July 17, 2010.

322 G. Hancock, "How GE's 'Treasure Hunts' discovered more than $110M in energy savings," May 13, 2009; www.greenbiz.com/blog/2009/05/13/how-ges-treasure-hunts-discovered-more-110m-energy-savings, accessed July 17, 2010.

323 The Co-operative Bank, "Why we have ethical policies"; www.goodwithmoney. co.uk/why-do-we-need-ethical-policies, accessed July 17, 2010.

324 Walmart, "Associates' Personal Sustainability Projects" (2009 Global Sustainability Report); walmartstores.com/sites/sustainabilityreport/2009/s_ao_psp.html, accessed July 17, 2010.

325 D. McLeod, "Waving the Wand," *Financial Mail*, November 25, 2005; www. wizzit.co.za/media/wavinghand.pdf, accessed July 17, 2010.

326 GE Ecomagination, "Ecomagination Challenge: Powering the Grid," challenge.ecomagination.com/ideas, accessed July 17, 2010.

327 J. Ridderstråle and K. Nordström, *Funky Business: Talent Makes Capital Dance* (Upper Saddle River, NJ: Financial Times Prentice Hall, 2000): 97.

328 For deeper exploration on the role of meaning in business, see Pink 2005 as well as Brown 2005.

329 M. Losada and E. Heaphy, "The Role of Positivity and Connectivity in the Performance of Business Teams: A Nonlinear Dynamic Model," *American Behavioral Scientist* 47.6 (2004): 740-65.

330 Ibid.

331 C. Argyris and D. Schön, *Organizational Learning: A Theory of Action Perspective* (Reading, MA: Addison-Wesley, 1978).

332 P.M. Senge, *The Fifth Discipline: The Art and Practice of the Learning Organization* (New York: Currency/Doubleday, 1990).

333 Boland and Collopy 2004: 9.

334 Senge 1990.

335 E.E. Vogt, J. Brown, and D. Isaacs, *The Art of Powerful Questions: Catalyzing Insight, Innovation and Action* (Mill Valley, CA: Whole Systems Associates, 2003).

336 TED, "Chip Conley: Measuring what Makes Life Worthwhile," February 2010; www.ted.com/talks/chip_conley_measuring_what_makes_life_worthwhile. html, accessed July 18, 2010.

337 T. Kinni, "The Art of Appreciative Inquiry," Harvard Business School Working Knowledge for Business Leaders, September 22, 2003; hbswk.hbs.edu/archive/3684.html, accessed July 18, 2010.

338 D. Cooperrider and L.E. Sekerka, "Elevation of Inquiry into the Appreciable World: Toward a Theory of Positive Organizational Change," in K. Cameron, J. Dutton, and R. Quinn (eds.), *Positive Organizational Scholarship* (San Francisco: Berrett-Koehler, 2003): 229.

339 Cooperrider and Sekerka 2003: 225-40.

340 For an in-depth exploration of positive states in organizational life, please refer to K.S. Cameron, J.E. Dutton, and R.E. Quinn, *Positive Organizational Scholarship* (San Francisco: Berrett-Koehler, 2003): 225-40.

341 Losada and Heaphy 2004.

342 Kinni 2003.

343 D.L. Cooperrider, D.K. Whitney, and J.M. Stavros, *Appreciative Inquiry Handbook* (San-Francisco: Berrett-Koehler, 2008).

344 Innovation Center for U.S. Dairy, "U.S. Dairy Sustainability Commitment," www.usdairy.com/Sustainability/Pages/Home.aspx, accessed November 18, 2009.

345 P. Senge, C. Roberts, R. Ross, B. Smith, and A. Kleiner, *The Fifth Discipline Fieldbook: Strategies and Tools for Building a Learning Organization* (New York: Currency/Doubleday, 1994).

346 M.J. Wheatley, *Leadership and the New Science: Learning about Organization from an Orderly Universe* (San Francisco: Berrett-Koehler, 1994).

Chapter 7: Change management redux

347 For this quote and much more on the line between strategy and execution, see R.L. Martin, "The Execution Trap," *Harvard Business Review*, July–August 2010: 64-71.

348 Ibid.

349 A.L. Shapiro, "Coca-Cola Goes Green," Forbes.com, January 29, 2010; www.forbes.com/2010/01/29/muhtar-kent-coca-cola-leadership-citizenship-sustainability.html, accessed August 20, 2010.

350 To see the full video clip with this quote, and more interviews with Lee Scott, go to YouTube at: www.youtube.com/watch?v=MCeUET8mcVo (accessed January 12, 2011).

351 Deloitte, "Lifecycle Assessment: Where Is It in Your Sustainability Agenda?" (2009); online paper, available at www.deloitte.com/assets/Dcom-UnitedStates/Local%20Assets/Documents/us_es_LifecycleAssessment.pdf, accessed February 16, 2011.

352 B. Willard, *The Sustainability Advantage: Seven Business Case Benefits of a Triple Bottom Line* (Gabriola Island, BC: New Society Publishers, 2002).

353   For more information on Walmart's Sustainability Index, see walmartstores. com/Sustainability/9292.aspx, accessed January 12, 2011.

354   J. Andriof, S. Waddock, B. Husted, and S.S. Rahman, *Unfolding Stakeholder Thinking 2: Relationships, Communication, Reporting and Performance* (Sheffield, UK: Greenleaf Publishing, 2003).

355   Walmart, "Sustainability"; walmartstores.com/Sustainability, accessed July 27, 2009.

356   www.henkel.com/sustainability/raw-materials-12101.htm, accessed January 12, 2011.

357   www.chinadaily.com.cn/business/2010-05/31/content_9911034.htm, accessed January 12, 2011.

358   D. Fleischer, "Green Teams: Engaging Employees in Sustainability," Green-Biz report, November 2009, page 7; www.greenbiz.com/sites/default/files/GreenBizReports-GreenTeams-final.pdf, accessed January 12, 2011.

359   National Environmental Education Foundation, "The Business Case for Environmental and Sustainability Employee Education," February 2010, page 9; neefusa.org/BusinessEnv/white_paper_feb2010.pdf, accessed January 12, 2011.

360   www.trimo.eu/company/sustainable-development accessed January 12, 2011.

361   National Environmental Education Foundation 2010.

362   www.greenbiz.com/sites/default/files/Generating%20Sustainable%20 Value%20Through%20Employee-led%20Teams%20Final.pdf, accessed January 12, 2011.

363   Fleischer 2009.

364   Learn more about SOL Sustainability Consortium at www.solsustainability. org accessed January 12, 2011.

365   For more on the remarkable achievements of E4S, please visit www.e4s.org accessed January 12, 2011.

366   To review the full range of indicators for Rabobank Group, please see www. rabobank.com/content/csr/factfigures, accessed January 12, 2011.

367   Full GRI guidelines and much more can be found at www.globalreporting. org, accessed January 12, 2011.

368   For the audit, see page 29 of the 2009 MIT Sloan Management Review "The Business of Sustainability" at www.mitsmr-ezine.com/busofsustainability/2009#pg1, accessed January 12, 2011.

369   Discover the Sustainable Packaging Metrics at www.sustainablepackaging. org/content/?type=5&id=sustainable-packaging-metrics, accessed January 12, 2011.

370   For the full article, see J. Collins and J. Porras, "Building Your Company's Vision," *Harvard Business Review* 74.5 (1996): 65-77.

Chapter 8: Putting it all together

371 C. Laszlo and J.-F. Laugel, *Large Scale Organizational Change: An Executive's Guide* (Woburn, MA: Butterworth-Heinemann, 2000).

372 Epstein 2008.

Fruits of the future: introduction to Part IV

373 P. Senge, *The Necessary Revolution* (New York: Doubleday, 2008).

374 Pink 2005.

375 Pink 2005: 65-66.

376 J. Benyus, *Biomimicry* (2006; HarperCollins e-books, Kindle edition): locations 1,570-82. We are indebted to Janine Benyus for suggesting the examples and explaining the challenge of mimicking photosynthesis.

377 D.L. Cooperrider and D. Whitney, *Appreciative Inquiry: A Positive Revolution in Change* (San Francisco: Berrett-Koehler, 2005).

Chapter 10: Sustaining inquiry

378 See for example the work of Nobel prize-winning neurophysiologist Roger W. Sperry. His concept of "downward causation" suggested a process by which the whole exercises a determinant influence on the parts. As Sperry's work demonstrates, this is the kind of influence that happens in the higher nervous system where the consciousness exhibited by the whole brain governs the behavior of the brain's neuronal networks and subassemblies.

379 A. Koestler, *The Ghost in the Machine* (Harmondsworth, UK: Penguin Books, reprint edn, 1990).

380 B. McKibben, "Breaking the Growth Habit," a Scientific American excerpt from his book, *EAARTH: Making a Life on a Tough New Planet* (New York: Henry Holt & Company, 2010).

381 T. Nordhaus and M. Shellenberger, *Breakthrough: From the Death of Environmentalism to the Politics of Possibility* (Boston, MA: Houghton Mifflin, 2007): 5-6.

382 R. Goodland and H. Daly, "Environmental Sustainability: Universal and Non-negotiable," *Ecological Applications* 6 (1996): 1,002-17.

383 E. Laszlo, *Worldshift 2012: Making Green Business, New Politics and Higher Consciousness Work Together* (Toronto: McArthur & Company, 2009): 88-89.

384 Nordhaus and Shellenberger 2007: 28.

385 B. Commoner, "The Environmental Cost of Economic Growth," in *Population, Resources and the Environment* (Washington, DC: Government Print-

ing Office, 1972): 339-63; P.R. Ehrlich and J.P. Holdren, "Impact of Population Growth," *Science* 171 (1971): 1,212-17.

386 We are indebted to Ray Anderson, founder and chairman of Interface, Inc., for first suggesting this logic to us.

387 Nordhaus and Shellenberger 2007: 15.

388 G. Markowitz and D. Rosner, *Deceit and Denial: The Deadly Politics of Industrial Pollution* (Berkeley, CA: University of California Press, 2002): 172.

389 Markowitz and Rosner 2002: 173.

390 Markowitz and Rosner 2002: 176.

391 Markowitz and Rosner 2002: 178.

392 Markowitz and Rosner 2002: 192.

393 Markowitz and Rosner 2002: 204.

394 Markowitz and Rosner 2002: 207.

395 Markowitz and Rosner 2002: 214.

396 Markowitz and Rosner 2002: 223.

397 Nordhaus and Shellenberger 2007: 8.

398 Nordhaus and Shellenberger 2007: 18.

399 See also A. Hoffman and S. Bertels, "Who is Part of the Environmental Movement? Assessing Network Linkages between NGOs and Corporations," in T. Lyon (ed.), *Good Cop Bad Cop: Environmental NGOs and their Strategies toward Business* (Washington, DC: Resources for the Future Press, 2010): 48-69; A. Hoffman, "Shades of Green," *Stanford Social Innovation Review,* Spring 2009: 40-49.

400 J.R. Ehrenfeld, *Sustainability by Design: A Subversive Strategy for Transforming Our Consumer Culture* (New Haven, CT: Yale University Press, 2008): xix.

401 Ehrenfeld 2008: 24.

402 Senge 2008: 169.

403 E. Laszlo 2009: 75.

404 R. Gelbspan, *The Heat Is On* (New York: Perseus Publishing, 1998): 171.

405 McKibben 2010.

406 Senge 2008: 46.

407 C. Laszlo 2000: ch. 3.

408 en.wikipedia.org/wiki/Gifford_Pinchot, accessed January 12, 2011.

409 B. Commoner, "Unraveling the DNA Myth," *Harper's Magazine,* February 2002: 39-47.

410 Nordhaus and Shellenberger 2007: 239.

411 "Genetically Modified Rice Crucial in Drought Battle," Manila Bulletin Publishing Corporation, July 23, 2009; mb.com.ph/articles/212311/genetically-modified-rice-crucial-drought-battle, accessed February 16, 2011.

412 T. Nordhaus and M. Shellenberger, "The Death of Environmentalism: Global Warming Politics in a Post-Environmental World," quoted in Nordhaus and Shellenberger 2007.

413 See, for example, an article by the International Center for Journalists; www.icfj.org/OurWork/MiddleEastNorthAfrica/ConferenceIran360/FinalReport/

WhyNegativeNewsTurnsUsOn/tabid/872/Default.aspx, accessed January 12, 2011.

414 L. Brown, *Plan B 4.0: Mobilizing to Save Civilization* (New York: W.W. Norton & Company, rev. edn, 2009).

415 H. Kunstler, *The Long Emergency: Surviving the Converging Catastrophes of the 21st Century* (New York: Atlantic Monthly Press, 2005).

416 For more, see J.P. Kotter, *Leading Change* (Boston, MA: Harvard Business School Press, 1996).

417 J.P. Kotter, "Leading Change: Why Transformation Efforts Fail," *Harvard Business Review*, March–April 1995: 60-61.

418 D.L. Cooperrider and L.E. Sekerka, "Elevation of Inquiry into the Appreciable World: Toward a Theory of Positive Organizational Change," in K. Cameron, J. Dutton, and R. Quinn (eds.), *Positive Organizational Scholarship* (San Francisco: Berrett-Koehler, 2003): 233.

Afterword

419 David Cooperrider is Fairmount Minerals Professor of Social Entrepreneurship at Case Western Reserve University, Weatherhead School of Management, Cleveland, Ohio, U.S.A. David is pioneering new horizons in the AI Summit method – a large-group and network-based approach – for advancing business innovation and creative design.

420 J. Stavros, D. Cooperrider, and D. Lynn Kelley, "SOAR: A New Approach to Strategic Planning," in P. Holman, T. Devane, and S. Cady (eds.), *The Change Handbook* (San Francisco: Berrett-Koehler, 2007): ch. 38.

Index

About the authors

Chris Laszlo, Ph.D., is the author of *Sustainable Value: How the World's Leading Companies Are Doing Well by Doing Good* (Greenleaf Publishing and Stanford University Press, 2008), and *The Sustainable Company: How to Create Lasting Value through Social and Environmental Performance* (Island Press, 2003 [paperback 2005]). He is an Associate Professor at Case Western Reserve University's Weatherhead School of Management, where he is the Faculty Research Director at the Fowler Center for Sustainable Value. Chris is also the co-founder and Managing Partner of Sustainable Value Partners, LLC, an advisory services firm specialized in sustainability for business advantage.
Chris@SustainableValuePartners.com

Nadya Zhexembayeva, Ph.D., is the Coca-Cola Chair of Sustainable Development at IEDC-Bled School of Management, the European business school based in Slovenia, where she teaches leadership, organizational design, and sustainability strategy. Nadya currently serves as Vice-President of *Challenge:Future*, a global youth think-tank. She is a member of the Advisory Board of the Fowler Center for Sustainable Value at the Weatherhead School of Case Western Reserve University in Cleveland, Ohio. Nadya is also an Associate Partner of Sustainable Value Partners, LLC.
Nadya.Zhexembayeva@iedc.si